Happy Dogs...
Happy Winners

*The Complete Competition Obedience Manual
Fun Training with Winning in Mind*

Angela White

Revised Edition 2004

Rainbow Publishing · England

RAINBOW PUBLISHING
Happy Dogs Happy Winners
The Complete Dog Obedience Manual
By Angela White
Published by Rainbow Publishing
PO Box 1044, Haxey, Doncaster. DN9 2JL. England
Printed in England
ISBN 1-899057-05-6
Photographs by Michael White (unless otherwise stated)

Also By Angela White
Books
Everybody Can Train Their Own Dog (TFH)
Puppies - Your Successful Guide to Dog Ownership (TFH/Kingdom)
The Leonberger (TFH/Kingdom)
Dog Training Instructors Manual (Rainbow Publishing)
Glucklicke Hunde Gluckliche Gewinner
(German Version of Happy Dogs Happy Winners first edition)
Booklets
Clicker and Target Training (Rainbow Publishing)
How To Be Top Dog (Rainbow Publishing)
Home Alone Canine (Rainbow Publishing)
Training Your Pet Dog (Rainbow Publishing)

Acknowlegements

Grateful thanks are due to many people who contributed to the smooth running of life and gave help where it was needed most, whilst I indulged my favourite pastime next to dog training - writing.

I have never been totally away from the sport because I have continued to teach on a regular basis and judge periodically, but despite being hampered with illness I hope that competing will become a part of my life again. Returning to the ring after an extended break took a bit of getting used to. My training buddies, especially Janet Matthews and Julie Garnett and my friends at Bishop Burton College dog club. You have all been invaluable in helping me back into competition, pointing out the bad habits that I have acquired from a few years out of the competition ring and getting me back into competitive mode.

Thanks also go to the students at Bishop Burton College, (many of whom have gone on to become professional dog trainers and even instructors and counsellors following our courses), for acting as socialisers and distractions for my dogs.

To Janet Matthews, Sandra Pendleton and Jane Hanshaw for helping out with the last minute photo shoot and to everyone else who has allowed us to use photos of them for the purpose of illustrating this book.

Special thanks to 'adopted daughter' Sophie Fairfax for looking after my dogs with great care when I am away and posing for photographs with great patience and enthusiasm.

My son Daniel White and husband, friend and 'gopher' Michael White, thanks for being supportive, and for supplying me with endless hot drinks and encouragement even at the darkest times!

And finally... to all of the handlers from around the world, who have attended my training sessions, talks, courses and camps, and have listened with an open mind, learned and enjoyed training for competition and at the same time having fun with their dogs.

About the Author

Angela White has been involved in competition work with dogs since 1977. She started out with her first crossbred dog from the RSPCA and successfully competed and won at the lower levels. She then progressed to a first Cross German Shepherd/Border Collie who took her to test B. Having always wanted a Border Collie, even before discovering Obedience, the next dog just had to be her first Border Collie - Monteach Leika. Leika made the dizzy heights of test C. During her excellent career Leika produced a few notable litters of puppies, perhaps the most famous of her progeny being Sandy Wadhams' top winning Obedience Champion Collali Rocky (Ricky). Leika continued to enjoy heelwork until the very end of her life. Angela also owned and trained Leo, one of the last sons of Leika. Leo won out of novice, but tragically had an accident that resulted in him losing his sight in one eye. This trauma took him many years to learn to live with and caused the untimely end of his competitive career. The cover star of edition one of this book was Smudge, a rescue blue merle Border collie. Smudge was never taken into the ring due to pressures of work, but he was trained to competitive standards and Angela used him for demonstrating when teaching.

As a change from Collies, Angela took on a 9 month old Leonberger, Willow. She had a few behavioural problems, but these were soon ironed out and Willow went on to be Angela's PR dog for quite a few years - working with children and the general public. Willow produced 3 litters, a bitch from the first litter going on to break Leonberger records to become the top winning Leonberger in UK Obedience and as we go to press the only Leonberger working top level obedience in the UK, her name is Akamai Aroura, (Pat Leverick's Rosie). Sadly Pat past away rather suddenly but her husband Paul is keen to keep up with the training for as long as Rosie wants to work. Another pup went on to be a support dog for a disabled owner and many others are registered PAT dogs. Angela kept 2 from the litter, Scout who she trained to take over his mother's role as PR dog, and also to pull a traditional dog cart and his sister Minty - both became registered PAT dogs working with children and young adults who have learning difficulties. She now has a couple of young bitches that she hopes will carry on the Akamai Leonberger line.

Family (birth of her son Daniel) and business commitments took over and made keeping up with competition level training difficult. The business ventures included the development and manufacture of dog training equipment and also the creation of a magazine for Obedience 'Obedience Competitor Magazine' and another more general dog training magazine 'Smart Dogs', but due to the success of her other enterprises and unreasonable workload, these companies were sold. Amongst all of this she continued to develop her writing and added several titles to her portfolio, all on dog training, care and behaviour.

Angela developed her teaching becoming increasingly involved with Bishop Burton College in a quest to pass on kind techniques of training to a younger and more diverse audience. She continues to instruct at a competitive level as well teaching people how to deal with behavioural problems. She also teaches instructors so that the good practice can be spread more quickly. She has developed a keen following both in the UK and abroad (especially Germany) for her simple, kind, well-structured and fun approach to training and laid back attitude with her pupils.

As well as obedience, Angela has worked and acted as consultant in many fields of dog training including drug and weapon detection and security. She has trained her own dogs and helped others in a variety of fields including, agility, flyball, working trials, show, gundogs, guide dogs for the blind, search and rescue, demonstrations, heelwork to music, and media/TV work. She has had experience in teaching a wide variety of breeds and has adapted techniques to suit a variety of needs (both human and canine). She has also trained cats, horses, small animals, a goldfish and even cows!

In more recent times Angela has concentrated on developing educational packages. She has been a major influence and contributor to the development of a number of animal behaviour and training related courses, from entry level through to honours degree, at Bishop Burton College where she became Senior Lecturer in Animal Behaviour and Training and head of canine and specialist courses.

In January 2002 Angela and husband Michael took time out to spend time studying wolves under the guidance of 'wolfman' Shaun Ellis. They met and worked with various wolves learning to fine tune the skills and senses needed to read the language of wolves. This hands on experience helped enormously with their ability to read dogs.

In the Queen's jubilee year Angela organised and took part in a canine demonstration along with the equine department at the college. Angela and her very young Border collie Fizz were introduced to the Queen. The queen took great interest in their work.

Angela and her young Border Collie Fizz are presented to the Queen.

With her husband Michael she runs the International Animal Behaviour Training Centre. This enterprise involves a number of animal related branches including correspondence courses, the delivery of animal care and behaviour lectures, talks and hands on workshops around the UK for schools, colleges, care centres, the pet industry and other organisations.

As we go to press she continues to take on occasional judging appointments and is a qualified championship Obedience show judge. She has resumed competing with her home bred Border Collie 'Akamai Frosted Fizz', and is slowly re-developing a line of Border Collies for obedience. She also owns, breeds and trains Pyrenean Sheepdogs and hopes to help develop the breed in the UK as well as having the occasional litter of Leonbergers and Border Collies. She continues to write, to research, to instruct around the world and to further develop courses to increase knowledge and understanding of animals but more especially, our friend the dog.

Contents

Introduction

The approach to competitive obedience training has, over recent years, been gradually changing and, on the whole, for the better. It is the aim of this book to bring you up to date with the techniques and concepts that are open to everyone with any breed. So if you feel that you would like to enjoy the sport of obedience, you can now begin with confidence. The techniques are not fancy, nor do they require super human effort, and Olympic style fitness. What they do require however, is a fair approach, a dog's eye view, a sense of humour, some toys and/or titbits, patience, the will to succeed and a willingness to relax and enjoy.

In order to win in competitive obedience, very high standards are needed, particularly in the UK; therefore obedience in the competition ring can be very frustrating. With this frustration comes the fear of failure and sometimes, even aggression, very natural responses. However, a positive attitude and sound knowledge can change all of this.

Karen Pryor from the USA has influenced some of the concepts used in dog training today. Her work and the overall concept, operant conditioning, is based on the work of behavioural scientist B. F. Skinner. Dolphin/animal trainers like Karen can teach us a lot about how the concept is used. You would never see a dolphin being physically launched through a hoop by his trainer! The training is done using rewards, but to use them successfully trainers must gain a full understanding of how they work.

Reward based training is dependent on the careful timing and deliverance of rewards. The motivated intelligent trainer can gradually shape the behaviour of the dolphin, or any other animal, to achieve what the trainer wants - so long as the task is within the mental and physical capabilities of the animal. There is a gradual progression to the learning process, getting ever nearer to the goal. Of course there will be set backs, but a good trainer will not worry about these, in fact they will learn from them and get on with the job in hand. An aggressive approach would not give consistent responses and of course is not pleasurable for either the animal or the trainer.

Obviously with dogs we can manipulate the behaviour at much closer contact than the dolphin trainers can, but a reward based method of training still works the best. It creates in the dog's mind a desire to perform and work with you. Without the desire or 'want' to work, the performance in the ring lacks sparkle and natural style. Given the opportunity, the dog will choose to 'opt out' unless he enjoys and is confident in what he does.

This book is split into four sections; first the Concepts and ideology of training, second the Techniques - i.e. the methods of achieving the set exercises, and third Show Craft - how to succeed and give a confident, even professional display. And finally, useful information regarding competitive obedience, abbreviations commonly used, further reading etc.

The best way to use this book is to read part one - the Concepts section first. This will help you to understand about your dog, and the way that the techniques should be approached.

The aim is to enjoy - for both you and your dog. Set your sights high, but your daily aims low. To achieve the goals you must proceed with patience, perseverance, a pleasant and controlled frame of mind, but most of all understanding and compassion.

Section One
The Concepts

This section covers the ideas, underlying concepts and the information to give you the foundation and building blocks to a good working relationship with your dog. Competitive training is not just about understanding the tests and a technique of training, moreover the handler needs a good appreciation of how the dog's mind works, what motivates it and how to deal with individual traits. Some types of dogs have special characteristics that should be taken into consideration before and during training, these too are highlighted in this section.

Understanding the Dog's Mind

What's In It For The Dog?

If you can, imagine the dog's mind working rather like a slot machine or a one armed bandit in an amusement arcade. The machines are set so that they give just enough pay back (reward) to keep you interested. They don't give too much too soon, but just enough to keep you coming back time and time again. In dog training you should use your toys, treats and play times like this, giving just enough to keep your dog thoroughly enthralled and always expectant of further reward - stopping while the dog is still very keen and before the exercise becomes a bore. Always 'pay out' i.e. reward, just enough

to keep him keen, never overdo it, find the amount that he will willingly work for and use it. Tiring him mentally may seem like a good idea, but if it is done in the absence of stimulating handling, it will have a negative result and may send your dog looking for some refreshing novelty or even peace elsewhere.

Once the dog begins to learn that it is fun to be with you, you can start to take on more and more segments of exercises. It is normally best to have the dog on the lead, always using rewards - treats, toys or play to keep the dog close to you and always keeping the dog eager for the next move. It is important that the dog associates fun and enjoyment in close proximity to you. It will be of no use what so ever if your dog's greatest fun comes from chasing a ball down the garden or across the field - he needs to have fun next to you if you are to enjoy close work together.

Communication

Dogs are very aware of body posture and language because this is the main way that they communicate with each other. Therefore, it makes sense for us to use this to our full advantage. Ear carriage, expression, head movements, body posture, respiration rate, pupil dilation and tail carriage can all be observed and will tell us how the dog is feeling but, it does take practice to read the early more subtle signs.

A relaxed dog who is ready for work will have a relaxed yet alert posture - giving the impression that he is ready to spring into action without being over tense. His expression will show general interest, an attentive attitude and bright eyes (pupils should be normal size not dilated). His ears will be carried in a reasonably upright position (depending on the breed) - definitely not held right back. He will not be panting excessively unless he has just had very vigorous exercise (then it is probably not a good time to train anyway).

The old adage that a wagging tail denotes a happy dog is not necessarily always true. The dog wags his tail in anticipation of what is going to happen next. A wagging tail that is held low can be an indication of a very submissive dog - or it could be that he is feeling under pressure - despite the vigorous wag. A high slow wag is a sign of dominance, awareness and a possible challenge. Some dogs that are confident and enjoying the task may wag their tail but, others may hold the tail in a natural position i.e. not tucked and not over high, with more of a sway than a wag. Of course the natural position for a Collie's tail is different to the natural position for an Akita, and even within these breeds there will be variations - therefore individual and breed differences need to be considered too. Watch your dog and find out what is natural for him.

Dogs use eye contact as a means of communicating - a direct stare is usually seen as a challenge and should be avoided. A dog that is confident in his owner may look straight into their eyes with a quizzical expression, an anticipatory excitement, or awaiting command, but you should not enter into a staring match. If you do the dog will start to feel pressured and either look away or possibly even jump at your face. A common problem when teaching the dog to watch is the look away – handlers should consider the intensity of their own gaze – could you be staring and therefore putting your dog under undue pressure?

When the dog is feeling under pressure he will turn his head - an exaggerated way of showing that he is not staring and therefore not challenging. Your dog may start off with a simple flick of the eyes away from yours but, if you miss that signal the dog may follow up with more obvious signs in an attempt to get his message over. In effect he is saying 'didn't you see my signal the first time - back off!' More complex signals such as lip licking and yawning are also signs that the dog is feeling under pressure.

Using Canine Communication

Early detection and response to the signs given by your dog will improve your relationship and speed up the learning process. Animals do not learn effectively when under pressure - when you see the signs act quickly to find another less pressurised way of dealing with the situation. It is also important to try to anticipate the situations that might cause stress for the dog and avoid them by planning your training sessions well.

For example, if you are training a young, inexperienced, sensitive or submissive dog start at the dog's physical level. Sit down on the floor or on a chair, keep at this level for a few sessions until the dog is confident with you and you feel a good bond with the dog. Then gradually rise to an upright position over a few sessions. Any time the dog is unsure come down to his level in this way and give him confidence.

Be careful not to stoop over the dog because this can be oppressive - putting him into a submissive or even a defensive frame of mind. Keep your body upright and make sure you are not staring directly into the dog's eyes.

Look out for the signs of pressure and react straight away but without making a big fuss. Read those first signals and be ready with a different way, a more structured approach, or try to link to something the dog is already good at. If you are not sure what to do simply have a game while you think about it. Relieved of the pressure, the dog should move back into the confident mode straight away - and his confidence in you will grow.

Dogs are very good at picking up our signals, whether intentional or not - it is quite common to see dogs take a position in DC (distance control - test C), on the handler's intake of breath rather than the command. They also pick up signals relating to anger, distress, nerves and intention. We need to learn to control our signals in training and in the ring if we want to avoid confusion and lack of good performance.

Other Behavioural and Physical Influences

Dogs are also influenced by their own bodies - hormones, health, fitness, stamina, muscle power, diet and hunger etc. will all play their part - a competitive dog needs to be fit and feeling good.

The level of mental and physical maturity will also have an important role. Having an understanding of the physical and mental development stages of the dog will help in understanding why certain behaviours occur at various times during the dog's life. For example, most people are very aware of the importance of early socialisation. Around 4-12 weeks of age is the key time although it is very important to continue with this well into adulthood. However, it is less well known that dogs go through periods when they are naturally fearful. At around 8-11 weeks, linking with the time pups would be coming away from the safety of the den and again at 5-14 months, linking with adolescence. Your dog may show the first signs of testing 'who's boss' at around 12-16 weeks of age and then again at the onset of maturity. There are specific times (around 4 - 8 months) when the dog is more likely to want to run off and 'do his own thing'.

All of these stages are normal and important to the dog. Understanding that they will occur and supporting and guiding the dog through them instead of fighting them, will help bring the young animal into adulthood with a confident outgoing nature - much the same as bringing up children.

Instinctive behaviours such as predatory, territorial, social and hierarchical will all come into the equation too. Predatory behaviour is actually used quite a lot as we divert the chasing, possession and hunting elements of predatory behaviour into our retrieving, scent and play routines.

Our level of control is linked to the dog's perception of our hierarchical position - he should see us as under complete control. If this is the case, then territorial behaviours will cease to be important to him as the dog sees us to be looking after that side of things.

Giving the dog quality time and also allowing a certain amount of inter dog socialisation will take care of his instinctive need to be a social animal.

Ways of Learning

One of the most useful styles of learning when training dogs is Operant Conditioning. (Also known as Instrumental Learning or Type 11 Conditioning). The dog learns that his own behaviour will be the cause of an event.

Operant Conditioning - Clicker training is a system that uses operant conditioning and in the case of clicker training it basically means that the dog is working out the behaviour that will achieve his own goal i.e. reward. *(See Clicker and Target Training).*

Trial and Error - this can be linked to operant conditioning. The dog keeps trying different ways of getting to a goal and therefore learns by trial and error.

Observational Learning - this is also used by dogs - i.e. watching other dogs (or even other animals) do something and then copying it. Some dogs are better at observational learning than others. There is evidence of some dogs learning to play tug and to retrieve using this style of learning. However, sometimes it may seem that observational learning is taking place when really the dog is just obsessed by another dog or animal, (particularly if it is moving quickly). This is commonly the case when dogs are watching others doing exercises such as the Retrieve or Sendaway, but that's not to say that dogs can't get the idea by watching - some do.

Flooding - here the animal is literally flooded with a mildly frightening, but non harmful experience, by repeating it or keeping the dog in the situation until he ceases to respond to it. There are dangers in this. If the dog finds the situation particularly stressful, it may increase his anxiety instead of solving the problem.

A better style of making dogs less sensitive to situations would be by *habituation* or *systematic desensitisation*. This is similar to flooding but, done over time in a more gradual way, the dog can build confidence slowly.

Incidental and Latent learning – the dog will pick things up by going through the process, *(incidental)* even though at the time it may seem he does not have the idea. This learning lies dormant *(latent)* until a trigger appears that relates to the behaviour, he may then perform a perfect task, even though you thought at the last session he didn't have a clue.

Previous Experience and Learning

In an attempt to work out what is required, dogs and their handlers will draw upon a variety of areas as explained above, they will also use, to a large extent, the dog's previous experiences. These may be taught by the handler, learnt by trial and error, or indeed learnt as a consequence of other actions or events. Whatever the reason the dog may, if it seems appropriate to him, try to use these experiences to achieve the goal. Handlers can also use this to their advantage by setting up the situation. Sometimes this is useful for example in the case of progressing retrieve on to the scent exercise, but at other times it may cause us problems such as anticipation, apprehension, or confusion. Being aware of this is the closest step to being able to put things right.

Competitive Dogs Need Attitude!

Maintaining the right sort of attitude is important for competitive training - if at any stage the dog looses interest, then stop before you do any lasting damage. The most likely causes are that you are not motivating the dog sufficiently, going too fast and losing the momentum along the way somewhere, or perhaps you have missed out a stage or two. Take a break and consider your options and actions. Go back to square one and build up again slowly. It won't take so long the second time around; you may even be able to identify where you went wrong the first time.

The dog is not vindictive or naughty through choice - although it may be that sometimes he appears that way! The dog's biggest crime is that he does not understand our language - when the wires get crossed he can only save himself - he will react through instinct or previously learnt behaviours whenever he is confused, afraid, or lacks the understanding or motivation necessary for him to carry out the task.

Taking time out, or leaving the training part way through the process until tomorrow, can often result in a much more positive reaction from the dog the next time around. (Possible latent learning taking place). It is better to do this than to stress the dog by over-training and adding to confusion. Try to end on a good point even if it is not the complete desired response.

Chastising incorrect actions is counterproductive. It merely serves to release your tensions and unfortunately will confuse the dog even more.

When the dog has done something wrong you should stop, find a way of preventing the incorrect behaviour, and then start again.

The dog cannot think back in the same way that we can, he simply reacts to situations as they happen. We cannot explain to him which bits were wrong because he does not understand our language. If you teach simple commands such as 'leave' or 'off' or 'wrong' in a constructive way - then you can use them to prevent or deter unwanted actions. If you do stop him in mid flight with a command when he is on the wrong track, then that should be the end of it, and you must follow up with positive guidance and reward for the correct reaction to your command.

A dog trained by corrective means i.e. a dog that is allowed to go wrong and is then corrected stands out like a sore thumb in the ring. This is because he will be constantly correcting his own errors as he works.

Intelligence And The Competitive Dog

Trying to decide how clever the dog is always a difficult issue. Intelligence is relative and linked to survival and perpetuation rather than sendaway and scent! Different breeds have developed different characteristics - the collie (Working sheepdog or Border collie) has become the most popular dog for competitive obedience because of its agile body, quick reactions and obsessive nature - does this mean it is the cleverest breed? In obedience we tend to measure intelligence by the speed of the dog's response to the set exercises and the style with which he performs. In a domestic environment the level of sensitivity may be a measure of intelligence, can the dog detect and react to the moods of its owner? Working trials handlers would be more impressed by a

good nose than a stylish head position. What you want from the dog and perhaps your experience of other dogs will largely govern how you rate intelligence.

Dogs are quite capable of linking two events or ideas, however they are not capable of making that link if the ideas or events are separated by time unless there is some way of triggering the connection.

True, not all dogs are extraordinarily 'competitive obedience bright' and some of us will be lucky and experience that 'dog of a lifetime' that seems ideally suited to our situation and desires. However, obedience is not so difficult - almost all dogs can achieve if taught in a way that they can understand - some will take longer than others, some will enjoy more repetition than others. Some might not have the stamina or drive (even if it is a Border collie) to go right to the top - but that shouldn't stop you enjoying the dog you have. One should think of dogs as we do people - all very different. Finding the way through to create a good working team - is truly the mark of a good dog trainer, the more difficult the dog the more you will learn.

You must learn to take time out, to sit back and think about your errors as well as your achievements, to back track and to start again takes a strong will. But, when you have reached the stage where you can confidently start again - then you really are starting to understand the philosophy of training, and soon you will be on the road to a successful relationship with your dog and to ultimately become a 'Happy Winner'.

Starting with a Puppy

Where do you start when your pup is destined for obedience? If you are lucky enough to be about to start with a new puppy, then there are many factors that will have an effect on the ultimate attitude and behaviour of your dog. Moulding the pup in the correct manner can help to prevent problems later on. Much of this moulding can be done quite easily and sometimes quite inadvertently. However, if you are not fully aware of the pup's natural development you can mould him in the wrong way, not realising that certain problems could have been avoided, whilst other behaviours could have been positively enhanced with the correct start.

The perfect time to be reading this section is prior to getting your new dog, but if you have already got him, pick up where most applicable. Read through all the concept sections because this will help you to understand any behaviour that your pup is already displaying, and will also assist you to mould and form a suitable and enjoyable bond with your dog.

Before You Buy Your Pup

Do your homework. Of course it is helpful to study bloodlines and look at how dogs from those lines have performed, from an obedience point of view but, more importantly, from a health and temperament point of view. Look objectively at your proposed animals and discuss if possible, the lifestyle which has been adopted by owners of these types of dog. Don't be content to just speak to one individual owner, ask several. If possible, find someone of a similar age, time allowance and outlook on life as you, to discuss the dogs with. Some breeds are highly active and have an extremely strong working drive. Some lines within a breed have more of those characteristics than others. Even some individuals within litters have stronger versions of certain types of behaviour than their littermates. 'Fast to learn', means fast to learn both right and wrong! You have to be sure you are mentally agile and quick-witted, as well as reasonably fit to deal effectively with the sort of dog that may turn out to be a 'work-a-holic'. On the other hand, you may be the type of person who has the mental and physical capabilities to live and work with a live wire. It does not always follow that the hyperactive dog makes a good obedience dog. If the dog is very obsessive some people may struggle to get the dog to concentrate. A calmer dog may be more bidable and easier to train for some. Dominant type breeds will not suit some people's character, just as submissive types will not appeal to others - there truly is a lot to consider. So think carefully and don't forget you have to live with this dog as well as take it into the obedience ring!

Dog or Bitch?

In general bitches are a little easier to deal with than dogs, in that they are not driven to quite the same degree by the need to be in control. Having said that bitches are not an easy push over, there are very many strong character, challenging bitches. Fights between bitches are often more fierce than between dogs. A bitch with a strong character in the right hands will make a very good working dog, because that strength can be moulded in the correct direction. A very dominant male dog can be difficult for the uninitiated to handle, but the same rule applies to both sexes, if you harness the strength correctly it will work for you. If you are just beginning in the field of dog training it will make life easier for you if you choose a less dominant animal. But, basically it comes down to personal choice. If in doubt take a more experienced handler with you to look at pups and help you get a feel for the right sort of dog – but be careful – is what your friend likes really suitable for you?

Where to Buy

Once you are sure that you are looking for the correct type of dog to suit your personality and lifestyle, then you have to decide where to get it. The obvious choice is a breeder, but you may wish to help one of the many unwanted puppies or young adults by going to a rescue establishment. Unless you go for a specific breed, the problem with rescue pups is that you are never quite sure what you are going to get.

Choosing a dog tends to be a bit of a lottery, and even with the best advice in the world you can never be 100% sure of what you are going to end up with - if it were so easy the breeders would have all the best dogs!

Border collie/Working sheepdog types are very common inhabitants of rescue centres, particularly when they reach the age of 7 to 12 months. This is when - as they hit adolescence and the start of adulthood - they really start to become a handful for the ordinary pet owner. Obedience handlers can benefit from this, the collie at this age is ready to get started and raring to go! If it doesn't have too many hang ups the rescue collie can very soon be a dog to be proud of - particularly if you already have a bit of experience.

If you go to a specific breed rescue and tell them what you are after they will try to match the ideal dog to you. So don't discount the idea of rescue before you have had a look.

It takes experience, a great deal of study, and a bit of intuition to be able to choose the correct dog for you from a litter, or even several litters of pups.

Using puppy assessment tests can help you to identify the potential for strong play drive, social attraction, noise and body sensitivity, dominance etc. There are many assessors around the country some charge a small fee for their services and as with anything some are very good at carrying out the tests and analysing the results and others less so. The best and most reliable reports are done in conjunction with information given by the breeder about general character, experience etc. *(There is more information on puppy testing in 'Puppies, Your Successful Guide to Dog Ownership' Angela White, 1997. ISBN 185279023-7. Published by TFH/Kingdom.)*

When to Get Your Pup

In a perfect world, with the breeder doing his/her job properly, both from the point of view of general care and also socialising the litter with other animals, noises, environments, etc., the best age to obtain your pup is around seven to

eight weeks of age. The importance of early social learning cannot be underestimated. The pup must have the opportunity of learning correct dog behaviour and communication from other dogs in order to be able to happily interact with other dogs later on. You must help him to develop his hunting skills through play, just as his littermates would have done, because this natural behaviour will be needed later to help mould the obedience training.

The pup must learn bite inhibition so that he never bites and hurts. He would learn this from his siblings in the normal progression of play. If he bites too hard with those needle sharp teeth, the other pup will withdraw from the game, therefore, in order to keep playing, the pup learns to inhibit the force of his bite - a vital lesson for the future days living with humans.

Dogs descend from wolves, and they are, in their behaviour, extremely similar (and yet in many ways they are worlds apart!) We can make many comparisons to help us understand our dogs. In the wild situation the den or cave where the young are reared is a relatively safe environment. Therefore, the pups have developed an inherent, accepting attitude to this environment and during the early periods of their lives, accept that they would naturally remain in this safe environment. When they reach the age of around twelve weeks which is when they would, in the wild state, be coming out of the safe area, they are genetically programmed (as a defence mechanism) to be wary of new environments, animals and objects that they come into contact with. The reason for this is that in the wild habitat anything that the mother didn't introduce the pup to may in fact be a predator and therefore must be treated with extreme caution (at least until proven friendly, of no consequence or safe.)

If, during this early learning period, the dog has not had the opportunity of learning that meeting new things is a fun experience, then problems will, without a doubt occur. When you attempt to teach the dog that your environment and the objects and animals within it, are safe and enjoyable he may well be very fearful. That is not to say that it is an impossible situation to sort out, but it is much more difficult, time consuming and testing on your patience. However, it certainly helps you to deal with the resultant problems, when you understand the reasons behind them. Accepting that it is normal behaviour will help you to remain controlled and confident and hopefully pass this attitude over to your dog.

Adult dogs that lack the early social learning should be dealt with like puppies. They should be gently encouraged and introduced to anything new. You need to be constantly aware of the problem, use play and common bonds to help your dog to learn how to deal with new situations. At the same time it is important not to be over protective - if the situation is safe often it is good to just give the dog time to come to terms with it.

Armed with an understanding of normal dog development you can decide on the type of environment you would like to obtain your pup from, and at what age. If you are determined to have an older pup you must assess his attitude towards new environments, animals, sounds, objects and yourself. Decide whether there are any major problems. If so, have you the ability, knowledge and facilities to deal with them effectively and, will his attitude have a lasting or recurrent effect on his obedience career? If so does this matter to you? Remember; be fair to the dog by being honest with yourself.

Choosing the Pup

For some people, even some top handlers, choosing a pup is very straight forward - the one that looks right - the colour or markings suit their idea of a good looking animal - and that is the one for them! But for others, choosing a pup is never a straightforward process, preferring to take a more informed approach, but then there are still no guarantees!

You must give careful thought to what you actually want and expect. You must try to view the pups at various times of the day if possible, and listen to how the breeder describes their behaviour, in order to make an objective decision. Some pups may at first appear to be quiet, but you may have caught them after they have just spent an hour playing. To give you an example of this; I chose a dog pup for a handler saying that in my view, after many hours of watching, the pup was the best of the bunch for an obedience dog. He was very playful and often woke before the others and played with

toys or me before the rest of the litter was stirring. The prospective owner turned up each evening after work just as this pup was tiring, and finding a cosy corner to go to sleep, but the rest of the pups were just waking up. It took all my powers of persuasion to convince the handler that the pup was a real star. That dog subsequently became a superb and consistent Obedience Champion, and was Top Obedience Dog of the Year in Great Britain for two years on the trot!

What Should You Look For?

For an obedience dog certain behaviours, that can be detected at an early stage, (around 6 weeks of age) can give you a positive advantage:

a) A people dog - does the pup respond to people at least as much as he does to the other pups? Does he readily leave his littermates to come to say 'hello' to you?

b) Voice and sound sensitivity - does he respond to your voice? Try making differing tones and watch his response.

c) Touch sensitivity - we don't want him to jump out of his skin when touched, but on the other hand he should notice and turn to see what is touching him!

d) Movement aware - see if he will playfully follow a small toy, a leaf or a feather. Remember that very young pups have difficulty focusing upwards, so wave the article around in front of his nose to get his attention.

e) Playful - he must want to play and readily join in games that are instigated by you or the other pups.

f) Investigative - he should not be unduly perturbed by new introductions into his environment, and after possibly a moment to take it in, should be going forward to investigate.

When choosing a pup for an experienced, knowledgeable and competent handler to work the above factors should firstly be taken into account. Then, from the most likely puppies, (eliminating any that just didn't appeal because of appearance or just plain gut feeling) choose the one with the strongest character. The pup who instigates games, the one who the others give in to, the one who is at the feed bowl first, and stands his ground, the one who plays hunting games like waiting in ambush, pouncing, standing over his siblings etc. This pup whether male or female will make a good basis to create the type of working dog that the competitive handler wants; keen, lively, outgoing, yet bidable with sensitivity.

Choosing a pup for someone just starting out in training, for a more sedate, gentle or submissive personality or for a child, for a less agile or less knowledgeable person; again consider the first factors but then choose a much less dominant one. The quieter pup that is more inclined to cuddle may be more appropriate.

Try this test; pick up the pup, handle him positively and with care, turn him on his back and see if he accepts this restriction, if he struggles immediately and vigorously he may not be the pup for less experienced hands. All pups will eventually wriggle, but if they more inclined to accept your manipulation this is a good sign, particularly for the novice.

Where To Keep Your Pup

Before you go to collect your pup decide where he is going to sleep, where he will spend his days, and have food, toys and blankets ready for his arrival. It is important that you establish a bond with your pup. If you have other dogs in the household, obviously you will want the pup to spend some time with them, but on the other hand he must learn to be alone sometimes too. He also needs to play with you and learn that the fun and games do not come solely from the other dogs. Therefore, if he is to live indoors a crate or indoor kennel will be a good investment. The security will give him a safe environment away from the hustle and bustle of the house, and will double as an ideal travelling cage.

If the dog is to be kennelled, then it is best if he can have his own individual kennel and run - but this depends on whether you have enough time to give him social stimulus. Obviously you must not leave the pup crated or kennelled for hours on end; he is a social animal and needs company in order to develop correctly. If you do have to leave him for more than a couple of hours on a regular basis, you should seriously consider giving him a companion.

By having an arrangement where by you are able to control the dog physically, you will be able to also control his behavioural development much more, and he will learn to follow your lead. Your dog will know where he stands, and that you are in control. The crate gives him a retreat where he can safely go out of harm's way if he wishes or when you decide the time is right, when he is tired, when you go out, or when you are too busy to concentrate on him and prevent him getting into mischief. This control will help to make him grow into a well-adjusted individual. Ideally, if you have another social dog, your pup will get some canine company too.

Crate and kennel training is relatively simple, it is a matter of waiting until the pup is very tired, hungry, or he wants to have a good chew. Then just pop him in with the appropriate item, i.e. blanket, food or chew bone. Often a cover over the crate or an enclosed area of the kennel will make the pup feel more secure. A quiet setting for the crate or kennel is a good idea so that the pup does not become distressed watching activity going on outside. Build up the time he is enclosed, and always give him a treat as he enters the crate or kennel. Some pups adjust quicker than others do. Sometimes sitting with him until he settles works best, for others it works better if you leave quickly to start with so that he can't see you. Work towards the situation where he is in his crate or kennel and is content to stay there while you carry on your business outside. A supply of his favourite chews or biscuits often does the trick teaching him that it is rewarding to be in his own environment but, most of all, be patient. At 8 weeks the pup will be still very reliant on company, so any isolation needs to be built up very gradually. After 12 weeks of age the dog is more independent and can cope with a slightly quicker progression - but you will still need to build up carefully to give the dog confidence and avoid building in anxiety and its related behaviours.

Taking Him Home

The journey home may be your pup's first ever trip anywhere. Consider the trauma. Isolated from your family, strange people restraining you, you are placed in a moving environment, strange smells, strange shapes, strange feelings, in fact just about everything is strange and new. The competitive obedience dog will spend a lot of time travelling around the country in cars or vans, so don't make that first journey a severe trauma. Ideally let someone else drive, so that you can concentrate on the pup. Take along plenty of towels in case he is sick, nervous tummies are very common in young pups. You are very fortunate if the pup doesn't have a *little accident* of some sort.

If you have been going to view the pups on a regular basis you will not be completely new to the pup. Hold him gently but firmly and talk in a soothing voice, stroke him and help him to accept this frightening experience. A familiar smell can be of help too, a piece of bedding or soft toy from the breeder, even if it is one that you have supplied previously, to absorb the smell of the litter, will provide a familiar scent to help the pup settle.

The New Lead and Collar

All dogs that are to go out into a public environment must wear a collar and identity tag, (engraved with your name and address) and of course we need an anchor to which we can attach our arm extension - 'the lead'. Puppy collars should be soft and gentle, a soft webbing or nylon with a buckle fastener. Avoid hard bulky leather to start with, although the next collar (when he is bigger) which you purchase for him may be good quality bridle leather if you wish. Certainly avoid chain or any other harsh material as these are totally unnecessary, and may damage the pup's tender neck and vertebrae.

Some pups will react in an extreme manner to the first time they have something around their neck. Remember that the neck area is where another dog or animal would attack them and so they may react as though they are being attacked when you initially try out the new collar. As always be patient, leave the collar loose and distract the pup with a game, some treats or a chew until he realises that the collar does not pose a threat.

Once the pup has become accustomed to the collar and had a few days to adjust, try attaching the lead. Choose an appropriate soft leather, webbing or rope lead, with a safe trigger hook fastener. Again you may get an adverse reaction, but distract and play with him allowing the pup to drag the lead around and he will soon come to accept it.

Now you can start to teach the dog to enjoy the lead, producing toy and lead at the same time, hold on to the lead whilst you play with him. Every so often he will become restricted by the lead, distract and encourage him back towards you with the toy. Soon the pup will see his lead and know it is playtime. This attitude will be extremely useful when you start to mould his play into obedience exercises.

Building a Bond

You must make the first few days of the dog's new life with you as happy as possible. He must learn that you are someone that he can trust at all times. Take control of his life and start as you mean to go on. Provide him with a safe haven in which to sleep and put him there when you know that he is tired. Produce toys and play with him when you know he will be playful, and feed him when you know he is hungry. Notice the way that I am approaching the subject - putting you in control all of the time. This is how you and every dog owner should begin and indeed carry on throughout the dog's life. Don't wait for him to instigate behaviours, you must control his lifestyle. This approach will be beneficial in two important ways, firstly you will prevent your dog becoming dominant over you, (dominance is one of the most common behavioural problems.) Secondly your dog will look to you at all times, as his team leader, and will be constantly checking with you that he is on the right track.

Play, for an animal of predatory background, is the most important feature of learning. His reasons for living at the very basic level are food and sex, i.e. self-preservation and to perpetuate the species. His hunting skills are naturally learnt while he is still in the litter with his brothers and sisters. We normally take him away from this a little early and so we must continue to develop these skills. We can now take the opportunity to channel the play/predatory behaviour into the types of skills that will be useful to the dog's obedience career later on.

Play works as a reward in development and training, because it has a very basic link to survival. It is the primary behaviour behind hunting, hunting means food, food means survival.

Like children, dogs benefit from 'Quality time'. Time spent nagging and getting annoyed with the pup will be counterproductive. Time spent in positive play, socialisation and environment exploration will be of far more benefit to you both.

How to play with your pup is covered in the section on 'The Want', and this section will also help you to develop some of the skills needed to form a bond.

A bond is all about trust, confidence and enjoyment. If you control your dog and his environment you will be able to trust him because you will learn to predict his actions. If you are fair and do not try to trick your dog he will learn to trust you. In order to reap most benefit from these early days you need to learn about *'Understanding the Dog's Mind'*, *'Motivation'*, *'Timing'*, and *'Play Training'*, all of which are covered in the concepts section.

The more you understand your dog, and learn to implement that understanding, the more he respects and trusts you, and the greater the bond. Work with your dog until you know how he will react in any given circumstance, expected or unexpected. Play with him until you can turn him onto 'play mode' at any time and anywhere. Handle, groom and massage his body until he readily accepts your touch and enjoys it. Continue this throughout his life to maintain your relationship in tiptop condition.

The Want

What is the 'Want'?

The 'Want' is not about you wanting to win a ticket, a class or even to just win out of Beginners. No - the 'Want' is the mental and physical condition that you need to develop in your dog so that each time you use a keyword - for instance 'Watch', 'Heel', or 'Retrieve', the dog says - in no uncertain terms - 'Yes please, I want to work with you!'

All dogs are different of course; therefore the degree of power behind this yearning will be variable depending upon many things for example genetics, past experience, even hormones! If you have a more sensitive or quieter type dog he may not be in such a hell bent fury to get into the heel position. But, having said that all training should be aimed at teaching the dog to enjoy working with you, and therefore develop, in ever-increasing degrees, the 'Want'.

The 'Want' can only be achieved and maintained by teaching yourself how to keep the dog interested and excited in everything that you try to achieve. Even when you carry out a sequence of training or an exercise incorrectly, if the dog has the 'Want', then you can laugh and start again. The dog will not be unhappy and you will not have spoilt his spirit, as long as you have not lost your temper and blamed the dog for your error. Bear in mind that if the dog behaves incorrectly then your training methods and your timing should be carefully scrutinised. Dogs are not out to prove you wrong or wind you up (although at times it feels that way). Errors are caused by a number of things including; misunderstanding (on both parts – yours and the dogs), external influence, physical and emotional disturbances, frustration, fear, excitement, changes in your handling (often minute and hardly detectable by humans), etc. There are just so many reasons that it takes careful analysis to find them and sometimes you will not be able to identify the problem. It is far better to simply look at your technique, attitude and timing and try again.

Those who think that the dog is wrong should look carefully at themselves. The dog is being taught these exercises, which on the whole are most unnatural, and the teacher is the so-called intelligent animal at the end of the lead. A bad teacher will produce an ill-prepared pupil! There is nothing natural for a dog in walking to the heel and looking up at a human, sitting straight in a precise manner, or performing multiple position changes for no apparent reason. So, to teach these things you must gain the confidence and trust of your dog and teach him to enjoy learning new things with you and to perform with exuberance and accuracy the exercises that he already knows.

Teaching Your Dog To Want

With some dogs the 'Want' comes more easily than it does with others. Even the very keen, lively type of dog needs to be channelled into wanting what you want! Teaching your dog to play is a very important factor, but you must observe your dog's reactions carefully and try to see things from the dog's point of view. Be sure that he realises that he is playing and interacting with you and not just with a toy or other item.

The importance of learning to read your dog cannot be emphasised enough. Learn to anticipate your dog's actions then, steer him away from undesirable traits, and encourage him whole-heartedly in the things that you want him to do. It never ceases to amaze me how I can very accurately predict how other people's dogs are going to react in a given situation, just by watching the dog with their handler for a few moments. Yet, time and time again, the handler in question is taken completely by surprise by their dog's actions or reactions.

You must learn to think about your own reactions and those of the dog. If your dog always reacts in a certain way, and this is not what you are aiming for, then you must be doing something (or failing to do something) which makes or even just allows him to react so.

You need to consider how to change the behaviour pattern so that he performs in the right way, rather than what to do when he does it wrong. This will help him to have confidence and look to you for the next move – thus improving his attitude towards working with you.

How To Get The 'Want'

Achieving the 'Want' should be a carefully planned, yet natural procedure. You should make sure that you are always in a position to help the dog to enjoy and be confident at each and every step of your training. The chapters on *play training, toys, motivation* and *timing* will help you.

Assuming all of the above chapters have been read, put into use and thoroughly understood, then you can start your daily routine to teach your dog to 'Want'. Even if you think he is already keen, it will be worth following a set routine to make sure he really wants what you think he wants. It can take time - and a dog on which mistakes have already been made will often take longer than a young dog at the outset of his training.

All of the initial training can be done in the comfort of your own front room, or a quiet corner in the garden. So long as you and the dog are comfortable and confident in your surroundings then it's fine. This point is an important factor in the training procedure; the surroundings must not be frightening or distracting, at least not to start with, as this will make both the dog's concentration and your own, waver.

Having decided upon your location then you may commence your training by following these stages: -

Step 1 - First the dog needs to enjoy being on the lead. Therefore teach him to 'Want' to be on the lead. If he doesn't like the lead, then over a period of time you need to do pleasurable things like feeding him his meals, and playing with him while he is on the lead. Eventually, with patience, he will come to associate the lead with pleasure. Don't try to move on until this is achieved.

With dogs who have already gone through the sort of harsh, old fashioned 'heel - check' training procedure, this simple start of training on the lead may be a major stumbling block, because the lead may have an immediate negative influence on the dog. Therefore, if the dog is unhappy or frightened treat him like a puppy; sit or kneel down on the floor or at least come down to dog level. Let him trail his lead while you feed him his meals or titbits, play or simply have a cuddle. Vary what you do, but everything should be working towards building a trust bond with the emphasis of compulsion taken away from the lead. Take your time and be patient eventually his confidence will build. He must learn by your good handling and fair attitude that nothing horrible is going to happen just because he is on lead. In fact eventually he must realise that much pleasure can be derived from the lead and the 'new you'.

Read your Dog - only move on to the next stages when you are sure he is becoming happy and confident. If you have a young puppy, then this can be your first step, playing and cuddling on the floor, gently introducing little playful tugs on the lead to bring him towards you for pleasure and security. Tease him with a toy or knotted rag, keeping hold of the lead all of the time so that the dog is never far away from you. Encourage the dog towards you continually by bringing the toy or game close to your body and following it up with lots of cuddles. If the dog is more focused on titbits then use his favourite type to build up the attitude. Most dogs respond well to movement so even if using titbits, move your hand around so the pup follows the reward rather than just giving it to him. Start with small movements and short sessions and build up over time as the dog responds favourably.

You are now using the lead as an extension to your arm, and never should any aggression be forthcoming if you want your dog to enjoy being trained, to enjoy being by your side, and to 'Want' to be a team with you.

Step 2 - Progress with a few short sessions, as above, each day. Never going on too long so that the dog becomes bored. Read your dog so that you always leave him 'wanting' more. You will soon see the first stages of the 'Want' developing as the dog looks to you for fun.

It is important to realise that all dogs are different, and there can be no set time limit on training and developing a bond. Much depends on your ability to read your dog, to get your timing right and indeed, how many negative factors like bad training or loss of temper have occurred in the past. It may be the case that you must change your whole attitude towards your dog and then, you have the task of convincing your poor canine friend that you have changed! As one enlightened young woman on one of my summer camps proudly proclaimed to her dog 'You've got a new Mummy!'

Step 3 - The next stage of the training procedure is to get over the message to the dog that you are that same trustworthy person in a different place or environment, to once again win your dog's confidence and then, induce enjoyment and fun in varying circumstances. He needs to know that things can be fun with you in every situation and that varying environments are not to be feared or found too distracting. So choose another quiet place, maybe another room in your house, or any familiar area and start the training again - from **the beginning.**

Remember your top aim is to teach your dog to 'Want' to work in all situations; at any show, anywhere in the country, and not to find other external factors more stimulating, more rewarding or even just more comfortable and less boring. The dog must be happy and contented with you everywhere, so you must teach him that you are his best friend in any situation!

Developing this bond is the most important thing you will ever do, so take your time and make sure each step of the way, the dog learns to trust and want to be with you. This is not a time for lapsing into long stretches of heelwork or going through any other exercises which you may have already taught. It is a time for bonding, trusting and learning to play together as a team; you are laying the foundations for your future.

Once you are confident that you have achieved this you can then start to incorporate a few keywords, together with gentle guidance into physical actions that the dog will learn to respond to automatically later on.

If you have made mistakes in the past or, if you know you always get a submissive or negative reaction to certain words, then now is a good time to change some of those words. If in the past for instance, your dog has been yanked or harshly checked into the heel position on the command 'heel' - it might be easier for you to get a good association by changing to another keyword like 'close'. The fewer bad associations the dog has the easier it will be for you as a trainer to help your dog to enjoy his work.

Once the dog is keen, take him into differing situations to ensure he is keen no matter what the circumstances.

Step 4 - To incorporate formal teaching into the 'Want' attitude, probably the easiest word and action to start with is 'sit'. Making sure you have a hold of the lead, play with the dog in front of you, (sit or kneel on the floor if you are teaching a puppy or small dog because you don't want to over power him). Then, when the dog is in a good position place him into the sit position and simultaneously give your 'sit' keyword. Use a titbit or your toy in your right hand positioned above his head to motivate and angle him back into position. You can use the flat of your hand on his rump to help if you want to. If your dog has been roughly handled in the past it will be better to use the reward only and keep your hands off for now. *(See Teaching Static Positions - Sit)*. You should not say to yourself, 'Right I'm going to sit him now', and then attempt to do it. It is better to relax into the situation and place him only when you know that you can get a good and positive result - without being harsh, rough or having to over handle the dog. Even if it takes a little longer for you to get yourself organised, a natural and unforced approach will reap much better and more confident results than a fumbled, awkward and forced manner.

Just keep the dog in position for a very few seconds and then release by introducing a keyword that will, in the future, tell him that he can relax and come out of position - for example 'OK' or 'that'll do'. By introducing a word to say to the dog that you've finished, there is never any doubt in the dog's mind whether he should be still sitting there or not. By removing doubt you are looking to a future with a confident, accurate dog.

During these sessions you still have the dog on lead of course. Continue to play, cuddle and instil confidence and pleasure. You must work together as a team and build on the bond, which will give you the 'Want'. Don't - just because we have introduced a keyword - become all formal or revert back to your old rigid ways, keep your training light with fun. There should be no difference in attitude, from you or the dog, whether playing or carrying out exercises. Gone is the 'Let him know he's working' attitude. This has been replaced by a situation that is fun and enjoyable and so instils confidence in you and the dog and indeed to all who observe from outside. If you are doing your job correctly, the dog will be asking to be worked rather than having to be told.

The attitude and theory applied in teaching the 'Want' can be adopted in teaching all exercises. Each individual training exercise is covered under it's own section within the book later on. Developing the 'Want' by means of trust building, bonding, reward and play will help you in all of your training. It will teach you how to read your dog and even if it takes time, you will find that it is worth persevering, saving months - if not years of heartache and frustration later on.

Fun and Enjoyment

It is pointless entering into a sport as a free time activity, or even as a way of life, if you are not going to enjoy it, you may as well have stayed at home and bred gerbils or taken up flower arranging! Both of which I'm sure are fun, but the point is, if training and competition work is what you have chosen, then make up your mind to enjoy every minute!

The very fact that you enter a competition indicates that you would like to win or at the very least, achieve some degree of success. This does not have to be achieved with a negative or harsh approach and, as I hope you will appreciate, especially after you have read this book, training and competing should be and can be fun for both you and your dog.

Of course there are times when you will be tense. For instance those times when you are leading your class with only scent discrimination or the stay exercises to do. Similarly those occasions when you feel that you stand a good chance of winning or being placed because the particular judge whose class you are in likes your style of dog. But, you should not let your nerves or your desire to win get in the way of your good principles, nor take over to the detriment of your dog's mental or physical well being. There is always another show. If you want your dog to remain consistent,

you must take these things in your stride, particularly if you want to stand a good chance of winning next week as well! Good dog trainers learn to keep calm at all times, some even take up yoga to help maintain the equilibrium!

In schools nowadays, children are taught with a friendly, guided, constructive approach. Good teachers instantly earn the children's attention and respect. Corporal punishment has long been a thing of the past. In the schools where the teachers have understood the good practice of motivational teaching, it has been demonstrated that children learn quickly and thoroughly, much more so than those taught with a more negative attitude. The more laid back, gentle approach - incorporating play with learning, while still maintaining control and setting rules, brings out the individuality and confidence in young children as well as more mature students. Even within a single group of children, behaviour patterns are very different when the children are faced with a good teacher.

Likewise corporal punishment should be ruled out for dogs. It makes even less sense in the case of dogs, because of the type of memory a dog has, he rarely connects the punishment with the crime. *(See Understanding the Dog's Mind)*.

So let us enjoy our friend the dog. Take time to understand his abilities and limitations. Teach through play and reward, provide motivation and teach in a way that the dog can understand. Give the dog reason to 'want' to be with you, and create a team spirit.

Making competition work fun for both dog and handler gives the onlooker something worth watching. It promotes the sport and gives it meaning and credibility. No one likes to see animals under pressure or unhappy, so practise what you preach and keep it fun, and then sit back and watch the positive reactions.

All exercises - without exception - can be taught with a caring, no force, fun approach. In doing this you do not need to forgo the standard, in fact your dog will glow amongst the best. Understand your dog, don't be afraid to stand back and watch something that is not quite correct, because by doing this you can find for yourself new ways to make understanding the exercise easier and more fun for both you and the dog.

When things go wrong analyse and be objective. Teach with love, patience, care and motivation. The dog will follow what he thinks is the correct course of action; it is up to you to guide him into what you want. When he goes wrong, stop and ask yourself WHY? Count to ten and go back to the drawing board. Most of all remember the dog did not ask to get involved, he's there because you want it to be so. Treat him with respect, and enjoy one of the most rewarding relationships known to mankind.

Timing

Perfect timing can mean the difference between teaching the dog what you want to achieve and alas, teaching the complete opposite! Yes, it can be and often is, as crucial as that.

I'm sure that you can all think of friends, acquaintances or even times when you yourself have struggled week after week, month after month, sometimes even year after year, trying to teach the dog certain exercises with only negative results. Often despondent, handlers give up in desperation, ask someone else to teach the dog for them, or worst of all, give up on the dog all together, passing him on to someone else, labelling the dog stupid. Although I describe the last statement as 'worst of all', perhaps, in all honesty, the dog will actually be better off in more caring, sympathetic or knowledgeable hands!

One of the exercises that causes the most problems is the retrieve. Many handlers struggle needlessly through lack of understanding, or incorrect application of, 'timing'. Other exercises, it seems, can often be blundered through, over a period of time. Without good timing the results are not as perfect as the handler might like, but if he gets it right enough of the time, the dog starts getting the message - of sorts! The 'blunder' approach unfortunately is not so productive when teaching the retrieve.

Retrieve is a complex task requiring many different sections to be perfected, before the exercise can be carried out with the accuracy required for competition. Incorrect timing can often result in the exact opposite of what the handler is trying to achieve. More precise details are given in the section on retrieve but, this particular exercise is the perfect example to illustrate the importance of good timing.

Remember the way the dog's mind works - he is thinking of what is happening to him 'now'. Imagine yourself in the dog's place; your human prises open your mouth, pops in this 'thing', and says 'Hold'. He then takes it out of your mouth - he might say 'Give' at the same time. You release the article and he says 'Well done good dog' in a pleasant tone. So, the next time he again pops the article in your mouth it triggers your reaction for reward, which must be to 'SPIT IT OUT' as it was only when you gave up the 'thing' the last time that you were rewarded. You step back; wagging your tail, waiting for the praise which must surely follow.

Your human then goes into one of his rages, 'Bad dog, Stupid dog!' he says. What an unpredictable and confusing human you have! Eventually he calms down and tries again, this time you try even harder to give it up quickly, the human goes frantic! Perhaps the human does not want you to take the article at all; after all nothing pleasant has ever happened when it has been in your mouth! So the next time you turn your head away trying to avoid the nasty object, clamping your mouth tight shut, you didn't particularly like it anyway and absolutely no pleasure can be associated with it. The human tries to catch hold of your mouth, and ram the article in, you clamp shut - at last it has worked, the human walks away muttering something about tomorrow! Well at last you have got the idea; the human wants you to totally ignore the nasty thing! No problem!

So there we have a perfect example of how, by praising at the wrong time, the dog can totally misinterpret your actions. Think how you could teach your dog NOT to retrieve, it is not so far away from the above description? But this practice is seen going on all over the world under the inappropriate title of 'dog training'.

So when teaching any exercise or task, praise, motivation and encouragement must come at the very time the dog is performing correctly, or when he is showing signs of understanding what is required. When teaching something new or progressing a part-trained exercise, the encouragement must coincide with the guidance into the action to achieve the required results. It is too late afterwards, even half a second afterwards is too late. Remember the dog relates the reward, praise, or chastisement to what he is doing at the time it is issued.

The dog can be conditioned to enjoy the sound of a clicker which will mean to the dog that his reward is coming, and this can be a good aid to help the handler perfect their timing. *(See Rewards and Clicker Training)*

All of this can be rather a difficult concept for humans to understand. Our powers of forward and backward and indeed 'sideways' thinking are most advanced, but because of our powers we are able, with a little practise to understand, to some degree, how the dog perceives the world, although non of us will truly have all of the answers. Once we have good understanding, dog training comes much more easily to us.

It is a good idea to practise getting your timing right on an inanimate object. I often demonstrate using a stuffed dog puppet, 'Oscar'.

Oscar helps me to put things over without me putting a dog through the misery of mishandling. You can practise using the retrieve as an example. Pretend that your left hand is the dog's mouth. Place the article for him to hold into your left hand. Reward at the right time. See how hard it is to get your timing perfect, especially if you've been getting it wrong for a long time. It takes practise but it is better to get it right without the dog. The secret is to make sure that the part that you are rewarding is the part that you are trying to teach. Instead of using your own hand you could use a friend or partner. This timing of reward and keywords concept can then be transferred to all exercises.

If you are using clicker training the timing of the click is the crucial point. Rewards can come afterwards. *(See Clicker training.)*

Getting words, rewards, signals, even body movements in just the right places takes a lot of practice and perseverance on your part. The timing of where and how you place your feet in heelwork, the placing of your hands, your stance relating to the dog's action all have to be spot on to gain the perfection needed for the ring. A good way to analyse yourself is to have someone video you so that you can see for yourself. Also an experienced handler can pick up on the minor points that are difficult for you to spot yourself. However, when working with someone else be careful to not jump into change things in a drastic way – discuss and consider the options and although at times it gets pretty serious, remember to keep it fun.

The speed at which your dog will learn when you start to get things right could be dramatic. Your dog can be taught many new things, test exercises and tricks just for fun. Each task is approached in the same attitude of mind, perfect timing, motivation, fun and a clear idea of what you are trying to achieve. The end results will be exciting, satisfying and fun for both your and the dog.

Motivation and Drive

Motivation is what a dog needs to carry out a given task. In order to feel motivated he needs to see some sort of purpose and desirable end product. Motivation requires some sort of cognition.

Drive is more linked to a physical need, for example food and sex. The dog's predatory, pack and defensive instinctive behaviours will play a big part in the way he behaves. At times it may feel like you are struggling against these drives, at other times they will help you to achieve your goals.

Dogs vary in the way that these drives evolve. Some dogs have very high drives in some areas but not in others. For example a retrieve or chase mad dog could be said to be high in predatory drive. A dog that wants always to be with you or other dogs is high in pack drive. The dog that tends to run (flight) or stand his ground (fight) is said to be high in defence drive. All of the drives link together to aid self-preservation. All dogs need these drives to some degree to make them good workers. Reactive breeds such as collies and German shepherds are usually reasonably high in all of the drives – that's what makes them such good working dogs. Of course upbringing and socialisation will also affect the level at which drives manifest themselves.

Your understanding, and as a consequence, your handling of the dog when he is in one of these drives will affect the outcome. Your recognition of and reaction to situations that turn the drives on and off is even more important. You need to be a good observer and learn what promotes and controls the drives in your dog.

In order to carry out given tasks reliably, and to learn new tasks, your dog needs to be sufficiently motivated. Just like us the dog works to gain enjoyment, or at the very least relief, as a reward for his actions. Without motivation we can end up with dogs who 'turn off', or indeed never 'switch on', when required to work.

Food and play are directly linked because, as with most predatory species, play is the natural way of learning about life and to hunt for food. So the same survival instinct is driving both the need for food and the want to play. This is why these two motivational tools are the best to use in training. *(See the sections on Play Training and Rewards.)*

Motivation can develop in many ways; praise from you (links to pack drive), by reward such as a titbit or a toy (links to predatory drive). The dog can even be motivated just from the sheer enjoyment of carrying out a task that you have taught him to enjoy. Some dogs need far more motivation than others do, but all will respond favourably, when motivation is delivered at the correct time and in a way that the dog can connect with the given task. Motivational aids are useless in teaching, if given at the wrong time, as the chapter on timing explains. They are also useless if the dog is not motivated by them.

A dog can be taught to enjoy all sorts of tasks, with correct and timely use of suitable motivation; but motivation must be given in a way that the dog can understand. He needs to learn that every segment of what you are teaching is fun. If every segment is fun, there is no need for his instincts to take over in the search of release from boredom, apprehension, frustration or even fear. Without the correctly channelled motivation, the very release from a boring or frustrating action can be motivation enough for him to follow that same pattern of behaviour the next time. He will strive for the release and therefore, he will learn an action that is not the one that you were trying to achieve.

If things do go wrong, for instance if you are teaching a new exercise and the dog is not showing any signs of understanding within a few minutes, or is giving the wrong behaviour, then stop and give the technique and timing of reward some careful thought. Is your method of training correct for what your are trying to achieve? Is your timing right, i.e. are your actions and reward in the right place? Last, but not least, are you motivating your dog sufficiently, is there reason for him to 'Want' to perform?

Motivation is what makes the world go around. For some, motivation can come from just the basic need to survive, but for most, it provides a reason to go on. We as humans, are motivated to work, our motivation being to earn money on which to live, feed, clothe and house our families and hopefully, have enough left at the end of the day to provide for recreation, (go to the odd dog show perhaps!) In some cases our jobs provide motivation in themselves, giving us the desire to strive to achieve our aims. Animals, like our dogs, do not possess the power to look ahead in that manner; nor do they possess the mental ability for lateral thinking. Deprived as they are, of the basic motivational need to catch food, (it is always provided for them, by us, in a convenient dish) then motivation must be stimulated from things that the dog can enjoy. Pleasurable contact with humans or other animals; toys, titbits or tasty morsels, games and so on.

Because we are the providers of the food and safe accommodation, the dog never quite grows up. He maintains a puppy-like out look on life, (in comparison to his cousin the wolf). In the natural behaviour of most

predatory animals, play has a big role in the development of the puppy. In a captive situation the animal does not need this tool to develop his skills to find his prey and so the drive to play is an ideal tool for motivation because, in domesticity the animal is programmed to use it but lacks the need. *(See Play Training).*

Motivation is one of the keys to a reliable, happy, no hang ups dog. As handlers striving for perfection, we can become very repetitive and boring if we are not very careful.

Picture the scene; a handler is teaching his dog to walk to heel for the competition ring. He starts off by giving the dog a check around the neck and saying 'Heel'. The dog walks by his side, nothing special but it is OK. The handler proceeds to march up and down saying 'Heel, good boy. Heel, good boy'. The dog remains in the heel position. At the end of the training session the handler is relatively pleased with his dog and follows the rule of 'Praise your dog' at the end of the exercise. Then he releases the dog and allows him to 'do his own thing', or puts him back into the car. Feeling that he was successful in his training the handler repeats the procedure at the next training session, then the next and so on. Being a creature, like us, that aims for self-preservation or pleasure, the dog soon starts trying to eliminate the boring bits to get to the interesting bits.

Even if it is a physical impossibility to get away from the boring bits, the dog will go into autopilot, 'switching off' until the good bits come his way. In this case, reward, in the dog's eyes, comes only at the end of the exercise so that is what he feels he should try to get to. Even if the reward is only release from the monotony or boredom, it is worth aiming for if there is nothing else.

At this stage of the proceedings the handler may become annoyed and violently check, verbally chastise or even hit the dog. This may result in attention of sorts from the dog, most animals would watch if they were fearful of something or someone getting them. But, how long would **you** stay? At the first available opportunity, if it was you, you would be off - and so will the dog.

In this instance the dog has been systematically trained, all be it inadvertently, to switch off from the handler in heelwork and yet come alive at the end when he's finished. The result is the exact opposite of what the handler was trying to achieve. The dog, like us, is programmed to react in certain ways, and the more we understand about this, the better dog handlers and indeed the better people we will become. *(See Understanding the Dog's Mind)*

Rewards

We all work for something, very few are fortunate enough to work purely for the love of it. Even if we enjoy our work the fact that it becomes a necessity for our survival can turn it into a chore, and the rewards have to be sufficient for us to want to carry on. If the rewards are not readily forthcoming or at least anticipated from time to time, we begin to turn off and are less likely to respond enthusiastically to the task ahead.

Good employers recognise this fact and in order to get the best results from their investment, make sure wherever possible, that their employees are rewarded sufficiently to make them want to give it their best shot. Likewise dogs need a reward to make it all worthwhile.

Reward for a dog can come in many guises, but the important thing to remember is that the dog must want the reward and he must realise why he is receiving the reward, if it is to be of any use to your training programme.

The most common rewards are often given without thinking; a kindly word, a soothing voice, a pat on the head, or even just a smile. Given at the correct time in association with a correct action or during a training exercise, these can mean just as much to a dog as a bonus in your wage packet does to you.

It is a good idea to programme into the dog a good association with his name and any praise words that you use such as 'good boy'. This can be done by linking the words with rewards (cuddles, titbits, play etc.)

When teaching your dog to do more complicated and less natural exercises you may need some form of reward that is a little more positive, and can stimulate your dog's natural instincts. A titbit is fine but care must be taken in the administration. The dog must always think that there is another tasty morsel where the last one came from, (even if in truth you have run out!).You must learn to never give so many titbits that the dog is full or bored.You need to become accustomed to reading your dog and giving just enough to leave the dog 'wanting'.The best way to gauge this is by watching the dog, or by watching someone else with his or her dog. If the dog walks away or loses interest then the reward has been over done, or is not stimulating enough. It's rather like a human working in a chocolate factory, (even if you are a choc-a-holic!).At first you can't get enough, but after a while it becomes very boring if not a bit sickly.

The amusement arcades have rewards all sewn up; they know exactly how to programme the machines for minimum pay out and maximum profit.The game machine has that uncanny knack of paying out a little, just as you were about to walk away, and you are stimulated by the reward to stay a little longer to see what else will come your way. Reward training works on the same basis; learn when to give and when to withhold. It takes practice but once perfected it will be an invaluable tool to your training programme.

It is crucial to not become too predictable. If you become too consistent with your reward system your dog will start to work you instead of visa versa.The rewards must be given in a more random fashion with bonuses given for excellent work and lesser rewards given out for mediocre efforts.

You should work on the basis of giving only the minimum reward that the animal will remain interested for, and keep the big rewards in reserve for excellence. However, this depends on the dog.You will often need a high value reward to start an exercise off to get the dog really enjoying the experience. Once the task becomes fun, the rewards will be of lesser importance to the dog.

Using Rewards For The Best Results

Many handlers fall into the trap of slipping titbit after titbit into the dog's mouth thus achieving a status whereby the dog only pays attention if there is food just about to pop into his mouth.The dog may even start to throw in behaviours that you don't want, because you have used reward to bring him out of them. Similarly with toys, the dog is manoeuvred around in what looks like heelwork, with the toy attached to his mouth.When the toy is not there nor is the dog's attention.

In order to use food or toys effectively you must be strict with yourself.Approach the use of motivators in a constructive way just as you would teach an exercise.

To start, care should be taken in the selection of the reward. Food should be very palatable, small enough to be eaten quickly, and you should have a variety so that you can occasionally give a better reward when the behaviour dictates.

You will also need to consider diet; the smaller the dog the more crucial this can be. You may find it useful to have food allocations in a pot for each training session, this way you can be sure that you will not give more than you intended and upset your dog's system. It is often better to have the food in a container and placed on a chair or table within easy reach, but not in your pocket. This aids in the weaning off process and gets the dog accustomed from an early stage, to you going for the food to reward, rather than luring with it all of the time.

High value rewards might include freshly cooked meat, sausages, liver cake, hotdog sausages, beef burgers (avoid those with onions), cheese. Avoid human chocolate, grapes or raisins, as they can be poisonous to dogs. Commercially prepared treats are good too, but avoid high calorie or sugary treats. Some dogs enjoy chopped vegetables or fruit such as carrot or apple.

Toys should be safe, strong and preferably suitable for you to hold at the same time as the dog. Toys such as tug-a-balls, raggers, rubber rings, rope quoits etc. are ideal. Squeaky toys can be good too as they have the audible attraction, but are not so easy for you to hold on to. Work out what your dog likes best. Some dogs like a variety, others get hooked onto one type and still others will work of any type of toy.

Clicker training is an excellent way to use reward *(see Clicker and Target Training)*. You can also use the system in a similar way without a clicker, substituting a special word or other sound/signal in place of the clicker.

For ease of writing the explanation of the use of reward following is written as if you were using food but, exactly the same procedure would apply to toys - in fact is often best to use a combination of food and toys in training.

Teach your dog that when he hears the words 'Good dog', (or better still a word or phrase that you would not use indiscriminately for example 'Brilliant') that food will come soon after. Soon the dog will start to work to hear those words instead of just for food.

To programme this into the dog first say 'Brilliant' and then reward immediately. Next say it again and reward after one second, then after three seconds, then after two seconds, then after six, then after one and so on. Now the dog knows the food will come when hears 'Brilliant', but he is not sure when, and his attention will start to hold.

If you are predictable he will not have to try so hard or pay attention because he will know when his reward will arrive. Dogs are very good at learning our routines, as we know from our daily lives, so make sure your rewards come at random and big rewards come for the best work.

Chose a simple action to introduce your reward system - the sit for instance. Lure the dog into position or give your dog the keyword 'Sit' *(see Static Positions)*. Give a small food reward and say 'Brilliant' if the dog complies. Gauge the value of the reward on what the dog already knows. If you are sure he understands sit and does not comply immediately, give a very small or low value reward when he does. If he complies quickly give a better reward. Break the exercise and start again. This time allow a few seconds before rewarding with the food, but say 'Brilliant' - the dog will know the reward is coming. If he comes out of position simply re-command and reward when he complies. Build up the time that he remains in the sit, reward verbally but randomise the food reward.

You can introduce a secondary reinforcer like a clicker if you wish. *(See Clicker Training)*.

All rewards must be given, if they are to be of any significance, at precisely the correct time, i.e. in conjunction with the act that you are trying to perfect. *(See Timing)* However, your secondary reinforcer i.e. your clicker or the keyword 'Brilliant' will take the place of popping food into the dog or hanging onto a toy all of the time - but you still need to follow up with the primary reinforcer, i.e. your food or your toy. The time span between food or toys and actions should be randomised but also adjusted to suit the dog's ability, maturity, and level of competence.

If He is Not Bad - He Must Be Good!

Reward can be given to your dog not only when you are teaching something specific but also whenever he is displaying good behaviour. As I sit and write with my dog at my feet, I look down and smile and gently praise him as he lies there, and repeat my keyword of 'Settle'. I have taught my dog to understand that this means, 'Lie down and keep quiet whilst I am busy'. He slowly thumps his tail on the floor, and is happy and confident, reassured that what he is doing is pleasurable, I am pleased, and all is well. He lays his head back down and drifts off into a twitching, doggy sleep, chasing sheep in his dreams I guess! So just a small reward given at the right time in a way that the dog can understand helps to keep him happy and contented and makes your life easier. Of course if he was bursting to go to the loo, full of energy because he has not been walked or trained, or starving hungry it might be a different matter!

To keep your dog interested rewards should be varied, valuable and worth working for. But remember, if you want a calm quiet response then your reward should be soothing. If you want a lively exuberant response then the reward should be more stimulating. A Happy Dog means a Happy Handler and eventually a Happy Winner.

Toys

Toys are a versatile fun reward for competitive obedience training. They can always be available, never consumed totally and carried in your pocket and produced at just the right time. A toy to your dog can be a ball or pull, a rope knot, a squeaky toy, or simply a piece of rag, an old sock or piece of carpet - or even the end of your lead. Whatever you use, make sure that it is safe, and of a size that can easily fit into your pocket, and be carried wherever you go with your dog.

Some people have trouble with the dog not wanting to play with a toy, this can be turned around and the dog can be taught to enjoy a game with the handler and their toy. *(See The Want, and Play Training).*

Toys are a very important part of your dog training kit. To achieve the best results with toys as training aids, other toys should not be left lying around and available for your dog to play with at will. Remember you are using your toys as a reward and to increase motivation. If you have constant access to something, however desirable initially, it looses its appeal and novelty value after a while.

If you feel you need to leave something down for your dog, then a safe chew or pacifier would be a better choice, save the exciting toys for the training sessions when you will want to generate all the interest and enthusiasm. Few dogs that are trained and stimulated by their owners really need toys left scattered around and indeed this can lead to dominant tendencies in some dogs. *(Two of my books 'Puppies', published by TFH, and 'Dog Training Instructor's Manual', published by Rainbow, deal with behavioural problems).*

If you are carrying out your training programme correctly, your dog will be receiving plenty of mental stimulus and fun from you. Very young puppies perhaps will benefit from a few toys left for them to play with whilst you are out, but you must always make sure that these are completely safe to be left. The puppy must not be able to chew and swallow bits of them, make

sharp edges, nor throw them up in the air and then catch them in his throat. Even with young puppies leave only one or two well chosen chew toys, and then produce the exciting toys when you are around to control and take part in the game. When you leave or decide the game is over, the toys go with you leaving the dog wanting more, this is one of the crucial elements to achieving 'The Want'. *(See 'The Want')*

What Toys to Use

The types of toys that you use are much a case of personal or canine preference. Some dogs will be motivated by anything that moves whilst others will take a little more stimulating.

Toys that are specifically made for inducing team play between you and your dog are ideal. A game of tug with both you and the dog holding the toy will help you to develop a sense of team spirit. However remember, although the dog can win sometimes, you must always win in the end and the toy must remain yours, if you are to remain pack leader.

If you release the dog from the lead, the dog can go hurtling wherever he pleases and he is then no longer playing with you, but simply playing with the toy. This will not help your teamwork. You must teach your dog, and condition yourself, that play and reward are at their most exciting when you are working close together as a team.

Many handlers complain that although their dog will play, he lacks sparkle in his work and often the reason is that all the pleasure of the toy, all the sense of achievement and reward has come to the dog when he has been away from the handler. It may also be because the handler uses the toy only at the end of exercises rather than incorporating the toy into every step of the training.

It is important not to use solid balls or sticks for training. Solid balls can get caught in the back of the dog's throat as he reaches to catch them. Once there they are extremely difficult to dislodge. Sticks also can go into the dog's palate or down the throat. Both sticks and solid balls can cause fatal or serious damage so it is best to avoid using them.

So the main things to remember about toys as training aids are:
1) The toys belong to you not the dog.
2) They should not be left down for the dog to play with at will, (particularly if you have a problem with the dog not wanting to play with you, or with dominance).
3) The toys should be safe, non toxic and durable.
4) They should be compact enough to fit into your pocket but large enough for you both to hold for tugging games.
5) Toys should be used with care, learn when to give and when to withhold.

Keep play sessions close to you and maintain full control. Keep your dog on lead. Your reason for using toys is to help make training and working fun with you, not in the next ring, the next field or with another dog!

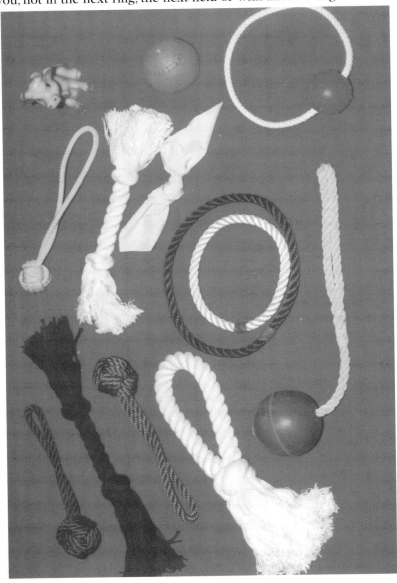

Play Training

One of the best ways to train a dog is through play. Children learn through play, and it has been seen in cases where children are deprived of play, that they develop all manner of extreme, compulsive, and unnatural behaviour patterns. Play training helps tremendously with motivation, it gives the dog the *'want'* to please and work for you.

Predatory animals like dogs learn through play to hunt – one of their main occupations in the wild. As they grow and develop they play and this helps perfect their motor skills. Practising behaviours like pounce, grab, stalk, tug, etc. all help the end product. Hunting of course, in their natural environment, is their means to survival. In the wild this perfecting and practising of hunt skills would be done with their siblings both from their own litter and older siblings or pack members who act as nannies. Domestic dogs are best compared to juvenile wolves, and so play remains an integral part of their lives and because they no longer need to hunt for food, we as dog trainers, can capitalise on this instinctive primitive behaviour.

Dogs That Won't Play

Sometimes dogs seem to lack the ability to play, possibly because of the way they have been brought up (lacking opportunities to play or traumatic situations). Often this is coupled with a placid temperament. Some dogs may not play because they are ill, overweight or simply just not fit. Also fearful, timid, aggressive or dogs with other behavioural problems may not play. Mental and physical health must be addressed before you can make progress. You may need to seek expert veterinary or behavioural advice to assist you.

Most of these animals (assuming they are fit) can be taught to play, even though it may take a long time, they can be motivated into enjoying a game with you. If your dog is one of these unenthusiastic individuals, then close attention to the following training programme will point you in the right direction.

Firstly, pick up all of your dog's toys, balls, chews, etc. This may seem harsh but you and your dog will benefit eventually. Observe your dog's behaviour patterns for a few days and determine when he is at his most exuberant. In some dogs this may be difficult to detect, watch carefully. During this observation time, ignore your dog as much as possible. Don't make a fuss of him, attend only to his basic needs and ignore his demands. But for feeding, watering and attending to his bodily functions, pretend that he doesn't exist for a day or two. Again this seems hard but you will reap the rewards in the long run.

When you have identified the time when the dog is most exuberant, (this may be before feeding time, or when you are about to go for a walk), take a tug toy or ball *(see Toys)*, and start playing with it on your own. Do not at this stage invite the dog to join in, just play by yourself with the toy. If the dog try's to join in then great, allow him to for a few moments only, (don't wait for him to grow bored). Then, put away the toy and resume ignoring the dog.

Follow the sequence as many times a day as you have detected excitement. Don't try to get the dog to join in, but allow him to if he shows an interest, just have a short game and stop while the dog is still keen. This procedure works particularly well when the dog is hungry as this heightens his excitement and anticipation (back to the basic hunt instinct). Always remember to put the toy away out of the dog's reach. He is only going to be allowed to play if he plays with you, ignore the dog the rest of the time.

Once the dog has shown some interest and you have created a desire in him to join in (this can take a while with older or more blasé dogs) the toy can then be left in sight, yet still out of reach. This heightens the anticipation of play as the dog can see the toy, but cannot get it until you arrive to have a game. Gradually the dog will want to play, but this method only works, if you refrain from pushing the dog into play, let him acquire *'want'*. Carry on keeping other contact to a minimum until you are confident that your dog will play with you on the production of his toy.

To 'wean' the dog onto other toys the procedure can be repeated, although it shouldn't take as long the second or third time around. You can start to incorporate the play into training, but very short sessions to start with.

This method also works exceptionally well with dogs that are possessive over their toys or will play only with the toy but not with you. If you have more than one dog, until you have mastered the play it may be advantageous to restrict the amount of playtime he has with the other dogs as he will be gaining all his enjoyment from them, and is unlikely to see any point in playing with you. It may seem hard but if you want your dog to play with you it is worth persevering. Once your dog is fully conditioned he can then gradually be allowed more play with the others but make sure that you always remain favourite - and if necessary repeat the procedure every so often. Do not lose faith, it can take a while but it does work.

Analyse your own behaviour too. Do you respond to every move your dog makes? Or does he have to try hard to get your attention? Is your dog given treats for no reason or does he have to work for them? Does your dog have free access to food or does he have to wait for you to supply it? You should be the one in control of all of this, not the dog. If the dog does not have to try – why should he bother?

How To Use It!

Play, particularly when it is incorporating a toy, can be used in all sorts of ways during training to aid motivation *(see Motivation and Drives)*. It can be used as an immediate reward for carrying out a task, or as an inducement to react to your command. It can be used as an incentive to heighten enthusiasm, and brought in at any time during an exercise to motivate the dog. It can also be used to distract the dog from things that you don't want him to do or as a target to show him where to go.

Avoid over using the toy to start with. If your dog has not been good at playing in the past, you don't want to bore him, and end up back at square one. Likewise with an over excitable dog too much of the toy will prevent him from concentrating on the task ahead - watch your dog and learn from his reactions. Don't be afraid to watch a training exercise go wrong, because by observing carefully you are able to put things right much more quickly and efficiently without distress and confusion being loaded onto the dog. It is far better to isolate a problem by watching and reacting correctly than to use a hit and miss approach.

Many dogs are happy to play with the handler alone, and do not need toys to motivate them. When bonding with a new puppy - it is always best to aim to teach him to play with you as well as a toy. If he will have a rough and tumble or chase after your fingers, as well as having a tug of war with a handkerchief, the lead, or a toy you will always have something available.

Make sure that you always have your motivation tools to hand, they must never run out, get lost or disappear. This gives you a great advantage at times when quick reactions are needed.

Training through play is a most satisfactory and pleasurable way of training. It brings pleasure to the dog, to the handler, and to all who witness it.

Toys and play can be used as the motivator to link exercises or part of an exercise together with another and so produce a stylish, accurate and highly motivated performance. *(See Linking)*.

Timing of course plays a big part in the ability to use play correctly. Playing at the wrong time can be distracting and counter productive. For instance when teaching the stay exercise you need the dog to be fairly calm, jumping him around with a toy is not going to create this effect.

However, depending on the dog's character, you may use your toy as a motivator to give confidence. Your play toy and your play attitude should become your lifeline and bond with your dog. If he shows confusion or apprehension at any time you can always pull out your 'Ace card' the toy, and lighten things up! But, there is a fine line between motivating and rewarding – be careful that the dog does not start an inappropriate behaviour pattern because it will result in a reward from you – when you think you are distracting from an unwanted behaviour! Learn to control behaviour patterns and be at least two steps ahead of your dog.

Teaching the Small Dog

Working with small dogs can be fun, but if you are not very careful, back breaking, especially for tall people! Generally small neat handlers make the best small dog workers, but having said that there are, of course always the exceptions.

The same principle of training can be applied in working small dogs as with larger dogs. Methods may have to be adjusted a little and the environment can be used to help. Upright handling is very important, as it is very obvious when the smaller dog has to adjust its position to work to the handler.

Some exercises like the close (heel) position, the watch, sit, down and stand etc. can be taught with the handler kneeling on the floor or with the dog on a table. If using a table, make sure that it is very stable and not inclined to shake or wobble. The surface should be non-slip; carpet or rubber matting is ideal.

Target training is ideal for smaller dogs as it allows the handler to remain upright while guiding the dog to where it should be. Clicker training is also good because it requires the dog to work things out for itself and is highly motivating. *(See Clicker Training and Target Training).*

All the techniques in this book are designed for all breeds, although some of them may need to be scaled down, or involve shorter distances to start with for the smaller dog. Use your own common sense and read your dog's reactions. Clicker and target training can be used in conjunction with any of the techniques.

Footwork must be extra neat using smaller steps, and it will probably be necessary to adjust your stride in order for the smaller dog to keep a consistent rhythm in heelwork. You must train yourself to have a gliding gait, placing one foot in front of the other pointing forwards, and keeping your knees as close together as possible. This style helps all sizes of dog to work neatly, but it is of utmost importance with smaller dogs, because every inch counts! Small dogs have less body mass to cover minor inaccuracies, but are often very quick to respond to minor body movements, therefore you must learn to be a very controlled handler.

Close fitting trousers are a must so that they do not flap in the dog's face. Your lead should be carefully chosen with two most important considerations in mind; for training a light lead with a dainty clip that doesn't hit the dog. In the ring, for the classes where a lead is needed, it may be necessary to use a slightly heavier lead, because the wind can catch a light lead and knock it into the dog's face during your work. A cord or fine rope lead is better than a flat one because there is less surface area to catch the wind. For a collar it is not necessary to use anything more than a soft leather or fabric buckled type, comfortably fitted.

When using food rewards, particular attention must be paid to quantity and quality of food used. The small dog has much less need for food and a treat for a large dog can be a meal to a small dog. Chop up rewards very small and always allocate content within the dog's normal diet. If necessary use meals as treats and don't give the dog an actual meal but, monitor intake carefully to ensure your dog has a good balanced diet.

Smaller dogs can be just as tough as larger dogs when it comes to fun and games, don't be afraid of playing tug and having a rough and tumble. Follow all of the pointers in the sections on *Play Training, Motivation* etc. to develop an attentive, happy working dog.

Don't be too repetitive, only the most obsessive of dogs can thrive on training based on a principle which involves doing things over and over again until it is right. For every time that it comes right there may have been twenty getting it wrong - which one is the dog to choose next time? He will take the easiest option no doubt, but I wonder if it will be what you want!

Be inventive and imaginative, think clearly before you begin to teach the dog and be sure of what you are doing. If you go wrong don't worry, simply smile and start again. If the dog goes wrong the same applies, start again and help him all of the way so that he can't go wrong again. Reward him when he is correct, and during the time that he is performing the stages of what you are trying to achieve.

Some dogs can be particularly sensitive or gentle in their actions, and you should not try to alter the dog's temperament, but you can develop the animal and help him to enjoy a more outgoing lifestyle and attitude to competition work. Do this by developing the play skills, and use distraction training to help the dog to accept unusual or difficult situations. *(See also - Teaching Sensitive dogs)*

Handlers often make the mistake of over-protecting smaller dogs, if you have done this then you will need to make a 'super human' effort in teaching your dog more about the social aspects of life.

If you have just acquired your dog, don't make social training mistakes. If allowed to mix with friendly dogs of all sizes he will learn to accept them all. Avoid situations that will overwhelm your dog and allow him to adjust to things from a distance - gradually building up closer contact where possible or appropriate. For some small dog owners, there seems to be a natural reaction to pick up the dog when the situation is perceived to have become a little too much, but you must try to avoid doing this. Let the dog stand on his own four feet, however small they might be!

Smaller, gentler breeds like Miniature Poodles, Shetland sheepdogs, Cavaliers, Papillons and the like have plenty of spirit, are normally very bidable and make excellent dogs for those new to the sport, for children or for those not wanting anything to powerful. Breeds like the Corgi and Jack Russell also make a popular choice but can be a little more powerful, both in mind and body. Some of the Spitz breeds can be fun to work with but can be a little independent.

The most important factors to be considered when training and working with your small dog, is to keep it fun, interesting, keep your handling neat and controlled and don't bore the poor dog's socks off!

Teaching the Large Dog

Large sometimes means slower, or more graceful both in body and mental maturity (at least in comparison to the Border collie!) But do not despair, the larger dog can be taught to move quickly and in a flexible way if you build up both his mind and his body tone. There is nothing more graceful or mouth-watering to watch than a large dog working attentively and with style.

Use toys and play to build up physical dexterity - not always in conjunction with the actual training, although this is part of it, but in exercise sessions too. A large dog makes a terrific dancing partner and a little and often gentle hind leg dancing can help to build up the muscles. Obviously much care must be taken in the physical growth and development stages of the dog; time must be allowed for the bones, muscles and particularly hips to reach maturity. When the dog is mature physically a little jumping, weaving and swimming, together with games that make erratic or unpredictable movements will strengthen and help the dog to improve mental and physical dexterity. The use of toys that bounce in unpredictable directions will do wonders for the dog's co-ordination and help to make exercise fun as well as productive. If there is any suspicion of hip or other joint/bone structure problems, then you should consult your vet on the type of exercise that your dog can have. It is a good idea to have your dog checked for any hereditary defect such as hip dysplasia so that you know what his limitations might be.

It is also important to monitor the dog's weight. If he is carrying too much this will give added burden to his joints as well as dulling his stamina. Keeping him slightly on the lean side will maintain a fit and lively animal.

In general people tend to make excuses for larger dogs saying they are too big to be able to perform some of the exercises. This may be true in some cases, but with general obedience exercises there is normally a way around the problem.

Straightforward heelwork doesn't normally present a problem, but sometimes intricate or repeated turns can cause anguish, especially left turns. Often this is because the heel position of the dog is too far forward, and when the handler attempts to turn her left leg the dog is already too far forward to achieve a neat turn. This usually results in the dog's position becoming erratic, surging, dipping, or in some cases the dog simply waits for the handler to turn and then rejoins the heel position.

It is imperative that you work on keeping the dog's shoulders level with your leg (not forward of you) all of the time during heelwork. You may find that this position feels a little too far back if you are accustomed to having the dog powering forward. Ask someone to watch so that they can tell you if it looks correct; remember the rules, the dog's shoulder should be level with your leg. Then, when you have perfected the correct heel position, you will find that you are able to introduce the correct footwork and training procedure, and so the turn can be performed well too.

There have been many examples of large or heavy dogs doing well in competitive obedience. Even if they do not possess the speed in a tight space that the more agile dog can produce, they should never the less work at a good natural pace, and will not be marked down by a fair judge. Obviously if you are content to let your dog amble around and do not motivate him sufficiently, then you should expect to be marked accordingly. The dog should be able to move at a speed, where appropriate, that would be natural if he were playing or self motivated - an important concept to keep at the back of your mind when training. If his work is sluggish you will need to analyse and work on motivation.

As with any breed that is not genetically programmed to be single minded, it is best not to repeat exercises over and over. Keep your programme varied and your motivation high. Larger dogs need to build up stamina like all dogs, but will take longer to do this than a breed which is built for endurance and has rapid and relatively early maturity. So take your time and be patient.

In Britain at the present time, German Shepherds are second only in popularity for obedience to the Working sheepdog or Border collie. They are so varied in type and workability that is quite difficult to assess the dog until it has started to mature a little. Some breed lines produce more of a working type than others, and it is worth watching progeny and looking at the family tree if you are thinking of purchasing one for this sport, although with the best research in the world nothing is guaranteed!

The environment in which the dog is brought up, and the way he is handled and moulded will have a lot to do with the eventual outcome. It is up to you to bring out the best attributes and not to dwell on comparisons with other dogs - nor allow others to do this for you.

Other large breeds tend to be less popular for one reason or another, but we do have in Britain a smattering of Rottweilers, Dobermanns, and the odd Standard Poodle, Old English sheepdog, Wolfhound, Great Dane, Newfoundland, Leonberger and others.

Outside of the UK it is pleasing to see many larger breeds working to a very high standard. Breeds such as Bernese, Airedale, Boxer, Schnauzer and even St Bernard can achieve good standards. However, there tends to be more encouragement to train all dogs in some countries than there is in the UK.

If you own and would like to train (or retrain) a large breed, you will find the methods described in this book quite suitable, they have all been tried and tested on a variety of breeds. You must encourage enjoyment and avoid too much repetition. Give your dog time to mature and develop, learn to go with the flow. Your dog may learn more quickly than you think, but the second you see confusion creeping in, stop and re-evaluate your actions.

Use obstacles to help you to guide the dog into the correct position. Sometimes it is near on impossible to reach the end of your large dog to correctly position his angled bottom! Use a wall or fence to help you. You can also use chairs, posts and rope or a line of poles to aid straight recalls or sendaways.

Use your common sense to make life easier, there is never just one way to train a dog. As long as what you do is kind, well thought out and will not worry the dog then success should come your way.

If you are particularly interested in working a larger breed then it is a good idea to compare a few breed lines, even within your chosen breed. Choose the lines that carry the more extrovert, lively types. Look at background, not just the parents but the grandparents and so on.

When you have finally got to the stage where you are choosing your pup from the litter, you should look for the most playful, (particularly with objects) and more importantly, voice and touch sensitive pup. The most dominant pup will not be everyone's cup of tea, although in the right hands a dominant dog will make a good working dog. If you are not 100% sure of yourself dominant dogs are better placed with someone else. Remember a dominant dog that becomes aggressive hurts more when it's big!

Some dogs, even within a breed or litter will have more of the attributes suitable to workability than others, spend as much time as is possible watching the pups both with your interaction and when left to play with their siblings. Look for the pup that responds well to people, other dogs, new situations and of course you.

When competing you need to consider your dog's stamina and tolerance levels. The heat will affect heavy dogs that are also heavy coated much earlier than the average dog. Use water on the dog's coat to cool him in hot weather. The heat will especially affect black or dark coated dogs. Also the actual stamina level may reduce as the day goes on. It may be a good idea to work early where possible. You will need to assess how much rest your dog needs prior to working and strike the right balance against socialising and training at the show.

It will normally take longer to succeed with the larger dog because they take longer to mature both physically and mentally. The good worker is often a character who will keep you on your toes, but all that hard work and determination will pay off when the wins

Pat Leverick with Akamai Aurora Obedience Warrant (Rosie) top wining obedience Leonberger in the UK. (Bred by Angela White.) Pat and Rosie were always a favourite on the UK obedience circuit. Rosie has competed at Crufts and was always great to watch. She was sure to create a crowd of spectators at the ringside whenever she worked. Sadly and unexpectedly, Pat passed away before she was able to fulfil her dream of working the championship class with Rosie.

Teaching Sensitive Dogs

All dogs have a degree of sensitivity but some are more sensitive than others. The sensitive dog is highly reactive to its senses – touch, hearing, sight, smell and even taste can affect the dog's behaviour. Our sensitive dog may have a greater reaction than the average dog to one or more if his senses and to varying degrees, this affects the dog's responses and general attitude to life.

Sensitive dogs need an especially caring attitude. You must be particularly careful not to become confusing in your approach to teaching, and indeed to every day life. It is very easy to go wrong with any dog but with a sensitive dog mistakes can be harder to deal with and put right.

Your attitude to the dog will have much bearing on the outcome. You must be positive, friendly and outgoing without being overbearing. The dog must see you in control of situations so that he can gain confidence from you. Many outwardly spirited dogs are quite sensitive underneath, and once you are able to observe and identify this, these dogs are a pleasure to work with.

Sensitivity is a human characteristic, in dogs normally the behaviour would be identified with a more specific name, submissiveness may perhaps be the category that they fit into, although not all sensitive dogs are particularly submissive. Sometimes they are socially insecure, fearful of the unknown, lacking in confidence, etc.

A little bit of sensitivity can be a positive asset in the training game, making the dog a very biddable work-mate. Where sensitivity is a problem, it is useful to try to understand what makes your particular dog sensitive, what situations trigger it off and then build on confidence particularly in those situations, using common bonds.

Being sensitive is often the label given to a dog who is confused and so withdraws, unwrap the confusion and the dog is more confident and ultimately becomes outgoing.

Of course every dog is different in character, even within the same litter of pups there can be terrific variations in temperament, which develop even before they go to their new homes. Sometimes it is extremely difficult to get the type of attitude that you want because, even with the best training in the world, many of the behavioural idiosyncrasies are genetically programmed, or learnt from the mother and siblings. Therefore it is best to accept your dog for what he is and build on all of the good things. Instill confidence as you go, and use the dog's natural behaviour to your advantage. Choose situations where the dog is naturally confident and build bonds that the dog can identify with to link you across to more difficult areas.

Touch Sensitive

Breeds like the Labrador are typically low in touch sensitivity - being bred to run through thicket without hesitation. Terriers also are fairly insensitive to touch - being bred to catch vermin touch sensitivity would be a negative attribution. Other breeds are far more touch sensitive; the German shepherd for instance is know for its vocalisation at the least little thing. Herding breeds such as the Border collie have highly developed sense of sight and are very sensitive to the slightest movement – it is in its survival interests to move quickly out of the way of a flying sheep's hoof. So it is best to find environments for training which are quiet with no sudden movements to keep the Border collie's concentration and increase its ability to learn. Of course later it is something which must be trained against in order to hold your dog's attention, but usually by then the training itself has become self-motivating, if carried out in the correct manner, and the dog becomes less sensitive to external movement. The use of movement within your training can have very positive benefits too.

Sound Sensitivity

Sound sensitivity can be a real problem when working in environments such as town shows. But this is not the only problem for the sound sensitive dog. If you try to teach a sound sensitive dog in a noisy environment his ability to learn will be severely hampered. Often a dog club environment is not ideal, unless you can work on an individual basis. Shetland and Pyrenean Sheepdogs are particularly sound sensitive, but many other breeds and individuals fall into this category too.

Mental Sensitivity

Mental sensitivity can be quite an interesting concept. Some dogs are particularly sensitive to their owners' moods. I know of one Border collie who whines in the back of the car whenever her owner becomes agitated by the traffic. Despite the best efforts of the owner to disguise her anguish, the dog always picks up on it. Mentally sensitive dogs soon succumb to stress in many ways, they will know when the owner is not pleased with their performance or when his owner is unwell or feeling down. Therefore mental sensitivity can be altered by confidence building and owner attitude.

With all types of sensitivity the dog is less sensitive to his surroundings and events when he is doing something he enjoys and is confident in, therefore it makes sense to find ways of increasing the dog's enjoyment in training and you will thus lower its sensitivity threshold.

A sensitive dog should be a pleasure for the less abrasive handler to train. In fact a more sensitive and intuitive handler will gain good results from a sensitive dog because they take the time to understand and work through the problems. Build on confidence, train methodically and yet with variation. With careful planning on your part you should make a great partnership.

Teaching the Keen Dog

Define keen; OTT (over the top), hyper-active, nutty, head strong, head in the clouds, head banger! All terms that people use to describe dogs which are more lively than the average. The keen dog is a super tool to work with, but generally the handler's biggest crime is that they try to suppress the keenness instead of using it, or transversally, allow the dog to become 'out of hand' for fear of losing the keenness! This especially occurs when the handler has had a quieter or flatter dog in the past because they are so keen to keep the enthusiasm that they fail to control and channel it.

You must learn to direct the dog's energy into what you are trying to achieve. Many dogs will become obsessive, particularly over toys or retrieve articles. They will seem to be uncontrollable in the presence of one of these items. The chapters on *eliminating aids* and *Rewards* will help you to learn how to use those toys to your advantage and to maintain control at the same time. Sometimes you will need to hide the toy behind your back or in your pocket until you get the dog's concentration on the matter in hand. Then quickly bring out the toy to use as reward for correct behaviour, which may be purely good concentration. Use the exercises that you teach the dog, not as a threat but as a part of the game.

Keen dogs especially should be taught that the words 'Good boy', mean that you are pleased. *(See Rewards)* The keen dog can then be rewarded by the handler, without even a toy or titbit being brought out, but make sure that you have built a good bond with your keen dog, and that he trusts you.

Dogs, like humans, naturally try to avoid things that are not pleasurable and will attempt to go on to those things that they can enjoy. So it is important to accustom yourself to making all sections of an exercise part of the whole, an exciting, rewarding and pleasant experience, instead of addressing threat to the static parts and allowing the dog freedom to be over keen in other more active parts.

The retrieve is once again a good example to use. Handlers who fear that they will lose control will yell and threaten when attempting to keep the dog waiting at heel. This makes the chase of the retrieve article all the more attractive to the dog! Not only is the out run and grab of the article fun, but it is a release from your nagging! Use your tools, your toy or your retrieve article, as an incentive to perform the control parts of the exercise. (The principles are explained in the section that deals with teaching the retrieve.) This principle will work in all aspects of training your dog.

The dog's behaviour is shaped into what you want with the incentive as reward. The secret is learning when to reward and when to withhold, when to keep the article out of sight and when to have it in full view and or in joint possession of you and the dog. Develop the dog's attitude to be just as obsessive over all parts of the exercise as he may be over the chasing or fast movement sections. Use one of the objects of his obsession as reward and motivation, but choose carefully, if something is just too desirable for words, put it away and use something else until you have better control, you must be able to control your rewards in order to use them.

Keen dogs often feel that they can control situations, and by applying some constructive rules to all aspects of the dog's life, you may find that the keen attitude becomes more easily controlled.

Often keen dogs work forward of the handler - if you observe carefully you will see that many of these dogs are forward of the handler even when not working. They will have a tendency to pull, to barge through doorways, and in the worse scenarios may become dominant. All of these and any other situations that could be construed as the dog in control should be worked on to give the handler the control of the dog's life. Otherwise, in their work they will take the lead.

To sum up; approach all exercises in a calm and pleasant manner, do not become hyped up yourself. Control all aspects of the dog's life including the more domestic situations, the dog needs a sound base on which to focus. With patient handling he will learn when to use his energy. The 'Watch' exercise will be of particular use to you, much time and effort should be afforded to teaching this in a calm, structured, pleasant manner, taking into consideration the dog's sensitivities.

The sections on *Timing* and *Motivation* will help you and in the *Techniques* section the variables of character have been taken into consideration when teaching each exercise.

Do not to suppress the spirit - use it!

Teaching the Hard Dog

What is a hard dog? 'Hard' is a term we hear banded regularly, normally accompanied by a callous statement regarding 'beating the hell out of the dog and it making no difference'! This kind of comment (if meant) shows total misunderstanding of dogs. Remember, the genetically programmed instinct of all dogs, is to survive and to reproduce. They, like humans can not alter this. Unlike us they do not have the mental capacity to ignore these needs unless we give them alternatives, based on those needs, on which they can focus their energies.

The term 'hard', when it is analysed in this instance, possibly means not very sensitive, dominant, and often bored or confused, although most people will be able to come up with an exception. There are always grey areas and terms like hard, sensitive, etc. are very broad bands, and after all humanism's.

With a dog which you feel fits this category you will find it easier to deal with if you give yourself chance to sit back and observe his behaviour. Identify what situations trigger the sort of drive that you find it difficult to deal with. Identify the times when the animal is easier and more biddable and use that knowledge to gain success by building your training patterns on the easier times and to create these instances where possible. Teach the dog that it is fun to be with you and to respond to you and keep friendly control at that point. The more you take control of his life, the more the dog will accept you in control, and so without a battle, you begin to reap the benefits.

Taking control, does not mean yanking the dog off his feet on a check chain, beating him with a newspaper or worse! All that is meant is that the dog becomes accustomed to, and enjoys you controlling things in his life not just in his obedience training, instead of the dog controlling things.

For most handlers the problem creeps up on them as the animal matures. As puppies the dogs are reasonably pliable if they are guided in the right direction, and any signs of problems in the behaviour are often passed off as 'cute'. But, as time goes by the dog matures and develops, handling is misguided, tempers fray and life becomes more difficult and sometimes a constant battle for all concerned.

Finding the right type of motivation, using the dog's natural behaviours to your advantage, and ignoring or better still blocking situations where it is hard to get through will help you to start to see success that you can then build upon. Read the chapters on *Motivation, Reward* and *Play Training* to help you to develop the dog's character into a more acceptable working medium.

Teaching Old Dogs New Tricks

Whether you are taking on the training and care of an older dog from someone else, or you have decided that you wish to retrain your own older dog, you must learn to edge your way carefully watching for confusion in your dog. You should be careful not to mistake confusion for disobedience.

Dogs have two main motivators, self-preservation and self-duplication, i.e. food and sex! Most correctly fed dogs find food in the form of titbits very welcome, and those who are not particularly interested in food extras often turn on to play. Food and play are directly linked because, as with most predatory species, play is the natural way of learning about life and how to hunt for food. So the same survival instinct is driving both the need for food and play. This is why these two motivation tools are the best to use in training.

When training an older dog you need to pretend that he is a puppy to a certain degree. You need to allow time to build confidence and to develop a trust bond between you and the animal. At the same time you must maintain control calmly and in a pleasant manner. An anxious handler will not help a dog that is anxious. Do not put yourself into situations where you are not confident that you can control the dog or others around you. Build on your own attitude, confidence, and self-control.

Approach difficult situations from a distance. For instance, if you have difficulty keeping the dog's attention on you in the presence of other dogs or people, do not go right into the middle of them and struggle with the dog. Stand on the outskirts, allow the dog time to take things in and then, when he is more settled, and the novelty has worn off, start a game. The duration of the game should be just a few seconds long to begin with. Try to instigate and also end the game yourself, so that you maintain control. *(See also Problem Solving - Counter Conditioning).*

Forget formal obedience exercises to begin with, just get that team spirit developing and enjoy your dog. Many is the time that new handlers to my class have been sent way down the field out of the way of the others, not

because we want them out of the way, but because it is much easier for the handler to get positive results. Then gradually over a period of time, the new handler and dog get closer and closer to the hubbub of things. In only a few sessions they are in the middle of the class playing with the dog. Now the handler has a tool he/she can use it!

Often it is easier taking on a second hand or rescue dog than it is to re-educate your own dog that you have made mistakes on, but both have their draw backs. With the second hand dog you are never 100% sure what has happened to the dog, even if in theory, you know where it has come from. Often the dog's previous history is distorted or down right untrue to make the previous owner feel better or more justified in parting with the dog. So you must allow time to assess the dog's character and learn how you can both feel comfortable in all situations. On the other hand you can't be too laid back and allow things to happen that you know in the long run are going to be unacceptable. Careful guidance of the dog, with calm control, will avoid these problems.

Teach ground rules without aggression, don't forget that a dog sees aggression as loss of control. A truly dominant animal never needs to assert more than the odd low key grumble in order to maintain his position. It is not in his interest to fight, he shows his authority in the way that he lives his life, to maintain proper control of the dog you must do the same.

With the older dog that you have made mistakes with, but now you have seen the light and want to put things right, you need to decide on your aims. Decide what you definitely don't want, and avoid situations that would spark off that behaviour until you have developed distractive methods to control the dog. Decide on what you definitely do want, read carefully and try to absorb information from the concept section. Learn techniques from the technique section that will promote the required behaviour.

Do not try to correct the behaviour or exercises that are wrong as this leads to confusion. Simply start over again once you have a clear understanding of what you want to achieve and how to go about it. Ignore and guide the dog away using distraction training (counter conditioning), from anything that you don't want. Putting all of the emphasis and reward onto what you are trying to achieve will make the dog home in on those things, and gradually by extinction the other behaviours will start to fade away.

Case Studies - In our class we had one handler whose dog was besotted with other dog's squeaky toys. She had struggled at shows for months, every time her dog heard a squeak his attention to his handler was gone. Much to her horror I suggested she stop fighting it and bought him a squeaky of his own. With careful distraction training and following the procedure to hide the incentives we soon taught the dog that whenever he heard a squeaky it could be his own. His attention improved and the handler now actually benefits from outside of the ring squeaks.

Another handler had a six-year-old Samoyed that had been taught obedience in a very hard handed fashion. The dog did not know how to play with the handler and was totally negative in his approach to obedience. After a short course using play, motivation, timing and understanding, the dog began to work through choice, and both handler and dog began to enjoy themselves. At the end of the course the handler burst into tears, when I asked her why she replied that she was just so overwhelmingly happy with the difference in her dog in just a few short days of positive happy training.

I have had personal experience of both second hand dogs and retraining my own older dogs that I had made my mistakes on ('Yes - non of us are perfect'!) The secret is to admit to yourself that even though you are supposed to have the superior intelligence, and are supposed to be the teacher, you are capable of getting it wrong. If the dog is going wrong then it is your fault. If things have gone wrong just learn to laugh and start again.

To sum up. Think clearly and positively before you start, be sure of what you *are* and *are not* trying to achieve. Build a bond. Be patient. Keep control. Admit that you can be wrong. Don't lose sight of your objectives, but most of all **keep it fun.**

Teaching Crossbreeds and Mongrels

Crossbreeds and mongrels can be a pleasure to train. When getting a dog as a pup, with a mongrel in particular, you never can tell what you will get and despite the best guesses it can be difficult to predict the end result in both size and attitude. It is very common in rescue organisations for staff to suggest that a pup is a cross between one breed and another or suggest at least one of the crosses. But these guesses are often way out. A very common assumption is that anything black and tan is a cross German Shepherd, anything black is a cross Labrador and so on. In most cases the assumption will have some truth, but there may well be many other breeds in the dog too. Many dogs found in a rescue situation are true mongrels with many breeds and crossbreeds in their family tree.

The term crossbreed more accurately relates to the crossing of known breeds or crossbreeds and so there is perhaps a little more foresight because you will normally know what the parents are. In obedience in the UK there is some purpose crossing with the aim of producing good, healthy dogs that are balanced and interested in work. Perhaps the most famous being the Coltriever line – a marriage of Border collies and golden retrievers producing many dogs that went into obedience homes and one winning Crufts. There have also been purpose cross poodle/collie and German shepherd/collie in reasonable numbers

If the dog comes from rescue then this may bring its own issues *(see Teaching Rescue Dogs)*, but in general you should simply 'go with the flow' and see what problems you hit. If you train with understanding in general, find the motivation that works, be prepared to adapt and use your head, training a cross or mongrel is no different to teaching a pedigree dog.

There may be some advantages in that they may not be so highly strung, they may be more healthy and live longer (although there are no guarantees – we do see mongrels with hereditary defects, just not so many).

You may be able to identify some of the traits of breeds that may be in your dog, for example the strength of the collie eye can come through in collie crosses, the tendency to dislike other dogs can come through in bull breed crosses and so on.

The best advice is to do everything as well as you possibly can – socialise well, train the basics thoroughly and motivate well and let the breeding take care of itself.

It is always a good idea to consider neutering mongrels and even known crosses if they are not part of a breeding programme. This will save any further breeding and will be an advantage to your obedience work as with bitches you won't miss any shows due to seasons or hormonal imbalance and with dogs you will not have them distracted by the opposite sex.

OB CH Coltriever Double Decker with owner, breeder and trainer Margaret Bradley, Winner of Crufts Obedience Championship 1991

Teaching the ABC Dog (Anything But a Collie Dog)

As with small and large dogs other breeds are often misunderstood or disregarded as not suitable for Obedience (particularly in the UK.) There are many excellent breeds that can do obedience, on the continent and in the USA we see some excellent examples. While the requirements may be a little different across the world the standard is often higher than you might think.

You need to consider the sensitivities and tendencies of your ABC dog. For example some breeds are easily upset or make long lasting connections that the collie might get over. Even if they don't at first appear to be sensitive many are, more so than you think. You will need to consider many issues and try not to allow your dog to make the wrong connections. For example, if your dog does not enjoy a particular activity like grooming, then don't do this in an area where you intend to train.

Consider what the dog was bred to do. Although it may be a few generations since the dog was actually used for its original purpose, there will still be remnants of the behaviour (and in some it will be quite strong). From here you can consider the strengths and weaknesses of the breed and your individual.

Most of the herding breeds have an over developed sensitivity to the environment and what their senses tell them. They can be flighty, nervous, and reactive and may seem to harbour a grudge or adverse reaction to situations they have found difficult. Of course they may react to movement and have a tendency to chase. However, they have also been bred to work closely with people and tend to bond well – thus making a working relationship that is easy to nurture. Some of the breeds that have done well include the Belgian shepherds especially Groenendael and Tervueren and the Malinois. The Pyrenean sheepdog is seeing a growth in popularity.

Briards are very bright and adaptable. The Samoyed can be worked to a good standard.

Guarding breeds build good relationships with their owners, but this can bring problems, as they often become unsettled if part of the family

Pyrenean sheepdogs are quite rare, but there is growing interest in the UK.

wanders off. They are powerful workers with a good level of intelligence and this makes them a super tool for obedience.

Terrier types react to movement with a powerful edge. Like herding breeds they may chase, but may be a little more difficult to get under control

German Shepherd dogs are particularly sensitive to family and like all of their people to be in sight. Therefore care is needed to build up self-confidence in the dog especially for the stay exercises.

once allowed to make their own decisions. They are strong tenacious dogs with bags of character and spirit.

Companion and toy dogs vary a lot in their character and nature. But what they have in common is that they have been bred to want to be with people. Some are more spirited than others – Papillon's are full of character love to learn, and are surprisingly robust for their size. But, you will have to have very neat feet to maintain good heelwork with such a small dog.

Gundogs – again lots to choose from and very different characters. Breeds such as the busy bustling Springer spaniel to the more methodical but clearly intelligent Labrador. Some of the less common gundogs can make good obedience dogs too: Portuguese water dog, flat coated retriever, Nova Scotia duck tolling retriever to name but a few.

Hounds are generally a challenge and some breeds in particular are notorious for being difficult off lead – the afghan for example. They have been bred to run, but of course hounds have also been bred to work with humans and so if you can tap into that inherent behaviour and channel it into your obedience you will be on the right track. Greyhounds can be a good choice of hound to work with although their lack of body hair means that it is very obvious when they make the slightest of errors in heelwork!

All breeds need a good level of socialisation to ensure that they do not react in an inappropriate way to new situations. The more sensitive the breed the more you will have to work at it. If you are just wanting an ABC but not sure what to go for, a breed from the working group will probably give you the best bet. However the official Kennel Club working group leaves out breeds such as the poodle (utility) that could also be a good alternative – a standard poodle won the Crufts Obedience Championships one year.

In general people who approach training the ABC dog as if it where a collie, but without the level of repetition that most collies are comfortable with, can have results that are very pleasing.

Teaching Rescue Dogs

Rescue dogs always bring along baggage, but then dogs that come direct from breeders are not always perfect either. When a dog is bought from a good breeder it is normally the new owner rather than previous history that causes any behaviour problems. Of course not all breeders give the dog the best of starts but most do their best to provide their customers with a pup that is sound in mind and body.

Most rescue dogs are in a rescue situation because of behaviour problems (although there are some other reasons such as death of the owner or ill health.) The rescue organisation may not be aware of problems because not all owners are honest about the problems just in case the organisation refuses to take the dog or worse suggests it is euthanased. Not all problems become evident in a kennels situation so it may not be possible for the rescue organisation to detect them. Of course some dogs are found roaming or dumped and picked up by the dog warden, police or members of the public so their history is rarely known.

Pedigree dogs are sometimes available through general rescue organisations, but if you want a specific breed it is best to contact a specific breed rescue who will be able to advice you of availability. Some breeds are very commonly found in rescue the 3 most common are Border collies, German shepherds and Greyhounds. You may be able to gain a little more of the dog's history from a breed rescue, but it is not always the case.

The first thing to do with any rescue dog is to build up a relationship and teach the dog to have confidence in you and any others that he will have to deal with on a regular basis. This is done with guidance, control, reward and love – love on its own is not nearly enough! Many new owners feel sorry for their rescue dog, especially if it seems that it has previously had a rough time. They offer it many privileges but all too soon the dog can begin to make himself at home and if the owner is not careful the dog may take over their life in a way that might not be appropriate.

It is easy to assume that a dog has been mistreated when it comes from a rescue situation, and obviously sometimes it has. But often, the dog has been simply misunderstood, even dogs that cower have not necessarily been hit it could be that they are naturally submissive and have never been given the confidence to develop more outgoing tendencies. Some dogs don't like men or children – it doesn't automatically mean they have been mistreated by them, they may just lack the experience of good associations. Without that positive experience some men can seem to the dog to be large or loud. Children may behave in a way that is alien to the dog for example, small children may be at eye level and may stare into the dog's eyes, others may be loud, excitable or move quickly etc. We can see the parallel in dogs that have been brought up without any beatings but are still wary of them just as some dogs are wary of objects – for example prams, wheelchairs, bikes, traffic. The way round it is to give them good associations to build their confidence.

Many behaviour problems in rescue dogs are linked to fear or underlying lack of confidence and or be naturally submissive or sensitive – at the other end of the spectrum dominance can be a problem too ironically the two are often linked. The dominant dog can lack confidence or fear for his assumed position and therefore become difficult to deal with or even aggressive.

Other common problems link to breed type for example chasing and nipping in Border collies and terriers, guarding and or territorial behaviour in German shepherds, Dobermanns etc.

A good way to help a dog to get over problems and build confidence is to apply a technique called *counter conditioning*. This gives the dog an alternative behavioural route to the one he normally would take and gives him a controlled 'get out' of difficult situations with you as the handler in good control. *(See Problem Solving)*.

You should also get your rescue dog veterinary checked to ensure that that is fit and healthy before you start training. Make observations on the dog's normal behaviour patterns and get to know its likes and dislikes as quickly as possible. The first couple of weeks are very important to the new relationship and problems can be avoided but also unfortunately created during the early stages of the settling in process. Make your household rules fair and stick to them so that the dog knows where he stands and what and where the behavioural and physical boundaries are set. Treat him with kindness and fairness but don't forget to maintain control.

Once you are ready to embark on the more formalised training programme, take things a step at a time, observing the dog's responses as closely as possible.

Don't treat problems as an excuse because he is a rescue, look at them as a challenge to be overcome to help the dog live a normal life with few or no hang ups. Every achievement will feel fantastic as it does for everyone, but will be all the more special knowing that the dog's fate could have been so much different.

Voice - Tones and Usage

What you do with your voice, rather than what you say and the commands that you use, will hold great importance to your dog training and ultimate performance. You need to develop continuity of voice control in training and in the ring.

Use of Tones

It is important to stay in control of your vocal chords. A change in tone, even if your are saying the same word, can mean a totally different thing to the dog, and may result in a missed position in heelwork or distance control, an incorrect drop in sendaway, or even something as simple as confusion over retrieve etc. Experiment by saying the dog's name in differing tones and watch his reactions. Some handlers even teach exercises such as distance control or sending the dog round to heel, (the finish), just using differing tones of the dog's name instead of a range of keywords. It is quite acceptable to do this, and the dog will learn to respond very well so long as the handler is consistent.

Voice tone can mean many things to the dog; for example it can mean pleasure, reward, interest, boredom, fear, or even something to be avoided. When using your voice in training you must make sure that the tone that you use to teach the dog is the same tone that you will use when you want the dog to perform the task in the ring. Many handlers make vital mistakes when transferring the trained exercise to a ring situation. Because of the distance, the handler needs the voice to carry, the tone of voice quite naturally changes when the volume level varies. It will also vary because of nerves or anxiety regarding the dog's, or indeed the handler's own ability to perform under the pressure of a ring situation. Whatever the reason handlers very often do not sound the same in the ring as they do in training. This is most confusing for the dog, often the dog ends up being chastised for his incorrect actions, when really the handler was not putting over their wishes in a way that the dog could understand, and therefore the dog should not have been expected to perform correctly.

It is with this in mind that, as a handler, you must train yourself to use the same tones in training as those that you intend to use in the ring. To create this, it is often best to put yourself in a mock up situation without the dog.

Let us take the sendaway as an example of when a keyword is needed at a distance, when the dog is in the correct area at the appropriate distance the keyword 'Down' is used to drop the dog. Natives of northern England may find it very difficult to project the word 'down' and make it carry any distance, whereas those with a Southern accent can give the word a more drawn out centre, 'D-a-a-o-wn'. Northerners may find the Southern pronunciation easier to use. But, everyone is different and you need to experiment, not just in the house or garden, but outside in areas that could represent a show ground environment. You will find that a voice that carries well in 12' x 15' room in the house is unlikely to sound so powerful out in the field with the wind against it.

Once you have decided on your keyword and tone usage, and have accustomed yourself to using it in the same way each time, then you can start to teach the dog. Use your play training, to associate your voice and tones with the actions that you would like him to perform. Remember, if you have had to re-think some of your pronunciations and tones, then you will have to give the dog every opportunity of getting it right. This means '**Training**', not just going through the motions of the exercise, but actually show the dog what you want, as if he had never done it before. This way he will learn very quickly, and you will prevent errors from creeping in. This will save lots of time and frustration for both you and the dog.

Use of Verbal Commands

An important thing to remember is that, there is no point in saying a keyword, unless you are sure the dog is in a position to carry out the desired action to that word, or that you are in a position to ensure that he does by guiding him. Repeating a word and having the dog not do the appropriate action is paramount to teaching him to ignore or learn an inappropriate action to that word, (or to do the action only after numerous repetitions of the word). Therefore do not say the keyword until you are sure of immediately getting the required action associated with that word. This applies in the training of all exercises - make sure that you can achieve your aim and then put the keyword in. The dog does not understand our language, and therefore we have to find ways of showing him what we mean. Once he understands, by our actions, what we mean, it is a simple and painless task to link in a keyword.

Just about everyone, at the outset of training their dog, introduces far too many verbal commands, sometimes expecting the dog to understand whole sentences, and cluttering their keywords with lots of added extras for good measure. It is much easier for the dog, if we keep the keywords to a bare minimum; it is certainly easier having done this, to eliminate verbal commands ready for the higher classes. The typical heelwork vocabulary, with the inexperienced handler, consists of a variation on the following: "heel, close, watch, watch me, get in, come on, tight, back, turn, that's good, what have I got, bum in, what's this then, where's your squeaky, good boy, clever, rubbish, Oih!" All of this can be heard together with an assortment of noises that I will leave to your imagination! An incredible variety and quantity of messages being put over to the dog all really meaning one thing - follow my left leg please. Go along to any pre beginner/beginner/novice ring and listen to the cacophony of verbals. Then, watch out for the experienced handler with their young dog, competing in the novice ring. Often their dog will be among the youngest competing in that class, and yet the handler will not be uttering anything like the amount of commands and verbal stimulus.

Normally the dog who does not have to contend with all this 'verbal diarrhoea' will be much more attentive, and find it easier to concentrate with the aid of just a little well timed help from the handler. *(See Timing)*.

Some handlers may argue the point that their dog works attentively when they give lots of verbal stimuli however; what will happen after a few attempts in the higher classes without the aid of the voice? Nine times out of ten, when the handler shuts off the noise, the dog is confused and less motivated. The handler then becomes frustrated and, if we are not very careful, loses their temper with the dog into the bargain. Of course the dog then sinks even lower. This common fault could be one of the major reasons for the high drop out rate of handlers or rejection of dogs after the lower classes. Many new handlers come into the sport with non-standard breeds, (as far as obedience is concerned). Perhaps this basic problem is a contributory factor as to why so many of them give up. If they do come back into the sport it is often with the almost obligatory collie, alas many will make the same mistakes again even with a collie! Get it right in the first place and perhaps we will see more persevering with ABCs.

If you are recognising yourself at this point, please do not feel that you must be one of the dropouts, all is not lost. Because you have recognised the problem you are half way on the road to solving it.

As you work through the exercises in the next section of the book, you will see that one keyword only is necessary to trigger each action. The dog will learn to follow through the exercise solely on that one keyword (and the linked body posture from the handler) with just added encouragement and motivational tools in the early stages, or at any time that you feel the dog needs an extra boost of confidence.

Breathing

You will need to control your breathing. It is common for dogs to anticipate keywords because they learn to associate the intake of breath that precedes a keyword with the desired act. This is particularly evident in distance control. This is because we tend to take breaths differently to make different sounds – the more confident the dog gets the more likely he is to pick up on this. Therefore try to breathe quietly through your nose and avoid great movement of the chest. Breathing through your diaphragm pulling the breath from as low down as possible will also help prevent coughing or the catching of breath. Also teach the dog to wait for the command, it can be very cute when your dog first reacts to your intake of breath, but it must go unrewarded and trained against if you want to eliminate this type of point costly anticipation.

Controlling your breathing will also help with general self-control. It will help you to overcome nerves and maintain control during fast pace.

The sections on *Understanding the Dog's Mind, Motivation, Rewards* and *Play Training* will help you to know when, and how intensely, to give reward and encouragement, and the sections on Linking will explain how the dog is able to understand how to perform, following one keyword only, a complicated task.

Problem Solving

Most problem solving is better tackled by retraining. If you try to correct problems by corrective training methods, blocking etc., it often confuses the dog and you can end up with a dog that thinks that the original behaviour pattern and the newly introduced corrective lesson are all part of the desired end result. For example if your dog goes wide in heelwork and you correct him by bringing him in closer following a wide, he may learn that the wide and the correction are all part of the exercise. With a number of repetitions in training, the dog will learn to go wide and then correct himself. Often handlers see that the dog is 'trying' to get it right and feel that they have succeeded. However, the dog will show the fault in the ring and may be marked by the judge as inconsistent, erratic in its it position or simply wide each time it drifts. Therefore almost always it is best to train the exercise using your aids to ensure that the dog can't go wrong and reward him for the correct action that occurs straight away – which is after all what is needed in the ring.

Problem solving cannot be achieved without the handler's ability to anticipate and identify the starting point or triggers of problems. Reading the dog's body language (posture, tail and ear carriage, expression, and eyes) is of paramount importance and cannot be underestimated.

The dog's past experience (training and lifestyle) and natural drives will play a big part in his behaviour, therefore careful thought should be given to any problem before you begin searching for the answer.

Counter Conditioning (Distraction Training)

Sometimes problems can be quite severe and obsessive. Behaviours such as diving out at other dogs, barking at people, dogs or other animals etc. can be a problem even when your dog is trained for obedience competitions. One of the most common and effective means of re-focusing a dog is to counter condition (sometimes termed distraction training). This means to teach the dog to focus onto something else, instead of what it is that causes him to behave in an inappropriate manner. This technique can also be used to focus dogs onto the handler even when faced with their ultimate distraction. For example if an another person's squeaky toy distracts your dog, use one yourself and follow this technique. *(See Teaching the Older Dog – Case study).*

Before you start tackling any problem behaviours the dog must be ultra confident in you as his handler and partner because you are going to be taking control of situations and he must feel you are capable of doing so. If you lose your temper easily or are inconsistent or unpredictable the dog will not have confidence in your ability to deal with situations and will try to deal with them himself.

The handler needs to be aware of the triggers that will make the dog go into the undesirable behaviour. The handler must be able to predict possible problems and learn to act before they become a problem. If the handler only reacts when the behaviour goes wrong this technique will not work effectively. As a rule of thumb, if you are not sure if the situation is a possible trigger for the behaviour problem, take it as is if it is – it is better to be safe than sorry.

For problem areas like chasing, interaction problems and so on, where the handler fights a loosing battle every time they come into that situation, teaching a new and powerful behaviour will give them the control and confidence they need.

Powerful is the operative word. The new behaviour needs to be powerful, i.e. the dog needs to want to do it at least as much, preferably more, than he wants to do things that are inappropriate.

During the retraining process, try to avoid any of the problem situations if at all possible. Every time the problem arises, you are in effect condoning it, no matter what your reaction is, so it is better to try to avoid the problem for a while until you have a good strong positive tool to work with.

Step 1 You need to find a toy or a reward that the dog will 'sell his soul' for. A squeaky toy is great because it is audible, but it is more important that the dog wants it.

Step 2 Next take other toys out of the way so that the dog cannot look elsewhere for his fun. Also, do not follow an adlib feeding routine that allows the dog to have food available all of the time. At the same time, work on mentally and physically distancing yourself from the dog so that the dog is craving your attention instead of getting it on demand.

Step 3 *(Using a toy)* - Once steps 1 and 2 have been achieved, you should begin your training, start by playing with the toy. If the dog offers to join in he should be allowed - if not he should be ignored and you should make an issue of having some fun on your own, all the while ignoring the dog. Have just a short session of this and then the toy is put away. Make it fun, don't always give him the toy straight away, tease him with it, make him follow and make an effort to get it. Once he has the toy enter into a game with him and the toy. Take it away while he is still keen.

Step 4 *(Using food rewards)* – take some of your dog's favourite food, this can be anything he really likes e.g. roast chicken, sausage, cheese, fish, liver. Pretend to eat some yourself, if the dog comes to you asking for the food make him wait and want but then after a few moments give him some. Give only very little at a time and in any one session to start with. Make the food fun, don't always give it to him straight away, tease him with it, and make him follow your hand and the food so that he has to make an effort to get it. (NB do not use chocolate, grapes or raisins as these can be poisonous to dogs.)

Step 5 The session is repeated. Soon the dog will start to be keen to join in. The handler should always be the one to finish the game, and to maintain control of the dog and the toy/rewards. As the dog becomes interested, draw him towards you by backing off a few paces before giving the reward. This way he is learning to come away from distraction and put his faith in you. The game should be finished leaving the dog wanting more.

Step 6 Once you are sure the dog is keen, it is good idea to give the game a name or a sound cue, so that the dog can easily be turned on to the fun both by using his eyes and his ears, and probably his nose too. Use a word that is not often used in your day to day language and not included in your training so far. It is also a good idea to give a physical cue if you can, a couple of gentle tugs on the lead followed by reward will soon have the dog making a good association with that action and this will aid your control. The lead training can be progressed to a longer line when and where appropriate.

Keep working at this, with careful planning and control, until you reach the stage that the dog will turn towards you and have a game or enjoy your reward anytime you give the cue.

Step 7 It is now important to train the game in a variety of situations. Try in different rooms of the house, the garden, and other quiet areas. Once you are confident, the dog can be taken to a mildly distracting place and the same game instigated.

Step 8 Once the dog is working well in all of the above and you feel confident that you can predict his behaviour pattern, start to take him closer to situations that have been problematic in the past. Take it slowly to start with and go only as close as you feel you have control. Do not over do it, keep the sessions short and positive.

It should be remembered that the dog would easily lapse back into his old behaviour if you allow the situation to occur. You must act before the situation becomes a problem, anticipating the problem and guide the dog away to have some fun rather than fighting the problem. Soon the dog will make the choices that bring him the best opportunity to enjoy life and feel comfortable.

Punishment

Is there a place for negative training techniques such as chastisement, raised voice or smacking? On the whole the answer to this is no – lack of understanding cannot be altered by threat or punishment. However, if your dog is used to you working with him in a calm way, in an emergency a raised voice can stop him in his tracks – if he is used to a raised voice on a daily basis it will not have the desired effect.

Chastisement is not a good way of training a dog. Your dog will only try to avoid contact with you rather than take the chastisement, or worse still you could find your dog taking out his frustration on you, another member of the family or even an innocent third party, (redirected aggression).

Training in a negative manner is not pleasant for the dog or the handler and could be deemed a welfare issue so is best avoided.

Control Measures

Teaching your dog the meaning of words such as leave and off in a controlled and constructive way will help you to control and guide away from problems. Use what the dog knows and teach him what you do want rather than dwelling on the problem behaviours. Develop a positive attitude towards any behaviour the dog gives you and consider the difference between what he does and what you want a challenge rather than a problem and you will be well on the right track.

Section Two
Techniques

There are very many techniques for training dogs. You may be using differing techniques to those described in this book – this does not mean that the either is wrong – just different. As long as the technique is humane, motivational and it gets the desired results then it is okay to use. Try to stay with a technique for reasonable amounts of time to give it chance to work. However, if there seems to be no improvement or the dog is becoming confused it is best to take a break and consider whether the technique is ideal for you and your dog.

Akamai Frosted Fizz (Photo by John Midgley)

Before You Start...

Before embarking on any of the techniques described in this section you must first consider several points:

1 Do you really understand the concepts?
2 Can you easily recall the importance and apply split second accuracy of timing?
3 Have you formed a true bond with your dog?
4 Does he respond the second you appear and give him motivation - whatever the circumstances?
5 Does you dog truly 'Want' to play and to be with you?
6 Do you have a good understand as to how the dog's mind works?
7 Are you prepared to have fun and keep your patience with your dog?
8 Have you the right equipment and motivation for your dog?

If you can confidently answer 'Yes' to all of the above then you can now move on to learning the techniques for teaching your dog the exercises. If you have any doubts, then it won't hurt, in fact it will be beneficial to go back over any grey areas, make notes as you go through if it helps, and treat your work as if you were studying a subject that you were to be examined on. This may seem a little extreme but, after all, if you are to be entering competitions then you are offering yourself up for the scrutiny of others, so you really should know your subject as well as possible.

If you are pleased with the results of a technique that you are already using to teach your dog, then there is no need to change just because the technique described in this book might be different. Most techniques used in teaching for competition today will be effective, as long as they are kind and fair to the dog, and used in conjunction with the concepts described in the first section of this book.

Don't complicate matters, all techniques should be kept as simple as possible, both for you to be able to implement correctly, and for the dog to understand and learn. Obviously some techniques suit different characters of dogs, and some suit different characters of people. In this section of the book are some methods that you might like to try, some you will have heard of before, or at least a variation on the theme, and others may be new to you.

Any harsh or forced methods of teaching are neither necessary or desirable. Take time out to understand your canine companions and work mate and leave aggression or temper out of the equation. During teaching, a dog learns nothing by being physically abused, bar the fact that you are not a very nice person, and that it might be as well to try to keep out of your way in the future.

Too much repetition can be mind numbing. Practicing the same exercise over and over again will not improve the dog's performance, if anything it will make it worse, the dog becomes confused, you will become frustrated, and then things go from bad to worse!

Teach all techniques step by step, and make sure that you understand what you are trying to achieve at each step, as well as the ultimate goal before you start on the poor dog. Be positive and well motivated in everything you do, and you will get a positive, motivated response from your dog. If his response is not what you want then stop, check, and carefully scrutinise what you are doing.

Remember you are the teacher, the dog is but the pupil. He can only learn if you show him in a way that he can understand. If the dog goes wrong do not chastise, simply start all over again and make sure that you get it right this time. Help the dog all of the way and enjoy the learning process together. Imagine if your child came home from school and said, 'Mum/dad, my teacher says the world is flat and if we get too near to the edge we will fall off'. Would you chastise the child for being wrong? No, it would be the teacher's fault for giving incorrect information. Likewise if a dog performs incorrectly, then we should look carefully at ourselves, to examine where we are going wrong.

Before starting to teach your dog anything, think carefully of the ultimate aim, then split the exercise into easy steps that you can follow. Approach each session with the view that you must retain in the dog the 'want' to work with you. Make sure that you are in a position to help the dog to achieve the keyword so as not to put him under any pressure. Be clear of your goal before you start, (both future and immediate). If you go wrong simply relax, play with your dog and start again.

The methods in this section are, on the whole, a basic guideline, and will serve to give you a structure to set you on the right track. They are simple and easy to follow, and almost all handlers, from sprightly teenagers to more sedate senior citizens and their dogs will be able to cope well and get good results. All you need is to have a pleasant attitude, and to give yourself and your dog a fair chance.

So enjoy yourself, training should be fun. If you are not in the mood, just go out and have a game with your dog, you might find the dog will get you in the mood, if not there is always tomorrow!

Deportment and Attitude

There is more to dog training than simply teaching the dog some tasks, especially if you wish to compete. It is important to work on your own attitude and body posture in order to give the dog a fair chance of understanding what is required.

When teaching any exercise, it is very important that you maintain as upright a body stance as physically possible. Accepted, you will need to bend to the dog, especially the smaller dog, but you must constantly tell yourself to keep upright, bottom tucked in and shoulders square pointing in the direction that you are going. If you don't do this in training, when you come to work your dog in the ring, it will feel so different to the dog that he will think you are in a totally different mood, or that the circumstances are different. He will not understand how you want him to work, and then all of that training, no matter how good, is wasted. Therefore, you must aim to have the same body stance and attitude in training, as you will have in the ring.

It is easy to identify someone who is not behaving in the same way as usual. Nerves and tension can change the handler's deportment. You need to get a good friend to watch and to yell at you if you are not upright, if you are leaning into your dog, or have the famous 'collie shoulder' i.e. the handler's shoulder dropped back and down in an attempt to hold the dog back using posture. (Whatever your breed this can be a problem!)

When you are trying to perform a good piece of flowing heelwork you need to be able to identify if your training posture is different to your handling posture. If you have worked on deportment in training then, even if you are nervous in the ring, to some extent you will be giving off the right signals to the dog because your body stance will be correct. The dog will then have something concrete to latch on to and will feel more confident – this in turn has a knock on effect to you.

Some handlers are very verbal and lively in training, but then are unable to react in the same way when someone is watching. Adjust your training to suit your personality. If you know that you find it hard to be

extrovert in public then learn to handle in a quieter manner in training. The dog's hearing is far greater than ours, you don't need to screech and shout, try whispering to your dog, see how he responds. Use your toy - your common bond, to reward the dog. Once the dog is hooked on a toy your input can be minimal giving you time to concentrate on yourself. Find a happy medium where you can cope in public and train in the same way. The dog will soon learn to respond to the 'quieter you' in training, and so it will be easier for him to read you when you are in the show ring.

The same attitude and procedure applies in all of the exercises, as your training progresses work on maintaining the upright body posture that you will use in the ring. Use the same sort of actions, words and signals each time, don't change your routine of setting the exercise up when your get within the ring ropes. In training don't let the dog fly off in-between exercises, you won't be able to do that in the ring, keep the fun next to you.

Practice on your own, just as you should with the footwork for turns etc., to get a natural, even, balanced gait until you feel comfortable with it. Use a pacesetter (electronic metronome or even a piece of marching music on a portable CD or Cassette player) to create a regular pace. The more you do it, the more natural it will become.

Make sure you are starting out in the correct manner too. Your feet should be together, the dog sitting straight and neatly by your side. You should be standing up straight and holding a loose lead (if attached). Your hands should be positioned in a natural comfortable manner that you can hold through out. In the lower classes you will be able to move your arms as you wish in the UK but at test 'A' any hand movements will be construed as extra commands. In the UK you are allowed to either loosely swing your arms or hold them still. In other countries it may be compulsory to swing your arms (or suffer the subsequent point loss of course!).

Watch other handlers, see how the good ones bend and straighten in a natural progression, and their body is upright most of the time, always becoming upright when the dog is in a working position even when training. The best place to watch is in the car park when handlers are warming up or training prior to going into the ring. But beware, don't take on board everything you might see in the car park, some handler's attitudes to the dog leave a lot to be desired!

So to recap - Keep upright. Develop a natural, even, gait. Be the same in training as you intend to be in the ring. Shoulders back, body facing the direction in which you are going, tuck your bottom in, don't slouch into the corners, turn keeping your body square. Aim to flow!

The Watch

Before you start teaching the watch you must have achieved 'The Want'. The dog must be interested in communicating with you and motivated by your rewards.

The watch is probably the most important single exercise you will ever teach your dog. Before starting this or any other exercise, you should first have established the 'Want'. If your dog does not 'want' to be with you, to work with you as a team, or to bond with you, then you will have an uphill struggle and probably never reach the level you wish to attain.

Firstly we need to establish just what we want from the dog when we say the keyword 'Watch'? It should mean 'Pay attention to me whatever you are doing, look and listen ready for your next command or signal'. This is a lot for a dog to take in from one single command. But with patient guidance and a lot of love and play, it can be achieved. Obviously some dogs and handlers will find it easier than others will and past experience will have a bearing on speed and ease of teaching.

Teaching the watch is a good 'hearth rug' exercise, i.e. you can do it anytime that you and the dog are together, e.g. at home on the hearth rug! To start with it should be done with no distractions. When the dog becomes competent and confident, distractions will be added and worked with and against. You can start this exercise at any age, but you must be sure first that the dog is happy and confident with you.

Clicker Tips
Click on the behaviour you want – this is usually eye contact at least to start with. However watch is going to mean pay attention and as long as the dog is doing this, direct eye contact is not always necessary.

Keep sessions short and fine-tune your timing to ensure you are clicking on the right thing. Don't fall into the trap of using the clicker to get the dog's attention.

Keyword Choice

The ideal keyword is 'Watch', but if you know that you have already frightened or confused your dog with this word, or if you use this for another activity then use a different word to make it easier for the dog to understand what you are trying to achieve. Choose your word carefully so that it cannot be confused with any others that you use.

Step 1 - As with all teaching, have the dog on a soft lead and collar. Start off with a game and a cuddle. Use a titbit or a toy to get the dog switched on to you.

Go down to the dog's level, i.e. on the floor with a smaller dog or puppy, (sitting on a chair, or standing with a bigger dog). If you are standing, be careful not to stoop over the dog - keep an upright body posture bowing only your head where necessary.

You can start to teach the watch when the dog is most receptive.

Talk to him in excited tones; stimulate him with his toy or titbit. Hold the motivator up towards your face, as soon as you have eye contact, say the keyword 'Watch', immediately reward with your incentive, then break the exercise giving your release command, 'That'll do'. Keep up the momentum and the 'want' by playing.

Repeat the procedure when you are sure that you have the 'want'. The initial eye contact need only be for a fraction of a second, the object is to get it right and give immediate praise so that the dog knows that he has done a correct action, and that you are pleased. If you try to hold the eye contact too long, the dog has the option, and it becomes increasingly tempting, for him to look away,.

Eye contact could be construed by the dog as a dominant stare, and he will have no option but to look away if he feels dominated by you. (If it were any other way you would have problems). So make sure that your eyes show friendship and fun, never threat.

It is not necessary for the dog to look at you eye to eye, the word 'Watch' could come to mean watch my hand, or simply watch my body stance. The dog will be reading all of these signs, and acting on his learnt responses to them. He picks up far more from your body than he does from words. So, as long as he looks at you in connection with that word then you are going in the right direction.

Remember your aim, which is to teach the dog to look at you and pay full attention when he hears the keyword 'watch'. Fractions of seconds of perfection are worth months of corrective training.

Step 2 - Once the dog is happy to watch you for a fraction then you can progress to a full second. If your timing is correct and you are truly praising the dog at the correct time, he can then associate your praise and play with the action.

Analyse yourself, be sure that the dog is being praised at the exact time that he responding correctly. If his eyes are looking elsewhere then you are either going on too quickly, he is confused, or you are not portraying the correct attitude and/or body posture, and the dog may feel dominated.

Step 3 - Once the dog is happily watching in the play sessions you can progress to having the dog sit by your side. Start off at dog level, kneel on the floor or sit sideways on a low chair if you have a larger dog. Place the dog in the sit position by your side, guide his face up to look at you, stroke the velvety part of the dog's nose and calmly teach him that it is

Guide the dog's head into the correct position and teach him to enjoy being there.

a pleasant and soothing place to be, as well as a fun place. Then, when the dog is watching put in the 'watch' keyword, release and play.

Spend time at this and the above stage, repeating several times at each play or bonding session, or anytime you feel you will get good results.

Step 4 - When you are sure the dog knows what you mean when you say watch, you can start to introduce some distractions. Start off with something not too attractive, like a person sitting quietly, or a quiet but new environment. Repeat as above from the beginning.

Step 5 - Once the dog is coping with all of the above you can introduce your own more realistic distractions, one at time of course. Drop the lead, sneeze, have someone speak, work against another dog, another handler training, etc. Be fair to the dog, tell him what you want, don't try to catch him out all the time. That is not what it is all about. You are teaching and should make the atmosphere stable and enjoyable, not threatening.

If the distractions are too great and you are failing to get the right response, put some distance between you and the distraction. Work gradually nearer as you get the right response. (Not necessarily all in one session).

Step 6 - Teach the dog to watch from a range of situations not just in the heel position. Once you have stable static positions i.e. sit, down and stand, the dog can be taught to watch while he maintains the position.

Put him in the sit, tell him 'Sit, Watch'. Gently leave him to a lead's length, repeating both words. Use your toy/titbit to keep his attention. Go back still talking and reassuring. Gently position yourself back in the heel position. Praise, reward and release. Repeat for the other positions. This will be a useful exercise for DC, recalls, stays etc.

Step 7 - Repeat any and all of the above, anytime, anywhere, to continually remind the dog what is required when he hears the keyword 'Watch'. Ideally have this training exercise at the start of every training session, as part of the warm up routine. It is important that you do not neglect this important part of the training in favour of corrective methods, as too much correction will de-motivate the dog towards the action.

Trouble Shooting

The main problems are caused by the handler asking for the dog to pay attention for too long a time in the initial stages of training, poor timing of rewards, fear (of the handler or of an outside influence), distraction.

No Obvious Reason

Start your training from the beginning and ensure the rewards are high and the time span short. Reward perfect seconds rather than holding off for longer periods. Build up the time slowly. It may be necessary to vary the rewards to keep the dog's interest.

Fear or Apprehension

If the dog is apprehensive, you must tackle that problem first before expecting him to watch you unconditionally. Some dogs are naturally more wary or sensitive than others and these will find it hard to concentrate.

A submissive dog may be reluctant to look you in the eye as this is a dominant act.

All of these issues can be tackled by a combination of confidence boosting and association with good things. Take time out to tackle the problem. For example if the dog is wary of other dogs he will want to keep an eye on them and will not be able to concentrate. Take him to good well controlled reward based training classes and allow him to learn how to socialise or deal with other dogs being around. Don't keep asking him to do things allow him time to take in the situation and learn that it poses no threat.

If the dog is fearful of the handler then there are a lot of bridges to build. The relationship must be mended before any progress can be expected.

Distraction

If the dog is easily distracted because of his/her interest in outside influence then he needs to spend a lot of time amongst those distractions until they become less appealing.

When this has been achieved the training should start at a distance away from the distraction to gain the dog's attention and then work gradually nearer as the dog learns to enjoy the game of 'watch'. You will also need to make yourself very appealing to match and better the outside influences.

You will find that use of your leave command exercise comes in handy if you have taught it well. When using the leave command, make sure that you remember to reward the correct behaviour.

You may also find counter conditioning of use in cases where the dog's behaviour has developed into a habit. *(See Problem Solving)*

Don't avoid distractions seek them out and work against them.

Leave on Command

Before you start - The dog need not know any formal exercises, although an understanding of what is meant by 'Sit', will be a useful tool to help keep him under control and make him focus on the job in hand. He must however, be confident in his handler, and happy to be on lead.

This exercise, although not a formal obedience test, is a very useful discipline to teach your dog. It will be used to tell the dog to leave other dog's, to ignore incorrect articles, leave people alone, keep off furniture, and has all manner of other applications within the competition world as well as at home. It will also help you to have control of your 'want' aids and other rewards. Use it when you need it, taught as a proper exercise it will serve you well.

Step 1 - Have the dog under control on his lead. Hold the lead a short distance from the collar. Try to have the lead loose so that the dog is not relying on it for his messages, but just a turn of your wrist will give you control when you need it. It doesn't matter what position the dog is in (sit, down or stand) as we are teaching a leave not a position.

Take a titbit, or part of his dinner. Give him a small piece so that he gets a taste. Take another piece and show him what you have. He will assume that it is for him, so this time, as he reaches forwards, say the keyword 'Leave', in an authoritative, yet pleasant manner.

Prevent him from getting the titbit by using your lead to pull him back away from the treat and then relax the lead again. It may be a bit of a struggle to start with and the dog may be puzzled by your actions, but persevere in a pleasant and controlled manner, repeating the pull back and relax technique until he sits back away from the treat on his own.

As soon as he does this, reward him with the treat, but introduce a keyword to say that he may have it, e.g. 'Take it'.

Step 2 - Repeat as above, this time the dog may start to get the message. If he sits back and pulls away from the treat straight away, go immediately in with the reward. This is the behaviour you are striving for - so reward it. If he tries to get to the treat, pull him back, (as above) and keep him there a few seconds, and then reward, 'Take it'. Remember he will not learn if you keep the lead tight all the time – so relax the lead as soon as you have pulled back.

Step 3 - Repeat again, by now most dogs are starting to understand. As you approach with the treat, tell him 'Leave', count a few seconds after it is obvious that he is trying, then reward him. 'Take it'.

Step 4 - Build up the length of time that the dog is sitting or withdrawing from the titbit. If he does really well reward him sooner. Now the rewards should start to come at various, unpredictable times. Count to yourself to see how you and the dog are improving. 1,2,3,4, 'Take it'. 1,2,3,4,5,6, 'Take it', 1,2, 'Take it', and so on. Remember to reward in a random fashion, the dog will soon learn a pattern if you become predictable. You will be surprised how hard it is for we humans, creatures of habit that we are, not to start building up a pattern - so work hard on randomising yourself.

Step 5 - Now you can transfer the dog's newfound control not to differing circumstances and objects. Choose an object in the house that the dog is not to have, control him whilst you wave it in front of him. Give him the keyword 'Leave', when he pulls back away from the object, reward him with a high value treat.

This can be broadened into all sorts of situations. The dog can be taught not to jump up, not to go on furniture, to keep away from the gate, all using the same basic procedure, simply adjusting for each situation, and controlling the dog so that he knows what you do or do not want. You may wish to introduce a different keyword, depending on the circumstances, but apply the same psychology.

Static Positions
Sit, Down and Stand

The teaching of statics can be a much-neglected discipline. Generally some positive structured time is taken when the dog is a puppy, but then, as he grows older, the tendency is to rush to go on to more interesting things like heelwork, retrieve, etc.

The three static positions, Sit, Down, and Stand are the basis and control element of many of the teaching exercises, so it is of utmost importance that the dog is happy and confident in these positions, and truly understands the meanings of the three keywords and/or signals.

Some breeds and types of dogs are more prone to anxiety, are more reactive to their senses, and/or have highly tuned instinctive drives that make them strive to keep the family together. These types are more likely to break stays than others. For example the German shepherd dog is a highly reactive breed. He will soon become anxious which also leads to problems such as mouthing of retrieve/scent articles.

One shouldn't feel defeated by this fact, but being armed with this knowledge helps you to understand that great time and patience must be taken, particularly when training and working with this type of dog.

The more anxious the dog, the more likely it is that he will want to break and come to find you, or simply to run out of the ring in panic causing chaos around the show ground.

The dog needs to be taught the discipline in such a way that he will become stable, feel content and confident when left, and will understand to stay put until released or given further instruction. This means, as with all of your training, that you must be patient, confident in your approach and thorough in your training technique.

There are a variety of techniques for teaching statics, handlers and dogs will vary in their ability and appreciation of them. It is a good idea to work with the dog and try out a few to see what suits the pair of you as a team the best. The most important thing is that the dog does not feel pressurised or confused. Some of the 'hands on' techniques (modeling) are quite manipulative, but done in the correct manner the dog can learn to enjoy being handled – in fact some dogs thrive and learn quickly with these methods, others fair better with a more 'hands off' approach. Many handlers like to use a combination.

Think about your aim all of the time, even when going about your household duties and normal daily activities, these times can be moulded into training sessions. However, don't ask your dog to do something and then not be in a position to make sure that you can enforce it (in the nicest possible way of course). If you are busy, preoccupied or too tired to bother then put the dog out of your way or just ignore him. Never expect a dog to perform correctly if you, as his teacher, are not in a position to help him along the way.

Clicker Tips

Clicker training is great for building a confident static position. The dog will soon start to take up the required position quickly and smartly. The click marks the behaviour but also tends (in most cases) to end the exercise as the dog comes to get his reward on hearing the click. This procedure is fine at the starting point. As you develop the time in which the dog maintains the position you will need to withhold the click for increasing lengths of time to hold him in position. However you can reach the point at which you can use the clicker as a confidence boost while holding the position – this is discussed in the section on stays.

The Sit

Teaching the sit position is often taken for granted. It is almost as though people think that dogs should come ready programmed. True, the sit is a natural position for the dog, but he has to be taught our concept in conjunction with the keyword.

Some methods will work better than others for teaching this position, much depends on you and your dog, and your experiences so far. If you have been spending time getting the dog into the sit position in front of you for Distance Control, then the dog may try to avoid being in the sit position beside you and is more likely to want to sit to the front. He may have a tendency to try to wriggle away to the front when he hears the keyword 'sit'. If you have this problem allow the dog to sit in the position he has become accustomed to and then *you* move into the side of *him*. Stroke him and soothe him with your voice. When he is settled gently move away again. Build up the exercise as you would any other, a little at a time. Doing this will prevent him from becoming confused or feeling pressured.

You may find that changing the keyword and/or signals, including body stance for this control exercise, will help if you have spent time on the DC type of sit before teaching the sit at your side. (It must be said that this is a fault that occurs more often amongst competitive handlers who are working on their second or third dog, because it is very enjoyable for the handler teaching the DC style positions, they can be introduced quite early, and practiced just about anywhere. Less experienced handlers are usually content to work on the basics!)

For the best results in competition, 'Sit' should mean just that to the dog, i.e. whatever you are doing, whatever position you are in, if you hear the keyword 'sit' then that is what you do, immediately, irrespective of anything else that is happening. Most people think that they are teaching just that, but confusion and frustration can soon set in.

The techniques described in this section will normally encourage the dog to bring his front feet backwards and his bottom straight down to achieve the sit. This is ideal for stays, DC, ASSD. But you will want to adjust the technique for presents and heelwork halts where you will normally want the dog to pull his back end into the sit while keeping his front legs still in the correct position. *(See relevant sections to achieve this).*

Keyword Usage For The Sit

The keyword that most people use for the sit exercise is not surprisingly *'Sit'*. It is not usually necessary to have differing words for the sit position in different exercises. However some handlers do prefer to use alternative commands because the body movement required from the dog varies, i.e. sometimes tucking the bottom in as in the present position and at other times taking a backward sit (drawing the front legs back) as in the case of DC. Some handlers make the difference clear by tone, for example in DC the word can be said in an elongated fashion to make sure that the word travels the distance. A quietly spoken person may prefer to use the hand signal for distance control.

For the sit in the 'present' position (retrieve or recall) it is not allowed to use a command beyond the Novice class in the UK. The position will be achieved on one commencing keyword only, and the dog must be taught the series of moves and to link them together. Most handlers very quickly drop (or don't even bother to introduce) the sit command for presents, using posture, lure, and positioning to get the dog into the correct place. This also applies to the sit at the halt in heelwork.

Starting The Sit With A Puppy

There are a variety of ways that you can get the dog to sit and enjoy being there. Following are some of the easiest:

1 **Reward/Incentive Based** - Use a treat and move it above the pup's head until he naturally sits, then give him the treat. Once you have the pup doing this quite naturally and easily you can introduce the keyword 'sit'. To lengthen the time the dog stays in position, simply withhold the titbit a few moments. Not too long to start with otherwise the dog will launch out of position. You can also use your 'leave' and 'watch' commands (if taught) to aid concentration and keep the dog in position.

2 **Modeling** - The sit can be introduced with a young puppy during play and bonding sessions. Wait until you have the puppy in a position where you know you can gain success, then simply place him into the sit position by putting one hand on his rump and the other guiding his front end up, a positive yet gentle action. As you do so, give the dog's name and the keyword 'Freddy sit'. Hold the position for seconds only, and then give the release word, ('OK' or 'that'll do') and continue playing.

This can be repeated a few times at each session, and pretty soon (as long as you keep getting your co-ordination and timing correct) the pup will be going into the position automatically as soon as you start to go through the motions of guiding him.

Always make sure your are in a position to be successful, never get complacent thinking the pup can do it on his own, otherwise you will be taking one step forwards and three steps back.

Be careful when handling the dog in this way to use gentle manipulation. Too much force may cause damage to the dog's developing limbs or he may be put off being handled.

3 **Feeding Time** - You can use dinnertime ensuring that the puppy sits for his meals each time, and of course with a puppy that gives you three or four training sessions each day. Be careful that you don't fall into the trap of waiting for the dog to sit after giving the command several times, all

you are teaching him then is 'In your own good time buddy!' Then later, you will wonder why you have a slow sit, or a dog that does not always respond on the first command.

Hold up his dish and wait for the dog to sit, then give him his food, this can take a while to start with. Alternatively take a small morsel from his dish and use it as described in technique 1. This can be repeated several times until the dog starts to be more responsive. His best response can be rewarded with the remainder of the food.

4   **Natural Behaviour** - You can also use the dog's own natural behaviour. Each time you observe the dog sitting simply put in your keyword and verbal praise and/or reward if you have one handy. Every little helps!

Older Dogs (Sit)

You can use all of the above techniques for older dogs, but your positioning may have to be different. Depending on the size of your dog it may be necessary for you to bend or go down on one knee to guide the older dog into position using the same procedure as described for puppies.

1   **Reward/Incentive Based** - The idea is the same as the puppies' section - technique 1, but stand up straight with larger dogs particularly. Dogs who are new to training, or those that have been harshly handled in the past will respond especially well to 'hands off', reward based techniques. This technique can be used in conjunction with modeling too.

Photo J. Midgley

Use a titbit or favourite toy to lure the dog into the sit. The position that you hold the food is important if you are to get a smart sit. Take your hand up slightly above his head and backwards. Too far forward and he will be encouraged into the stand or walk towards your hand, too far down and he may just do that - go down, too high and he may try to stand on his hind legs or beg. So experiment with the dog to find the perfect place to achieve the position. Give his keyword 'Sit' as he goes into the position and give the reward once he is there.

2   **Modeling** - If you have a larger dog try to keep your back straight as you position the dog, i.e. your torso should be facing front, bend at the knees, and guide the dog into the sit position. Obviously you may have to turn

towards the dog to start with, in order to gain control but you should aim to keep as straight as possible. You can use the titbit or toy to help, bringing it up in line with the dog's body to guide him straight.

With an older dog, you must still adopt the same sort of attitude as you did with the pup. The sit should be fun to do and not be associated with a threat.

2a Placing - Play with the dog get him relaxed and 'wanting', hold your lead in your right hand with your toy or 'want' aid ready in your pocket in case you need it or in your hand with the lead if it helps.

When you are ready, shorten up your lead so that you can gain better control, i.e. as near to the collar as possible. Then, with the dog's name, and the simultaneous keyword and action, lift upwards with your lead and press down with your left hand on the dog's rump. If you are sure of getting the position, add your keywords 'Freddy Sit'. Keep it there a few seconds only, praise whilst the dog is in the sit position and then give your release word, release the dog by pulling or encouraging it gently out of position and play.

At this point you must be careful that the dog does not learn to jump up out of position in order to get rewarded, therefore the abundance of calm yet meaningful praise should come whilst the dog's bottom is firmly on the floor.

It does not matter whether the dog is by your side, in front of you or at any angle in between, remember what you are teaching, an 'instant sit'. Differing angles will actually be an advantage, helping him to understand that wherever he is and whatever he is doing when he hears the keyword 'SIT' then that is what he does.

2b Stroking Legs - Some very large leggy dogs can be helped into the sit position by running your hand down the back of the hind legs. As you come to the knee joint apply a little pressure, you will feel the dog start to bend forward into the sit position, encourage and give confidence as the dog may wonder what is happening to him to begin with. Help by pushing back on the chest to ease the dog into the sit if necessary. This technique works particularly well with breeds like the Great Dane.

2c Using a Wall - With long bodied dogs the use of a wall is an added bonus. Sometimes it is a virtual impossibility to reach the back end of the dog with your hand especially if he wants to swing away to the side in an effort to see your face. Position yourself and the dog so that the wall acts as a barrier, preventing him from going to the side. This is a good technique to use on heavy dogs, or for people who are not as strong as they would like to be, it takes away the strain on the handler, and gives you much more control. Then use a lure (toy/titbit) to bring him into position.

3 Feeding Time – As with puppies you can use feeding time to aid your dog's understanding of the keyword 'sit'. It is a good time to help you gain better control of your dog, and extended sessions with food from the dog's rations will help build your bond.

4 Natural Behaviour – Again as with pups, whenever your dog takes up the position naturally you can add your keyword and reward.

The Down Position

The down is a submissive position, and many dogs feel vulnerable when manipulated at the outset. If, when the dog is first introduced to the command and action, or when asked to do it in the presence of another dog, he shows any awkwardness or aggression, it could be a sign of the dog being uncomfortable with his status. It could be that he is unsure and feeling vulnerable, or it could be that he sees himself as higher ranking and is taking aversion to you putting him into a submissive position. You must think seriously about your dog's position and where necessary go about applying dominance control rules in the home as well as in training. This will involve a combination of training and lifestyle changes that aim to get the dog into a lower ranking frame of mind. If allowed to continue, or the signs are ignored, elevated dominance can become a major problem that may creep up on you unawares. *(This is covered in some of the other books by the author, "Dog Training Instructors Manual", "Puppies" and the booklet "How To Be Top Dog". See appendices at the back of this book.)*

There are very many techniques to help you to get the dog into the down position, even with older dogs the methods described for puppies are good to start with. It must be remembered that this is very submissive position for the dog to find himself in. He will feel vulnerable and may become a little distressed to start with. You must give him courage and confidence and create a calming effect with your attitude towards him. If you become irritated or angry he will worry that something is indeed wrong and will not settle easily, if at all!

Keyword Usage For The Down - The keyword that most handlers use for the down is 'Down'. Other keywords you could use include 'Flat', 'Lie', or you could make up your own. There are a variety of situations where you will require a down but the actual body position will vary. For example in a stay situation you will want the dog flat on the ground or at least in a relaxed position. For DC it is best to train a sphinx shaped position and this is normally best (although not so concerning) for ASSD as well. For lying down in the house many handlers introduce another command (usually 'Settle'), which is a command that means go down where you like.

Starting The Down With A Puppy

As with the sit you can start training the down from a very early age. It is a good exercise to achieve early as it helps put you in control.

1   **Reward/Incentive Based** – Bring a titbit down between the dog's two front paws. Hold it in position until the dog follows it down. Once he is down release the titbit to the dog. Be careful to keep your hand still and close to the dog. If you draw it forward the dog will creep forward, too high and you will get a sit. If the dog does not go down straight away simply hold your hand still and entice with the titbit until he does.

2   **Modeling** - Starting with a young pup is always the easiest because they are so pliable and simple to manage. Place your right hand at the front of the dog, under and to the side of his chin. You may wish to slip your hand into the collar of larger or more powerful pups. For the smaller or less robust pup simply cup the dog around the shoulders, and with one hand on the dog's back, simply slide him back and slightly sideways into the down position.

Have the lead attached to his collar just in case you lose control whilst trying to manipulate him into position. You can then get a hold of the end of the lead before the dog disappears, and encourage him back to you, giving you the added bonus of retaining complete control. You shouldn't need to use the lead to get a small pup into position, kind, gentle hands can do all of the work.

To give the dog added incentive you can use a titbit or toy to entice him into position, but often it is not necessary if the dog has confidence in you, your own presence will be incentive enough for him to want to work with you.

If you use a titbit it should come straight down between his two front paws as above. Make sure you have perfected your handling technique and then introduce the keyword 'Down' to teach him the connection of word and action. Your hand position pointing down towards the floor, together with your body stance will become a signal to use later if and when necessary.

3   **Natural Behaviour** – As with the sit, you can also use the dog's own natural behaviour. Each time you observe the dog going into a down simply put in your keyword and verbal praise and/or food reward if you have one handy. This is especially useful to help train the dog to settle in the home.

Older Dogs (Down)

1   **Reward/Incentive Based** - Immature adults or adolescent dogs often go through a wriggly stage, where it becomes difficult to control them with your hands and the more you touch them the more wriggly they become. This is when a 'hands off' approach to teaching will be of great benefit.(Technique as above.)

2   **Modeling** – If the dog is unsure of being handled or has had a bad experience, you can use a combination of modeling and reward. Bring the motivator straight down between the dog's front paws as described above, and then, introduce your hands to gently soothe him. You will probably have to build up any touching of the dog fairly gradually, teaching him that your hands don't automatically mean a rough and tumble game or unpleasant correction and that they can be very soothing.

With all modeling techniques you must be careful that the dog does not come down with a bang as this can damage his limbs, or cause him fear or pain that constitutes a welfare issue, and will no doubt put him off too. This is especially a problem with heavy breeds. In all cases have the dog on a soft surface for these techniques. If in any doubt it is better to use the reward/incentive method. There are many modeling techniques for the down, here are just two.

2a **Side and Down** - If you can imagine the dog as if he were a roll of carpet. If you were to push straight down you would be unable to knock it over, but push to the side and it goes over easily; the same principle applies to your dog. Hold the dog on lead, have your hand up by his collar, preferably with the dog in the sit. Push gently but firmly on the shoulder sideways and down.

2b Weight Advantage - With larger dogs you should use their own weight to your advantage. One can learn a lot from watching the martial arts experts, and the way in which they use weight and balance. Place your hand on the dog's shoulder and feel the direction of his push, if you apply gentle pressure, he will usually push back. You can learn to use this, in that you can release the pressure and pull the dog towards you and into the down. You must learn to get the timing just right, and with practice, you will be able to apply this technique to the largest of dogs. When you know that you can get the procedure correctly, introduce the keyword *'Down'* and the dog will start to connect the word with the action.

The Stand

Of the three positions, the stand is the most neglected and those not actively needing the position tend to forget to train for it. However it does come in quite often and can be challenging to teach as the dog easily paddles out of position.

Keyword Usage For The Stand

The word that you choose is not as important as its usage. Many handlers use different words for different types of stand. For example in DC 'Back', for a temperament stand 'up', and for the stay 'Stand'. The different words are used because slightly different things are required from each of the positions. However, the dog is capable of learning that there is a difference in what you require simply from your body posture, physical gestures and set up, even if you do use the same words. When teaching a young dog many things, and requiring so much precision, you should try to make things as simple as possible for the dog and yourself!

Starting the Stand With A Puppy

1 Reward Incentive Based - The titbit should be held in your right hand marginally above nose height, (dog's nose that is!) Then move your hand and titbit gently, horizontally forward to bring the dog up into the stand position. If you hold the titbit too high, the dog will just look up, go into a sit, or even try to come up on his hind legs, too low and he will go down. Trial and error will help you to get this right. Don't put in any keywords until you have the procedure correct.

Your left hand should contain your lead coupled up and held close to the dog's collar to make sure that the dog does not paddle too far forward. This of course will be further prevented if you make sure that you stop moving your right hand (and the titbit), as soon as the dog is on its feet. If your right hand keeps moving the dog will keep following, so you must learn when to stop.

To begin with the dog should be rewarded immediately when he comes into position, but as he grows more confident the titbit should sometimes be held back in your hand. You may wish to use your keyword for 'Leave' if the dog is particularly persistent, but don't introduce this restriction too soon, the dog must be happy to come into position before you build on and randomise the time that he is in position.

You can then show the dog the flat of your right hand, as he rises into the stand, your thumb and forefinger holding the titbit, and this will become your hand signal for the stand position.

2 **Modeling** - Another favoured method for teaching the stand is to have the dog in the sit position, stand at the side facing the dog. Hold your lead in your left hand, sweep your right hand forward as a signal, and push your left foot under the dog's body, encouraging his hind legs backwards, and thus he will come into the stand. This is not meant to startle or hurt the dog, and no pressure should be a burden upon the dog. The action should

be more of a gentle teasing of the legs from the ground. Later, you could use the leg signal to bring the dog into the stand, because if your training is correct he will comply as soon as he sees you shifting your weight onto your right foot. Be careful that the action does not appear too fast and so be misconstrued by the dog (or spectators) to be a kick. Once again introduce the keyword once you have perfected the technique and you are sure of what you are doing.

Alternatively you could use your arm to sweep the dog's legs back instead of your foot. This is of particular benefit for smaller dogs.

3   **Natural Behaviour** – as with the other positions you can use the dog's natural; behaviour, but this is more difficult as you can't normallty be quite so sure of the dog holding the position.

Progressing the Positions

Whenever you aim to make some progression, always make sure that the dog has every opportunity to get things right. Even if you have achieved off lead work or further distance, if you are introducing some new element to the task, go back and help or put the lead back on. It is worth starting from scratch at the beginning of any session, resist the temptation of going to the top level of achievement at the start of your training session. Do not be in a rush to take the dog off lead, expand distance or add too many distractions – aim for success.

Dropping Aids - Eventually, as the dog becomes confident aids can be dropped one at a time. You will need to drop the actual keyword 'sit' for some exercises, but not others. You can teach the dog to work to the command or the hand signal as required – this is usually personal preference. He will easily learn the hand signal as an extension of your upward arm movement with the lead when placing him into the sit position. Teaching hand signals for the basic positions can be of great use if you are not blessed with a strong voice when it comes to control at a distance.

For heelwork, it is best to incorporate the help by hand and incentive, and spend less time on the command, because after the Novice class you will not have the option to use the command except when leaving the dog in a position during heelwork in test 'C'. Also the same applies to the sit in the present position, but the dog soon learns what is required from your body posture and the situation.

The dropping of lures etc is dealt with in a separate section.

Expanding Time - Gradually the time that the dog is kept in the sit position can be lengthened, and randomised. Take it a tiny step at a time, if your dog begins to get agitated or tries to break the position then you are going too fast for him, and you need to build up more trust and confidence, before extending the exercise. The time span that the dog is left in the position should only be lengthened, (but don't forget to randomise) when the dog is ultra confident, and not because you feel you should have progressed further, or because others around you have had more success. Patience in these early stages will stand you in good stead for the future, when others around you are struggling with problems, you will be streaks ahead.

Adding Distractions - The next step is to put in a few distractions that might naturally occur, like dropping the lead, sneezing, coughing etc. You can gently test how solid the sit position is by first repeating the keyword 'sit' and then giving a very cautious, gentle tug on the lead, a little gentle pressure on the dog's shoulders, or pointing down towards the floor. If he goes to move, gently reassure him of the sit position and help him to stay put. Give your dog confidence and be careful not to frighten him into thinking he's got it all wrong.

Don't forget, short sessions to start with, with plenty of play and motivation in between, but not to a degree where by the dog derives more fun from the end of the exercise than he does from the actual thing that you are trying to achieve.

The teaching of this exercise should be approached in the same light-hearted manner that you approach your play sessions, but with a calming influence to help gain the stability.

Introducing Distance - When you are sure that the dog is confident close to you in the sit position, then you can start to introduce a little distance between you, one step at time. With the dog in the sit position gently reinforce the keyword 'sit', hold the lead in your left hand, up above the dog's head for the best control, and carefully take one step away from the dog. The lead should be slack so that there is no pressure on the dog's neck, but it should be short enough for a turn of the wrist to give you immediate control.

Continue talking to him in a gentle reassuring voice repeating the keyword several times. 'Sit, good boy, that's clever sit, good boy, sit'. If the dog goes to move, your hands will be in position to gently make sure he stays in the sit. This can be done either with gentle lifting of the lead with your left hand, or if the dog lunges out of position your right hand can come over to take hold of the lead by the dog's collar, releasing your left hand to reposition the dog.

If he becomes very fidgety you are perhaps trying to achieve too much too soon, he needs to be reassured and to gain more confidence. Shorten the time he is left by going back to him after only a few seconds, gently praise him, keeping him in the sit position while you do so. As the dog gains confidence you can increase the distance one step at a time until you are at the end of your lead. Remember also to do this at random so the dog does not learn a set sequence, i.e. sometimes longer and then go back to shorter distances and so on.

Off Lead - To teach the dog the statics off lead we go back to step one, very close to the dog making sure that you are there to help him every step of the way. Off lead work at a distance needs much consistent and confidence building training to be sure of success. Be satisfied with rock solid work on lead before you consider detaching your extended arm – the lead!

You can, however, practice getting the sit off lead at any time that you have the dog under close control, but train for success, do not put yourself in a position where you will invite failure. Informal play sessions are a good time, but even most of these should be done on the lead to make sure that the dog is close by you and enjoying himself in close proximity with you. **Further Development and Application** - Building up time and distance are covered more fully in the section on stays as the principle applies to all three positions, sit, down and stand.

Ring applications for this exercise are covered in the various sections where relevant, e.g. Stays, ASSD, Retrieve, Recall, Scent, Sendaway, Distance Control, and Heelwork.

Heelwork
Introduction

Heelwork is for many the most interesting and challenging of all the obedience exercises. In the UK the precision required is very advanced even in the lower classes. To gain this level the handler must have an excellent relationship with the dog, they must want to work together and have fun breaking down the test into minute sections in order to get them all as perfect as possible.

The dog must carry out heelwork on the handler's left hand side (unless the handler has some disability that prevents this). The perfect heel position is with the dog's shoulder level with the handler's left leg and reasonably close. This allows the dog to watch the handler without impeding the progress forward. Any deviation from the position or impeding will normally lose marks.

However, some judges allow a little deviation from the KC description as long as the dog holds the position consistently. At all times the dog should work in a happy, natural manner.

The lower classes include some heelwork on lead, but the lead must be kept loose, any tension or use of the lead will be penalised.

Heelwork comes in 3 differing paces, normal walking pace, fast and slow paces. There must be a clear distinction between the three and all must be performed with the highest level of accuracy. In the UK normal pace only is needed for the lower classes. Once into test 'B' fast and slow are introduced. In test 'B' the paces are changed at the halt, but in test 'C' the change of pace can be from a halt or while on the move.

The judge can include a variety of turns; in the lower classes right and left turns (90°) and right about turns (180°) are the only turns allowed. In the Novice and 'A' classes diagonal turns are permissible. In test 'B' a left

Sandy Wadhams and OBCH Collali Rocky (Ricky)
competing at Crufts.

about turn (180°) can be added at slow and normal pace. It test 'C' weaving, figure of eight, circles and double about turns (360°) can be included.

It is permissible to encourage, talk to and give multiple commands in the lower classes, but at test 'A' this changes; a simultaneous command and signal are allowed at the start of the heelwork and following any halts within the test. In test 'B' and 'C' a command or signal is allowed (but not both).

Good and consistent attention is the key to good heelwork, the precision required is so much easier to achieve if the dog is paying good attention. He will need to listen to commands, but more importantly he must watch your body language for the key to what is required. This is especially important in test 'A' and above, because commands are limited to the starting point only. However, good attention should be aimed for, right from the beginning to ensure the best results.

Heelwork should not just purely be broken down into the simple teaching of turns, the heel position, and then working on the move, although this is a basis, it is much more complex if you want the top results. For instance once the turns are taught at the static position many handlers then assume that the dog will be competent enough to automatically put things together in the ring, or even in training. It must be remembered at all times that the dog is not a mind reader (although he often appears to be one step ahead of his handler!) He needs to be taught and reminded all the time, about the sort of precision that you require. Reminding him does not mean going through the motions of a pattern of heelwork at each training session! Reminding him means going through the basic steps, breaking down each exercise as you did when you initially taught him.

This basic step by step training should be done at each training session and where possible on the show ground before entering the competition. *(See Routines)*. Of course you should always be striving to maintain 'the want', any time you feel this slipping you should abandon whatever training procedure you are doing, or are about to do, and go back to square one - playing with your dog and working as a team. It works rather in the same way as giving a child encouragement or reward in the middle of a difficult project, it helps give him the will and the drive to carry on.

Sometimes your dog may be a little puzzled at the outset of a new exercise, but continue to break it up into small step by step segments and keep him keen by using your 'want' aids, then he will trust you. Each time he learns to trust you a little more, it makes teaching the next exercise so much more easy. He then knows that he has nothing to fear and that pleasure is always connected with you, thus he will become more receptive each time, and enjoy 'learning to learn'.

Heelwork comes very naturally to some dogs and handlers, to others it seems like an uphill struggle. Each dog is different, each handler different, so you must learn to be adaptable. You may be lucky enough to have a dog that, without any formal teaching, automatically takes up the watchful heel position. However many more will take a time to mature and then teach. So even knowing how to do the right things does not always mean that you can do it straight away. It will all come together with trust, maturity, and a willingness to learn, on both sides of the partnership.

Heelwork
The Heel Position

Before you start - You should have achieved with your dog the 'Want'. It will also be beneficial to teach the sit and the watch.

Keeping the dog in a consistent and correct heel position in the ring can be the difference between winning and losing in these days of super precise handlers and dogs. So the keyword for 'Close' or 'Heel' must mean to the dog, much more than just, 'walk to heel'. 'Close' must mean, 'follow my left leg, whatever it does, wherever it goes, and stay in a precise and consistent position'.

Step 1a - To teach the word and position 'Close' we of course first need to be clear of what we are trying to achieve. Secondly, the dog must be in a receptive state, so you must work with him to get him in play mode and achieve 'the want'. Then you can guide him into the heel/close position and gently, encourage and motivate him to put his head up to watch you. He will of course be on his lead so you will have complete control. As soon as you have him in the perfect position, give your keyword, 'Close', praise while he is correct and then release.

Initially 'Close' will mean 'come into the heel position, and watch me'. You should also, at this time, use your keyword, 'Watch' to gain eye contact, gently guiding his head up with your hands or using your toy/titbit to get a positive result. Remember to keep this light and fun.

Play with the dog to get the 'Want', keep the momentum going, hold your lead in your right hand and slide your left hand down towards the collar to guide by sweeping the lead out behind you to the left and then bring the dog forward into the perfect heel position. When sweeping behind try to keep the lead as close in line with your body as possible – this is not always easy to start with but you should aim for it as soon as possible. When the dog is in the correct position, give the keyword 'Close'; guide the head up with your left hand, or use your toy or titbit as an incentive for the dog to look up. Talk to him to keep his attention on you and use the keyword 'watch'. Then give the release word, 'That'll do', and play with the dog.

Repeat this several times to get the dog enjoying the action and to gain momentum. Each time you do the exercise the dog should become more confident, and eager to launch himself into position. The more laid back, quiet, or sensitive the dog the longer you stick to step one, teaching the dog that it is OK to have fun and to work with you.

It is up to you to guide the dog into the correct heel position. His shoulders should come level with your leg. Do not be tempted to allow him too far forward, especially if he is a keen dog. He should not be wrapped around you, or be lying heavily onto you, although it is normal to feel some body contact, particularly whilst the dog is at the early learning stage. You will avoid problems associated with 'Laying on', 'Crabbing', 'Surging', 'Dipping', and so on, if you follow the techniques carefully. You should also refrain from checking the dog across your body with a lead, or making him unsure of himself by expecting him to cope with things that you have not taught correctly.

Step 1b – The above technique can be done by using a titbit for the dog to follow instead of manipulating with the lead. This especially useful for dogs who are less comfortable with hands on methods of training. Simply

hold the lead in your right hand and a titbit in your left – get the dog to follow the titbit as above into the correct position.

Step 2 – Repeat as above but this time take just a couple of steps forward, praising the dog when he is in the correct position.

Step 3 - Once the dog is happily coming into the correct heel position, you can add the sit position at the end or beginning. Therefore steps 3 and 4 can be done in any order. With the more exuberant dog, you may find it easier to put in a sit at the beginning, with a dog that becomes more excited the more you train him, starting at this step gains the initial control.

So we are simply following the instructions above, but adding a static sit. Start off with the dog in the sit position, go to the end of your lead, and then call him into the close position, take a few steps forward, reward when the dog is in the correct heel position, release and play.

Careful positioning of your toy or titbit will help to keep the dog in the correct position and to keep his eye on you, so try to keep the reward just above his head.

Keep repeating the above steps until the dog is accurate and keen to come into position.

Step 4 - Now you can introduce a sit position at the end of the exercise. You need not do this every time, but it will start to teach the dog that close means 'follow the left leg, if it stops you do too'.

Follow the instructions as step 1 and 2, and then instead of just

breaking and playing after you have taken a couple of steps, reach back with your left hand and place the dog in the correct heelwork sit. His shoulders must be level with your leg. He should be positioned square behind and in front. He should be watching and happy. It takes a little practice for you to get it right, but once you have got it, you should be able to place the dog accurately every time. Now he is learning correctly, and not by correction!

All of this should flow, with no obvious breaks. There is no need to give the sit command, as we are teaching a whole procedure on one keyword, 'Close'. The dog is quite capable of achieving this position without even the 'watch' command, as you can encourage the head up and he will come to associate 'Close' to mean 'Head up and watch', as well as the rest. The 'Watch' keyword will be useful later on when you need to gain the dog's attention in differing circumstances. It is a tool for you, an extra keyword that the dog understands, and can be used when your handling or the circumstances necessitate.

The sit command is not needed because we are teaching the dog to stop and sit immediately the left leg stops, and to come into a perfectly positioned sit. If you have been training the 'Sit' position separately you should be getting an instant sit on that keyword. Therefore if you give the keyword 'Sit' in the heel position you may indeed get a quick sit, but it could also be a crooked sit because the dog should sit wherever he is. So it is better to keep the procedure and the keywords as uncomplicated as possible.

Never prolong the teaching session just because it appears to be going well, this will only be inviting error. Be contented with one or two perfect steps so start with, only increase when you are sure that your dog is understanding, and also enjoying the close position... **Read Your Dog!**

Step 5 - Once your dog is ultra confident in the close position, you can practice some of the following tightening up exercises in conjunction with your daily routines.

A Always start off with play to achieve the 'want'. Using the 'Close' keyword, move forward and bring the dog into the close heel position. Use your hands, lead and voice to guide his head and body into the correct position leaving nothing to chance.

Next step sideways away from the dog whilst still moving forward. Run your left hand down the lead to the dog's collar to guide him into the close position. Just do it once to begin with, but as the dog progresses you can add to the exercise by taking another step forward, and another step sideways, guiding him each time. When the dog becomes confident you can link several paces at a time. Give no aggression or harsh handling just a playful attitude and clear concise movements and words.

B Another exercise is to take a few paces with the dog in position, take a quick yet playful turn in the opposite direction, to the left or to the right, again guiding him into the correct position, telling him 'Close'. The attitude must be that by your side is the best place in the world to be. Never be domineering or forceful with your voice or handling.

C You will find many other exercises throughout the book that will reinforce this close position. All of the heelwork exercises will be dependent on it and in turn help to teach it. Exercises for the test 'A' Recall, (recall to the heel position) the Finish, and various others all have components within them which will help.

D Short spurts, broken with play, never over doing it and never tiring or boring your dog will improve the overall desire to work and keep the accuracy.

E Try left and right handed circles, large ones and then getting smaller, weaving or figure of eight with imaginary or placed markers to help you.

F Circuit training will also help you to keep your dog in a happy and stimulated frame of mind. *(See Circuit Training)*.

Trouble Shooting

Wrong Position - If the dog is going wrong, stop and go back to the early steps or change direction and bring him into the correct position.

Lack of Motivation - The important thing is not to make it boring, keep that toy or 'want' aid ready all of the time, giving the dog lots of motivation and fun. Keep sessions very short to start with. Consider clicker training as this is based on high motivation.

Poor Attention – Work on attention as a separate exercise before bringing it into the heel position training. Make sure you keep the training sessions short and highly motivated. Work on getting rewards away from your person *(see Eliminating Aids)*, this will help the dog to understand what focusing on you can bring.

Remember Read Your Dog!

Footwork

Before starting on teaching the dog to do any turns in Heelwork it is important to make sure you know what you will do with your feet.

Footwork is a very important factor of good handling. In fairness to the dog, it is a good idea to perfect this on your own, i.e. without the dog, rather than drag him around whilst your try to perfect your walking rhythm and foot placement.

The foot patterns included here are just suggestions but many handlers find these the best. Some handlers may choose to use other patterns because of physical abilities and/or training techniques. The objective is to make sure that the dog understands where you are going from your body posture and foot positioning, so the main criteria is that the footwork should be consistent – i.e. the same every time both in training and in the ring.

The techniques used for teaching the exercises in this book match up to these footwork patterns. If you use others, you must make sure that you are using the correct training techniques. The idea is that, in training you will over exaggerate the body posture and footwork that will be used in the ring.

You must concentrate on keeping your body upright, and your head should at all times be facing in the direction that you are going. *(See Deportment and Attitude).*

Starting and Stopping

Often neglected in footwork is the beginning and end of heelwork. Your start should be smooth and gliding. Avoid tipping your body forwards. This is a particularly common fault at the start of fast pace.

Practice taking your first steps - setting off with your left leg, as this is the first signal to the dog that you are going somewhere.

Stopping should be equally smooth. Bring one foot up to the other, normally handlers like to stop on their left foot, and bring the right up to it, but you might like to see which is best for you and your dog on this. Once you have perfected the smooth gliding halt, it probably won't matter which foot you stop on.

Stamping of the feet is quite common at the halt; this will lose marks and may also worry the dog – bring your feet together quietly. Another fault is stepping sideways into the halt, often in an attempt (conscious or unconscious) to hide a crooked or wide halt. Make sure you are aware of

Heelwork Turns

The Left Turn

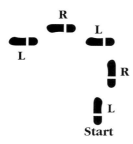

The Left About Turn

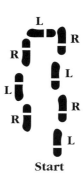

The Right Turn

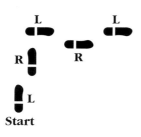

The Right About Turn

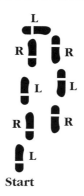

where you are going and keep straight. This fault often creeps in during training because you are looking down at the dog instead of where you are going. Of course you will need to look at the dog in training to start with, but as you progress, you must quickly accustom yourself to standing up straight and allowing the dog to do the work. Do not shuffle into the dog to make him feel straight, bring him into you so that he gets used to this procedure.

It is important to take small steps during the turns. A slightly smaller stride than normal out of the turn will help the dog keep his position. A good guideline is to remember to try to keep your knees as close together as possible during the turn, this way the steps will become naturally neat, and you will avoid staggering or side stepping which would result in sending the dog wide.

Keep your body posture upright and look where you are going. Set a target to aim for, that you know will bring you out of each turn in a straight line and will, emphasise any over turning faults so that you can correct yourself.

Practice the turns until they become second nature and you can do any combination without having to think about where your feet should go. Once this is achieved you will be able to concentrate on the dog rather than yourself.

Curves for Weaving, Circles and Figure of Eight

The footwork for circles, weaves and figure of eight, is just the same as normal, except that you should be curving your feet in the direction of the pattern. Keep your steps as flowing and neat as possible.

Obediance trainers in Sweden practicing footwork.

General Tips

Footwork can be practiced anywhere. If you go out to work practice your footwork on the way or when moving around the building. It can even be practiced in the supermarket behind a trolley. Turning up and down the isles, placing your feet can be great fun, no one realises what you are doing, and who cares if they do!

It is useful to practice with possible distractions as you will need to do it with the pressure of the ring set up, judge and others watching.

The more you do it the more natural it becomes. When you have perfected it on your own, get someone to call for you, or take a tape recording of a ring steward's voice to follow. It is somewhat harder to start with, when someone else tells you when to turn, but with plenty of practice this too will soon become second nature.

Heelwork
Sits

If you have taught the *'Close'* keyword correctly *(covered in the 'Heel Position')* you will not need to worry unduly about sits in heelwork, except to make sure that you are always in a position to ensure their accuracy.

In teaching the word *'Close'* we have taught the dog that whatever the left leg does - he should follow. If the leg turns he should go neatly with it and if the leg stops then he must sit squarely by its side. We have, as a separate exercise, taught him that *'sit'* means just that - sit *(see Static Positions)*. If given the *'sit'* command in heelwork, then that is what he should do, i.e. sit immediately. If your timing is not impeccable, or the dog steps onto an uneven piece of ground and his body wavers slightly, this could mean a crooked sit. But, by giving him his *'Close'* keyword as you come to a halt, he will learn to tuck himself neatly in, by your side in the correct heel position. Of course your hands will be there to guide him.

Remember to keep your body upright and to bring your feet together smoothly to give him the best chance of understanding what you want. *(See the chapters on Deportment and Attitude and Footwork)*.

Clicker and Targeting Hints

If using a clicker as usual it is important to be clear which element you are working on. It is not easy to use the placing technique, as you will run out of hands! Some handlers can manage but if you are struggling it is perhaps better to use the lure.

You can shape the behaviour, but it will take time. You can short cut this by using a lure to get the dog in more or less the correct position and then make gradual progress to the exact place that you want the dog by gradual repetitions nearer and nearer to the correct place, ceasing to reward lesser approximations.

You can use your target stick or your hand as a target to draw the dog up into the sit position in the same way that you would use a lure. If using a stick make sure it is the right length or held short (with larger dogs) so that you can guide the dog with it into the correct position.

Step 1 – Play with your dog and get him into the right frame of mind. Hold your lead in your right hand leaving your left hand free. Bring the dog into the heel position, take a few steps (2 or 3) and then glide to a halt. At the same time, reach down with your left hand and place the dog into the sit position.

Alternatively you can use a titbit or toy to bring his head up and back into a sit position. Hold the lure in your left hand, close to your body and as you come to the halt raise your hand up, keeping it well back and your elbow tucked in. Picture the movement that is the ideal for the dog and hold the lure just slightly above this so that the dog follows the exact movement that you want.

It is not necessary to use a keyword for this as later (in the ring) you will not be allowed to use one, but if you feel you have to, just use your 'close' command. Reward and break the exercise.

Step 2 – Repeat as above for a few repetitions and then break and go onto something else, come back to it later. Put in some training sits at every training session, irrespective of the dog's level, to ensure that he continues to keep the correct position and to prevent faults creeping in.

You should find that the dog's level of precision and speed will improve the more you do this, it almost becomes a race between you and the dog. He will try to sit before you come around to place him. However this won't occur if you are harsh or bad tempered with your dog. Keep it fun

Try to avoid doing long stretches of heelwork and lots of sits. When training for sits, do a few paces and then guide the dog into the correct heel position. Place him each time with your hands, or use your titbit/reward to guide his head up and keep his body straight. With larger dogs you can use a wall to make sure that they do not topple over to one side. Use your knowledge to ensure that the dog is always correctly positioned in training, and this will avoid him assuming that anything else is acceptable.

Trouble Shooting

If the dog develops faults along the way look to your basic training of the *'Close'* command. Probably you have become a little less thorough than you should be in your warm up training routines, and need to do more regular ground work. It does not hurt; in fact it has very positive results if you refrain from putting the heelwork together at every session.

Faults may include sits that are slow, crooked, wrapped, wide, hesitant, backward, forward or missing altogether - go back to the basic routines only, and then progress slowly eliminating aids one at time, keeping up the momentum in training, before putting things together ready for the ring. Remember your masterpiece can be unveiled in the ring you do not have to keep having sneak previews to see if you've got it right!

Heelwork
Left Turns

Before you start the dog must already understand - how to play - and know what to associate with the keywords 'Sit', 'Close', 'Watch' and any praise words such as 'Good Dog' (see Rewards). Before teaching the dog the turns, it is a good idea to make sure that you can do them yourself. (See Footwork)

Step 1 - As always start with play and achieve 'the Want'. Once you have the dog keen and receptive place him in the sit position by your side (on lead of course). Tell him to *'Sit'*, *'Freddie SIT'*. Leave him, taking a pace to your right and a pace or so forward. Stand side on to your dog, hold the end of your lead and your toy or 'want' aid in your right hand, now simultaneously step back with your **right** leg, run your left hand down the lead near to the dog's collar, and guide the dog into the heel position. Take a step or two forward with the dog in the heel position, and then use your toy to reward as you release and give your keyword, *'OK* or *'That'll do'*. Follow with lots of enthusiastic praise.

If preferred you can follow this procedure, but instead of using the lead to guide the dog, hold a titbit or toy in your left hand and have the dog follow it into position.

When you have mastered the technique introduce the *'close'* command.

During the exercise use your reward words *'good dog'* to give the dog confidence. There is no need, at this stage, to put in a sit position at the end of the exercise, because what you are trying to achieve is a good, neat, flowing left turn not a sit!

Many handlers will be used to moving the left leg back to teach this turn. Whilst this does work, moving the right leg is imitating and over emphasising the body stance that the dog will be working to when you are competing in the ring, therefore it is more effective at getting the message over once you introduce the turn on the move.

Step 2 - Once the dog is happily coming into the heel position from approximately a lead's length away, you can shorten the distance that you leave him, a step at a time. Eventually you will be just turning side on to him, and ultimately turning left on the spot.

Always use all of your aids, your voice, your lead, your hands, and your 'want' aid. Never go too fast for the dog, only progress as fast as you and the dog are comfortable with, and at each session start from the beginning, working up to the previous session's level, and then moving on a little when you and the dog are ready. Even when you consider that the dog is completely trained, always start from the beginning at each training session to remind him of what is wanted. This way you will maintain the accuracy ready for the ring.

Step 3 - There are some variations on the theme that will help the dog to understand what is wanted from him.

Leave the dog in the sit position, go to the end of your lead, take a couple of steps to the right, stand side on to the dog. Run your hand down the lead to the collar, take a step back with your right leg and guide the dog into the heel position. Once you have perfected the technique put in your keywords.

On the Move

Once the dog is well on the way to performing the turn accurately from a standstill, you can start to teach him to put it together in heelwork. This is a most important stage of the left turn that is often forgotten by handlers in their rush to be ready for the ring.

Remembering, and being well practiced in your footwork, will make it so much easier for the dog to perform accurate turns. Making the procedure the same each time will give both of you a much better chance of getting it right.

Step 4 - Make sure you have the dog's full attention by getting 'the want', and then, with the lead and your 'want' aid in your right hand, give your heel command and take a few paces forward with the dog, encouraging him to join you in heelwork. When you feel comfortable, simultaneously give your 'close' command *'Freddie close'*, turn your left foot across the dog, and swivel your body to the left. Step back with your right foot, run your left hand down the lead, and guide the dog back with a circular movement into the heel position. Use your *'watch'* command and 'Want' aid to keep his head up and concentrating on you, take one or two steps forwards only, break the exercise with your release command and play.

If you have used a lure rather than lead guidance have it in your left hand. If you have a large or less agile dog it may be necessary to take a few steps back until you get him moving – this can be decreased as he starts to get the idea and feels more confident.

Again there is no need for any sits, either at the start or the finish. Be aware of what you are teaching all of the time and do not clutter the exercise with other things. It is not necessary to give a different command to teach your dog turns because we are aiming for him to take his signal from body posture and footwork only. Another command is another to be dropped at a later stage, so it is better to keep things as uncluttered as possible. You can use encouragement and excitement to motivate the dog.

It is important to make sure that your footwork is consistent and that you remain as upright as possible, otherwise you may well find that you have to completely re-train both your dog and yourself when you need to drop your commands.

To sum up: a few steps forward, the dog in the heel position, then foot across the dog for the turn, hand down the lead to guide (or use your lure/target) and sweep the dog back. Bring the dog back into the heel position, a few steps forward and break the exercise. The keyword is much less important than the body movement because the dog is more sensitive to this.

Clicker and Targeting Hints

When you first start this procedure the dog may be a little apprehensive, as he will be unsure what is required, therefore the clicker is very useful. If you click on any movement in the right direction the clicker-conditioned dog will soon start to get the idea. You can combine the clicker with either of the above variations on the technique (lure or lead guidance) with equally good results.

Instead of using a lure you can use a target (hand or stick) to guide the dog into position following the guidance above.

Dropping The Aids

At this point many people become unstuck, because they try to drop all of the aids at once, particularly if they are competing and have rather better success than they expected, winning out of classes quickly.

Remember, at each training session start from the beginning, use all of your aids, and work through. Then one at a time aids can be dropped. By this I don't mean a gradual progression leaving nothing to help the dog, but rather drop one, and then put it back and drop another. For instance, as you take the left turn on the move you would call the dog into heel, (still on lead of course and with your 'want' aid. These are always the last guidance aids to go), foot across the dog, hand down the lead guiding the dog back, step back, use the dog's name, but drop the keyword, 'close'. Your foot turning across in front of the dog, as well as your body posture, will always be the same, they are your signals in the ring so they must remain constant. Dropping the keyword 'close' first will probably be the least to be noticed by the dog.

Next time leave in the command but take out the step back, or rather make it less obvious by making it a small step instead of a pace.

Next time put back the pace and drop or make less obvious the hand movement down the lead, and so on.

Don't forget to keep up the 'want' using your toy and your voice, and you must break in between every section, sooner if necessary, and play. As the dog progresses these play sessions need only be fractions of the time that you spent originally, but only you can decide when your dog is ready, if you over do the play or reward it will become boring you must, Read Your dog.

Left About Turns

The left about turn is a progression of the left turn and is often unnecessarily feared in the ring. If taught correctly, with patience and following the correct procedure, all able-bodied dogs and handlers can perform the turn with style. The more agile dogs can even perform a good accurate left about turn at the fast pace, (although the rules do not necessitate this.) It really is just an extension of the left turn, and once your dog is happy doing lefts, it will be taken as great fun when you continue turning. The most important thing to remember if you want accuracy in the ring, is to make sure that you do the same each time. This means getting your body posture and footwork spot on. *(See Deportment and Footwork)*

Once you have your dog happily performing the left turn on the spot, it quite a simple matter to carefully place your feet, and turn a 180 degree turn. The dog may be a little unsure at first, but simply use your lead, voice and toy to give him confidence and guide him back. Most dogs will derive great enjoyment from completing a full 360 degree turn in this manner, and of course over emphasising the turn in training will mean that 180 degrees in the ring presents no problem at all. The 360 degree turn (double left about turn) can be included in test 'C' as can left about turn followed by left turn.

To help promote fluid and agile backward movement, which is necessary for the turn to be executed correctly, the following exercises can be added to your training routines.

The Twizzle - This can be done to start with just on its own as a game, but as the handler becomes more proficient it can be incorporated into heelwork and turns. It is simply as it suggests, the dog is taken in a 360° circle, in an anti-clockwise direction, guided by the lead or with a lure or target stick and in a fun manner. Using your toy/reward can start it. Allowing the dog to follow the toy around, keep the circle tight and yet wide enough to make sure the dog follows it. Have the toy and the lead in the left hand and guide the dog around, give it a keyword 'Twizzle', and have some fun with your dog. You can also teach the other direction for fun and to aid flexibility, but the anti-clockwise will help the dog become more flexible when turning to the left as it imitates that particular body movement.

The Incentive - On a similar vein, use the toy to give the dog the incentive to be fast on the turns. This is done by throwing the toy behind you as you turn left across the dog, the dog should follow the ball or toy by turning anti-clockwise away from your leg, as in the 'Twizzle'. Remember to drop the lead to allow the dog to get the toy, but immediately call him back to you. Do not throw the ball too far, as you want to maintain the 'fun as a team' aspect, if you give him too much distance fun could start to be more interesting when he is away from you.

Walking Backwards - This can be done on turns, i.e. instead of walking forward out of the turn, walk backwards and encourage the dog to do the same, this help to promote the close backward movements as will multiple left turns on the spot or at random during heelwork. Walking backwards, as in Distance Control training, will also help to make the dog more aware of this action. If the dog curves out, try doing it against a wall to start with.

All of the extra exercises can be done once the dog has the basic idea of the left, and remember, variety is the spice of life, keep it fun and keep it lively.

Trouble Shooting

Hesitant – Lack of understanding or confidence (or both). Break down and build the exercise slowly rewarding each step lavishly.

Waiting on the Turn – Usually due to hesitant movement from the handler. Make sure that your footwork is fluid with no stopping. Also could be due to insufficient training of any part of the technique or moving onto the finished product too soon and too often. Retrain spending more time on each element, and train at every session.

Wide – Similar reasons to waiting (see above).

Lagging/Dropping Position – The dog could lack confidence that he is correct. Include plenty of enthusiastic games as the dog comes out of the turn. Use the incentive technique described above. Make sure you are bringing the dog into the correct position in training, encourage with a reward. Keep your body upright and facing forward.

Surging or Erratic Position – The dog comes too far forward out of the turn, often dropping back to the heel position within a couple of steps, but sometimes maintaining the forward position. Or he could lag then surge etc. Use a lure in your left hand. Guide the dog into position and then hold it close and high on your body to encourage the dog's head into the correct position.

Impeding/Knocking – Usually due to either training the heel position out of the turn too far forward, or checking with the lead across your body. Make sure the dog is guided into the correct position, and not allowed to move his shoulder forward of your left leg. If he holds the correct position he cannot impede or knock.

General Point - Clicker training is ideal for working on the correct position as you can click on perfection and ignore imperfections. The dog soon learns which position leads to rewards.

Heelwork
Right Turns

Before you start - the dog must understand how to play - and know what to associate with the keywords 'Sit', 'Close', 'Watch', and 'Good Dog'.

The right turn (90 degree turn to the right) and right about turn (180 degree turn to the right) can be included at all levels of competition from pre-beginners to test 'C'. The turn should be taken as accurately as possible, showing acute angles and keeping in line with no drifting off to one side.

The right turn is often taken for granted until faults occur. The most common faults are going wide or drifting off the leg, losing position (lagging, forward working or surging) etc. Many handlers try to correct the faults instead of paying close attention to the correct training methodology. A dog that has been taught by correction rather than by guidance is very obvious to the judge. Even the good ones weave and drift in and out of position, and are constantly correcting themselves. They do this because this is what they have been inadvertently taught to do. Allowing faults to occur teaches the dog that it is okay to perform those faults. Even when he is corrected he has no way of knowing that the first part was wrong, and he will think that this is the procedure which you want him to follow, moving in and out of position as he has been allowed and then corrected. It is much better to teach correctly in the first place. It certainly saves some heartache on your part, stress on the dog and ink for the judge!

Clicker Hints

Use the clicker on the turn by shaping better and better efforts. You may wish to start by clicking on the sit, then the pick up into the heel position and then the actual turn. Once this is all in place, you can click on extra paces. Remember to keep breaking it down to stop errors creeping in.

Step 1 - Play with your dog and get him in a receptive mood. Place him into the sit, *'Freddie Sit'*; go to the end of your lead keeping your back to the dog. Take a step back with your left leg, slide your left hand down the lead towards the collar to get good control, and then with a forward movement call the dog into the heel position *'Freddie Close'*. Go into the turn

Janet Matthews with OB.CH. Charouska Kris Moss

by placing your left foot across your right, as shown in the footwork diagrams, *(see Footwork)*, and guide the dog. Your hand should still be low by the collar, and use your lead, voice, toy etc. to guide him into the correct position. Take a couple of paces forward and break the exercise. Remember there is no need for sits at the finish, as we want the timing to be right to reward for the turn.

If you prefer a more hands off approach you can simply put your left hand back and show the dog a titbit, and then encourage him into the heel position. Remember to keep your hand in a close line with your body to encourage the dog to come in good and tight. Raise your hand up and onto your side to encourage a good head position as he comes into place.

Step 2 - The distance leaving the dog can be lessened gradually until eventually he will confidently go with you as you place your feet for the right turn on the spot.

Step 3 – You can now progress the turn into a right about turn (180 degree turn to your right). As with left about turns, the right about turn is just an extension of the 90 degree turn. Commence as at the basic start of the right turn and simply place your feet, *(see footwork diagrams)*, all the way around guiding the dog with lead, hand, voice and reward.

Remember, take only a step or two after the turn and break the exercise. Reward the dog during the turn with your voice, and or encourage him with his toy or a titbit so that he knows he is correct. Do not sit him to finish, we are teaching turns not sits!

Further exercises can be incorporated, once the dog knows what he is doing, to help speed up and emphasise the turn: -

Play and Turn - Play with the dog and then call him into the heel position, take one or two steps, and then turn to the right, (90 or 180 degrees). Take one or two steps forwards, encouraging the dog, and then praise and play. Remember to place your feet correctly, keep your body posture upright, and help the dog every step of the way, rewarding him during the exercise with your voice to give him confidence.

Turn and Call - Take a few steps forwards with your dog, about turn and then back off, call your dog as if you were teaching him a basic recall, bring out the ball or toy to heighten the excitement. Swivel the dog back into heelwork for a few steps and then repeat the procedure. This will really help the dog that lacks confidence or motivation.

Back Steps and Side Steps - With more advanced dogs, go into the about turn, but then step sideways or backwards and quickly guide the dog into the correct position, this encourages him to be more attentive to the close heel position.

Incentive - A few steps of heelwork and then double about turn, as he completes the double turn, toss your toy in the direction that he has been following, i.e. round to the right, to give him a motivation boost.

As always keep it simple, fun and ever changing. Do not bore your dog. Even high fun activities will loose their appeal if you repeat them too often.

Trouble Shooting

The most common problems as mentioned above stem from lack of or insufficient structured training. Many handlers simply practice the turn, rather than going through the training procedure when training. It is tempting to do this, but you are inviting mistakes to creep in. So for any of the faults, rather than trying to correct them, go through the training procedure at every training session. Do not practice the end result until your training sessions are really strong. Then only practice one or two turns once the dog is competent and keep repeating the training sessions to prevent further problems. If problems tend to only occur in the ring then set up a ring situation and train through it.

Paces: Slow, Fast, Normal

Before you start - your dog should be happily working with you as part of a team. He should be confident and enthusiastic at a normal pace heelwork.

In classes up to and including test 'A' the pace for heelwork is 'normal'. Normal should be a reasonable walking pace. In test 'B' and test 'C' slow pace and fast pace are introduced. There are no rules that dictate the actual speed, but there should be a good and obvious difference between the 3 paces. In test 'B' the changes of pace are always from a halt, but in test 'C' they can be from a halt or while on the move.

The turns are incorporated into the various paces, but the left about turn is only allowed at slow and normal pace, this also applies to weaving and circling in test 'C'.

Pace Setting

Teaching your dog to do varying paces accurately, is very much an extension of normal, walking pace heelwork. For all paces it is important to develop a rhythm that the dog can come to rely on. There are various ways of getting your pace right. An electronic pace setter (or metronome) can be set to the perfect pace for you and your dog. It has a digital display that shows beats per minute, you can adjust it to suit your pace. Once you have decided on the best setting, you simply set the instrument and practice along with the rhythmic beat, both with and without the dog. Training yourself this way will help the consistency and quality of your pace. A good rhythmic piece of music can have the same effect, but finding the perfect speed is not always easy.

Although any serious fast and slow training should be undertaken once the dog is very confident at normal, it won't hurt to introduce them in a fun way while you are training the first stages of heelwork with your dog. It is a good time to be training yourself for the future. A little jogging speed, or slowing down, even with puppies, can help to break up heelwork and add interest to the session.

Clicker Hints

Break the exercise down and click on specific points that you wish to work on. With slow pace it is easy to take it a step at a time, but in fast you may have to get you and the dog moving and then click on the perfect bits.

Step 1 - To perfect your paces, and to ensure that the dog goes into them evenly, proceed as follows. Without your dog to start with, practice changing pace so that there is good obvious differentiation between the 3 paces. Consider what you will need in the ring, don't attempt to do the fast pace at a speed that you could not keep up for any length of time. (You may find that you may have to train and build up your own stamina to enable you to maintain an acceptable speed). It is better to get a good rhythm, a jog for example, than trying to run at full pelt if you are not built for it. Likewise with slow pace, do not be too slow, practice to become consistent. You may decide to change the speed slightly when you get together with your dog, but this self-training will give you a basis to work on.

Step 2 - Assuming that you have your dog working happily and confidently at the normal pace, and you have completed step 1, we can now start to train the dog to enjoy the variations of pace. Place the dog in the sit position or simply call him into the heel position using his name and your keyword, 'Close'. He will of course be on lead, because we are training, you can use all of your help aids, and of course your 'Want' aid should always be in your hand or in your pocket at the ready. Once the dog is happily and accurately trotting in a natural manner at your side in the heel position, gradually and smoothly glide (over two paces) into the slow pace. Just do a few steps reassuring the dog all of the time, and then, just as smoothly, glide back into normal pace. Break the exercise with your release command and then play. Repeat this several times playing and encouraging where necessary.

Step 3 - The procedure as in step 2 should be followed to introduce fast pace. Remember of course to keep your body upright and make sure your footwork is 'spot on'. The tendency is for handlers, particularly at fast pace, to let their legs fly all over the place. So remember, keep your knees together on those turns, and keep it smooth. It helps of course, particularly at fast pace, if you are reasonably fit, but you can train yourself to glide even if you are a little on the rotund side! Always be ready to break and play at any time that the dog needs it.

Step 4 - Practice the turns placing your feet just as you would in normal pace. Remember; take smaller steps out of the turn to help the dog hold the correct position. Keep it rhythmic and positive and the dog will hold position more easily.

Slow And Fast Pace From A Stand Still

Sometimes the change of pace is from the standstill, in some ways this is harder than the changes on the move. However, to perfect the differing paces from a stand still is a simple procedure, if you approach it in a simple manner.

Get your dog in the right frame of mind with a little well motivated heelwork. Halt and place him in the correct heel sit position. Before you set off into the slow or fast pace give the dog's name in a differing tone so that he is aware that something is to be different. The slow can be a calm slow tone, the fast a quicker more exciting one. Follow it up with the keyword, 'Close' in the same tone, and then smoothly glide into your chosen pace. Be careful not to lunge forward with your body in fast pace, because the dog is likely to surge forward with your posture; and be very positive as you move off in slow, to avoid hesitation and dipping.

Trouble Shooting

Many unnecessary marks are lost during slow and fast paces in heelwork. Major faults comprise of the handler launching their bodies into the start of fast, stumbling into the start of slow, being uneven in their movements, not taking turns smoothly. Handlers are often ring shy too, forgetting all that they ever learnt about footwork and deportment, not keeping a constant speed, not having good and obvious definition of pace, etc., etc.

You will notice that these are all handler rather than dog faults, therefore the answer is to practice and then practice some more until you don't have to think about it because it becomes so natural.

Dogs do tend to develop particular idiosyncrasies like getting over excited, barking, or lagging etc., but these faults are caused by the handlers not getting themselves organised in the ring and/or not being well enough structured in training. The more that the problems and inaccuracies are ignored or left to 'Go away on their own', the worse or more exaggerated they can become.

Go back to the basic training techniques and look at both your handling and your training to avoid problems and correct faults. If the problem seems to be related to the ring e.g. barking or whining with excitement, then you need to set up training rings with friends. *(See General Heelwork Trouble Shooting).*

Circles, Weaves and Figure of Eight

Before you start - The dog needs to have the want, and understand what 'Close' means.

Circles, weaves and figure of eight come into test 'C' in UK obedience, but in other countries they may be included at lower levels. Circles can be a variety of diameters from very large to about the size of a hool-a-hoop or even a little smaller. The rules do not give any guidelines with regards to the size. They can be in either direction, include any turn and be at any pace, but judges must ensure that all breeds entered in the class can accomplish them. Weaves or figure of eight can be at slow or normal pace.

Teaching the dog in circles is the way we often start in the early stages of training, to get a good flow of heelwork. But, when we come to use these techniques for working in the ring, it seems much harder. The reason is that once the dog starts to be able to hold a good position in the straight heelwork, the handler gets carried away teaching twists and turns, and the circles tend to be forgotten until suddenly they are needed when the handler gets into the higher classes.

The techniques for circles and curving heelwork are just the same as straight, but the handler will have to learn how to point his feet and body into the curve. *(See Footwork and Deportment).*

Start training with large circles, and accustom yourself to how it feels to not be going in a straight line. Try not to lean over the dog, keep an upright torso.

As you progress, you can go in slightly tighter circles. Normally the handler has more trouble coping with curving heelwork than the dog. Any turn should be done with exactly the same footwork as the straight turns.

You will probably find it easier, at least to start with, to teach the curves at slow pace. The dog should be very attentive and more easily controlled at slow, and there will be fewer tendencies for the dog to surge out of position. Once you get to grips with it, start to smarten your pace, until you are able to keep a consistent normal pace all the way around. It is important that you teach yourself to keep as consistent a pace as possible, *(see Paces)*, and then pass this over to the dog.

You must also accustom yourself to going into the curves from the straight and from a standstill. Sometimes judges will include in their tests, curves at the various paces, and also execute about turns to bring you back into the opposite curve.

All of this is really quite easy for the dog that has been taught correctly to start with. All of the techniques used in this book will teach the dog to follow the left leg. It is the handler who will have to learn to get good deportment and correct and accurate footwork. There is no easy option other than 'training yourself'.

When you start to get the hang of this, introduce actual markers to accustom the dog to ignoring the obstacle, and to accustom yourself to being more specific and structured with regards to which direction you go, and how you follow a set pattern. Children's hool-a-hoops are ideal training aids, but also bollards, poles etc., can be used to give you the right feel. Circuit training will help you with this, because you can set up your training area to either use or not use the obstacles. *(See Circuit Training)*.

Trouble Shooting

Drift in Position - If you feel the dog coming too far across you, surging or hanging back straighten up, revert to the opposite curve, or go into play mode to get the dog's confidence. Work on shorter amounts of heelwork so that you can reward the good bits more often. The clicker is ideal for getting the message over to the dog as it delivers a precise message when the dog is in the correct position.

Poor Differentiation of Pace – This is a common fault in the ring and can so easily be avoided by being strict with yourself in training. However, it is easy to fall into the trap when under pressure in the ring, especially if you are not well practiced. Work with your pace setter to ensure that the paces have a good range, and then get someone to video you or get an unbiased handler to observe you to be sure that the paces look different enough.

General Heelwork Trouble Shooting

There are many problems, associated with heelwork that can creep into your work, but all can be dealt with by applying the correct training procedure. This basically means, it is better to train from the beginning using a step-by-step approach than to try to correct things that are wrong. Corrected dogs tend to stand out as dogs that learn to correct themselves in the ring, rather than holding correct position. If the dog reacts in a way that is 'out of character', it is always worth considering possible problems with health, welfare and nutrition before assuming that training is at fault.

Clicker Hints

Clicker training is ideal for perfecting the heel position as it allows you to reward after the event, but the clicker gets the message over to the dog when he is in the correct position. Follow the techniques below, breaking down the exercise to give you greater control and click on the perfect position. Build up the time that he holds the position gradually.

Forward Working

Once upon a time, forward working was rarely a problem, as a judge, most faults witnessed were those related to lagging behind. However, there is now (thankfully) much more emphasis on reward based training, but the control element of the training tends to get lost amongst the high exuberance sometimes. Forward working is normally created by the fun approach to dog training being used without suitable control and sound teaching being implemented. The dog will be continually allowed to lunge forward for his reward, which the handler has a tendency to give at the end of the exercise. He is unable to perceive the correct heel position because he is rewarded when he is in the wrong position each time.

It is normal animal behaviour to try to get to the reward. When you withdraw a reward, the dog will try to get as fast as possible to the point at which the reward comes. The withdrawal of the reward will emphasise this, so although we need to learn to eliminate rewards, we must also learn when to reward. *(See Timing and Rewards)*.

Take the example of the very keen, over excitable dog. He will display all of the classic symptoms: keen, lively, and raring to go, but often will be really quite sensitive. The handler will have found that reprimanding the dog has no suitable effect, so it is obvious that there is need for a more constructive approach.

Technique one

Step 1 - The exercise must be broken down into segments. Set the dog up in the heel position and reward him calmly by stroking his head, or popping a titbit into his mouth whilst he remains in the correct position. Often, with over keen dogs, it is useful to use your voice a lot instead of continually rewarding with the toy, so that he learns to feel rewarded in a more controlled manner. But, you should not eliminate his toy completely, he must learn to give and take. *(See Teaching the Keen Dog)* and you must learn to control your rewards. *(See Rewards and Leave on Command.)*

Step 2 - Set the dog up again, and this time take one step with him, if he holds position reward him, (or click on it) whilst he is correct. This is the hard part to get under control, because the dog will have grown accustomed to surging forward to gain his reward. You may find, to start with at least, that it is easier to place the dog into the sit after one perfect step, and then reward him. Try not to do this for too long, otherwise the dog will start to think that reward comes only when he is sitting and this could lead to a dog that dips into the sit at every minor hesitation! If you miss and the dog surges, slide your left hand down his lead to his collar and hold him out away from you for a few seconds. He will want to come back to you so now is your chance to make it happen under control, bring the dog back into the correct position and reward him in position, *'Good boy'*.

Step 3 - You must now follow this technique, every time the dog surges forward, hold him away for a few seconds, bring back and reward the correct position. Keep going back to the beginning so that the dog gains nothing from his surge, but is rewarded in the correct position.

Technique two

Step 1 - Bring your dog into the heel position. Take a step forward, the fraction of a second that the dog starts to go forward from the correct heel position, start walking backwards, bringing the dog back towards you on your left. The keen dog will quickly try to get back to you, reel him in and make him go past you on your left, and as soon as he is heading past, start walking forwards again bringing him into the correct position. There is no need to say a word, whilst he is wrong, but as soon as he reaches the correct heel position, give him his keyword 'Close', and tell him 'Good boy'. Reward him when he is correct.

Step 2 - Set it up again. The dog will come into the correct position, but will soon start to race forward again, the second that he is forward, simply stop walk back and bring him into the correct position as above. The important part to remember is to act the fraction of a second that the dog is in the incorrect position. If you allow some forward work the dog will not know when to do it and when not, and will become confused. You must make up your mind that the dog will not forward work ever again, if you want him to maintain a good position in the ring.

The above technique can also be used on dogs that pull; even pet handlers can master it. The dog will learn with a minimum of input from the handler, that he can't go forward unless he does it in the position that the handler allows. It is up to the handler to decide on the position that is acceptable, and to only go forward when the dog is in that position. It may seem that you are not getting very far, especially if you are stopping a dog pulling on a walk, but it will be worth it and soon the dog will realise how to walk to heel.

Very often dogs that work forward, are dogs that spend much of their time forward of the handler, in many aspects of their lives, and are sometimes on the verge of becoming dominant, although it may or may not be obvious to the handler. They may be the dogs that get over excited, perhaps even aggressive, with other dogs. Handlers should spend time on this aspect of the dog's behaviour, teaching him that they, the handler, are in control and the dog's place is behind them in a variety of domestic and working situations. For instance they should not be allowed to barge through doorways first. They should not be allowed to dictate what the handler does.

In training they should be guided into working harder than the handler. For instance the handler should not swivel into the heel position, he should make the dog get into position himself and so on. It is important to build on this side of your dog's character and to maintain control in all aspects of his life. *(Other books by the author go into more detail on this subject - Dog Training Instructor's Manual and Puppies - Your Guide to Successful Ownership).*

Inconsistent Heel Position
(Drifting, Wide, Crabbing, Too Close, Crowding, Impeding, etc)
This is one of the top faults in the obedience ring, dogs that have a

fluctuating heel position. The only way to correct this is to make sure that you are teaching the dog correctly, and not by correction. Show the dog exactly what is wanted, and teach every part of the exercise step by step, rewarding each tiny piece and progressing to the stage where the dog is not quite sure what order things will come, but knows how to react to your signals and keywords. If the dog gives the incorrect reaction to your signal or word, simply go back to step one of the training exercise and teach the dog exactly what you do mean.

You must learn to be very controlled in you deportment and handling, so that the dog does not misconstrue your body or foot movement, but more importantly the dog must be given a controlled approach to all of the heelwork teaching.

By following all of the techniques the dog will learn the correct position, you must not teach with aggression, because this will make the dog very 'dippy', and inclined to drop out of position in case your hand is on the way down. Aggression will also produce a very frantic gait, or a poor ill-motivated style, depending on the type of dog it is used on.

Handlers not following the handling techniques that are compatible with their footwork and deportment in the ring cause many inconsistencies in position. In training your techniques should start by showing over exaggeration of the finished product. For instance, if you are doing a turn in training, your body should reflect this, but in an exaggerated way. Then as the training procedure progresses, you will tighten up the movement to leave only what the dog will see in the ring.

Problems such as crabbing are often caused by over excitement on the dog's part and checking across the body on the handlers part. Both can be tackled by teaching the basics again.

Broadly speaking, inconsistency comes with uncertainty, over excitement, incorrect training or training by correction.

Lagging and Lethargy

Dogs lag behind their handlers for various reasons; one of the major causes is that they are not motivated sufficiently to stay with the handler. Apprehensive and sensitive dogs are more likely to lag, as are larger more cumbersome dogs. Finding the right sort of motivation and applying it carefully, liberally and consistently will help change a lethargic dog into a keen motivated dog, even with the larger breeds. Many handlers try to take away motivators too soon in the learning process. You must always have some form of reward even when the dog is considered to be well trained. Every training session should include at least some of your dog's favourite motivator. When you train with lots of motivation, eventually the training and exercise itself becomes fun and the dog ceases to need the motivation. But be honest with yourself – have you really done enough to make him want to be there? If he clearly does not want to be there then the answer may be obvious!

You should also consider fitness and diet if your dog is generally lethargic. An unbalanced diet or food that is not ideal for the individual can cause lethargy and even depression. Generally speaking a good quality diet will not be cheap, but it will be worth it to see the life come into your dog. However, it does not follow that the most expensive diet will be the best for your individual dog – many dogs do very well on midrange diets.

Avoid giving additives to complete formulated diets unless advised to do so by your vet. Manufactures spend a lot of money on research to get the balance right, if you add more vitamins or minerals you will be creating an imbalance and may cause problems that can have far reaching effects.

Many handlers have had good results from feeding a more natural diet rather than a manufactured diet. If you go for this option think carefully about the balance of the food to keep your dog healthy.

Other problems such as hormone imbalance or ill health can make the dog lethargic, as can your own mood – if you are down the dog may pick up on this and match your mood.

These dogs cannot be taught by aggression, because this will make their motivation level even more difficult to uplift. The lagging dog needs a positive, controlled and highly motivated trainer. He needs to be shown exactly where he is meant to be, and what he is meant to do, in a manner that he can understand, and in the nicest possible way. His motivator must be chosen to suit his character.

Constant nagging on the lead will make the dog even more inclined to hold back. Often it is a good idea to dispense with the lead for a while, and teach the dog that the heel position is a fun place to be with the use of toys or titbits. Teach the dog that the lead has good associations, and even teach him to play with the lead, (as explained at the beginning of 'the Want.'). Constant nagging verbally will also de-motivate the dog, even monotonous praise words will have a negative effect.

Bad body posture will also cause lagging. If the handler looks down at the dog, with his head turned to the side, the rest of the body has a tendency to follow. This gives a false impression of the heel position and the dog ends up a few paces behind. The usual reaction from the handler is then to chastise verbally or nag with the lead, because he is annoyed at the dog, this is done by turning even further into the dog. Once this happens and the dog loses all continuity and faith, and it becomes more natural for him to get even further back than to come forward. Think about how you would teach a dog to lag, this is probably a variation on what you are doing, when you try to correct it!

To correct lagging you need to teach and motivate from the beginning. Do not try to make it right by correction because the dog will not understand, and will become even less likely to want to stay with you. Change your keywords if you have abused them, and teach the dog good associations. Lighten up your attitude and try to get the dog to work to you by walking forward briskly and in a positive manner.

Barking or Over Excitement In Heelwork

In highly motivated dogs, becoming too excited can create problems. Dogs often whine, bark or even snap at the legs of the handler during heelwork, all in sheer excitement. To combat this it is a good idea to take away the reward until the dog works in a calmer manner. For many dogs the reward can be the actual work rather than food or a toy. If this is the case the handler must set up the situation that creates the excitement and then as the dog begins to get excited simply put him/her into a down position and walk away. Then after a few moments go back to the dog and pick up the heelwork again. If he gets excited again repeat the procedure until he learns to work more quietly. Reward the quieter behaviour.

Wide Turns

Two things to look at here:

a) Is your footwork and deportment correct?

b) Have you taught the turns correctly?

a) Footwork and deportment must be compatible with your training methods. Check this first in the technique chapter applicable. The dog must understand what is meant when your body and feet take up certain positions. Even your head and facial expressions will make a difference. Make sure that your head follows the turn, and does not get left behind because you have your eyes on the dog. Make sure you are accustomed to turning when told to avoid errors, this means getting someone to call for you and practice without the dog to start with. Get others to analyse what you do or watch yourself on video if possible.

b) Often handlers start to teach turns but do not follow the procedure through and/or do not continue to train, preferring to 'handle' in training sessions. Progressing to the 'on the move aids' is often the stage at which training gets left behind in favour of handling, this must not happen if you want to keep your turns tight and accurate.

Crooked Sits

Three areas to look at here:

a) Crooked sits can be avoided or minimised by never allowing them to creep in training.

b) Bad body posture, hand position and footwork can once again be the culprit that sends potentially good sits crooked.

c) Use of incorrect verbal commands or signals in the ring will also confuse the dog.

a) In training always place the dog into the correct sit position at your side. The sits should be taught to start with as a separate exercise and only incorporated into heelwork in linking sessions. Remember to pay attention to what you are trying to teach, and make sure that your brain is in gear. *(See Linking)*.

b) Do not lean over, or stomp to a halt, as this will again affect the dog, and make him apprehensive or confused. Make sure that you glide to a halt and keep your body upright, bend back to place the dog, or use a wall to avoid the crooked position if necessary. If using a reward to guide the dog, make sure your hand comes close to your body and above his head (usually around your hip depending on the height of the dog). Do not have your hand across your body otherwise that is where the dog may end up.

c) Do not introduce the keyword 'sit' in heelwork if you have followed the techniques in this book, because you will have taught the dog to sit instantly on that word. So when he hears it in heelwork, if your training is good he will sit, irrespective of the position he finds his body in. If he needs an extra keyword in the ring then the word should be your heelwork command e.g. 'Close'.

Slow Sits

Both keen and not so keen dog suffer from slow sits. Keen because they are rearing to go, and the slower dog for obvious reasons. Both can be dealt with in a similar manner. The dog must have motivation to get into the sit position. Find what it is that your dog likes and use it as a reward for quick and stable sits. With the keen dog this is usually a fairly easy task as he is easily motivated, but the slower dog take more patience. Do not wait to do some heelwork to try this; teach it separately. When the dog is sitting reward him. Do your training little and often so that the dog starts to enjoy going into the sit, introduce a sequence of sit, stand, down and reward the sit more often than the rest. This shouldn't be 'Distance Control' style; just a bit of fun such as you might teach pet dogs with a titbit to reward the dog. Then transfer this sit signal that you have developed and use it when the dog is in varying positions including at your side. Reward in the same manner.

Clicker training is great for sharpening up the sits as you can click on the better sits and ignore others – the dog soon learns which sit leads to reward.

If the problem persists consider health – the dog may have poor hips or other problems that affect the sitting posture – consult your vet.

Other Heelwork Problems

We could go on forever with the variation of problems that can occur in heelwork and any other exercise for that matter. The secret behind having few faults is good constructive training techniques, coupled with reliable motivation tools, patience, and the ability to reward what is right, when it is right, so that the dog can understand the connection. You must resist the temptation to use training sessions as workouts on completed exercises, and condition yourself into using them for good quality constructive training time.

Always incorporate your step by step approach at each training session rather than practicing finished heelwork as the latter will allow the faults to creep in.

Advanced Stand, Sit and Down (ASSD) Heelwork Positions on the Move

Before you start - The dog must understand the meaning of the keywords for heel, watch and must have achieved the want. He must be happy and confident in the heel position, with no signs of apprehension or confusion.

This exercise is introduced in test 'C' in the UK. In other countries it may be introduced (in part or in its entirety) in lower classes. During heelwork, on a command or signal from the handler, the dog will be required to take up a sit, down or stand position, in the place and order decided by the judge, while the handler continues forward without the dog. The handler will then be directed back to the dog to collect him with one command or signal and then the handler and dog continue together with heelwork as directed. The positions and pick up must be smooth and clean with no fidgeting, shuffling or surging etc.

The first part you must achieve, is for the dog to stop, and assume the position given; for this the dog needs to understand fully what is meant by the keywords, stand, sit and down, or signals that mean the same. So this must be concentrated on first. Normally, by the time you come to teach ASSD, your dog will have already been taught the three positions in conjunction with other exercises, so the transition to taking up the position from heelwork should not be difficult.

Your dog must be very happy and confident when working in the heel position before you start introducing this exercise, otherwise he may become unsure and hesitant in his heelwork. Having said that, you don't have to wait until you qualify for the standard. If you have an ultra keen dog, teaching ASSD can help to keep him under control, giving him something more to keep his mind occupied, and preventing heelwork from getting boring.

Clicker Hints

The clicker will help you to give confidence in this exercise. Make sure you click on good non hesitant positions and clean pick ups but split the exercise up and work on one thing at a time.

Step 1 - Make sure that your dog is happy doing all three positions on the spot, using whatever technique you have found best to get a quick precise result. For the sit and the stand the techniques using your hands to place the dog, or clicker training are usually the best. These are covered in teaching statics section. For the down, the technique used in the sendaway will be useful, as this promotes a fast and confident down. So practice getting the dog into position quickly and accurately with a minimum of fuss, making sure your signals or commands are given in a clear and precise manner to the dog.

Step 2 - Take things, as usual, one step at a time. Decide on what position you would like to start with, the sit or the down are probably easiest, but if your basic training is good, then any position will do. Let us say that you will start with the sit position. Remember your general training procedure, get the dog 'wanting' before you start, use your 'want' aid, and of course keep him on lead. When you are ready, call him into the heel position to join you as you walk forward, *'Freddie Close, Good boy'*. Shorten your lead up in your right hand, and then, when you are confident that you are going to get a good result, simply but swiftly raise your right hand with your lead upwards keeping the lead short. Place your left hand on the dog's rump, just as you would in basic training. The secret is that you should not come to a formal

stop before you place him. The object is to imitate as much as possible the position and body posture taken in the ring, i.e. leaving the dog behind as you walk forwards. Take a couple of paces away from the dog. Hold the lead high above the dog's head to make sure that he doesn't break the position. Reassure him, return to his side, break the exercise with your release command, and play. Repeat this a few times until you are sure of what you are doing, and can get it right most times, then introduce your keyword 'Sit'.

Step 3 - The other two positions are taught in exactly the same

way, using your basic teaching and aids to ensure that the dog assumes the correct position. You can use your lead to stop the dog in his tracks for the stand position, your hand signal may help, coming across the dog's face to make a very positive action. Some handlers use their foot to bring the dog to a stand.

For the down simply come straight down on the dog's shoulders with your left hand to physically manipulate him into position, or in front of his nose if you have used the titbit/incentive down method of teaching. Don't drag the titbit forward as this will create a paddle forward. Make sure that your physical signals and your verbal keywords are used in exactly the same manner as they will be used in the ring. If your tone or action changes, the dog will not understand. But, remember to keep your attitude fun and non threatening.

Step 4 - As the dog begins to gain confidence, you will be able to extend the time that you leave him in the position. First work on circling around the dog, again using your lead and your voice to make sure he remains static in the correct position. If he attempts to break, or shuffles around to see you, go back a few steps and be happy to just stand in front of him until he gains more confidence. Always complete the training session with a game, and of course, break in between each segment and produce your 'want' aid. Plenty of time should be spent on this stage of the training, to make sure that the dog is really attuned to what you want. Gradually you will be able to drop the aids, remembering that you should only drop one bit of help at a time, and then replace it before dropping another. *(See Eliminating aids.)*

Preparing for the Ring

Make sure that your keywords are precise and clear, and of course the same every time. Make sure your body posture is upright, and that you can give your commands without leaning over the dog. The pick up part is easy if your basic training has been thorough. To start with, pause as you come into the heel position, and then give the dog your *'Close'* keyword, encourage him forward in the heel position for a few steps.

To avoid anticipation in the ring learn to be varied in training, sometimes picking up by giving the *'close'* command, but more often walking past, sometimes taking an acute turn in front of the dog, or simply go to his side reward and release him. Don't always release and go forward, as this may encourage a surge forwards, sometimes release and go backwards or sideways. You will need to practice your own timing to get a perfect pickup.

Remember to always make sure that the dog is happy and confident, and at the least sign of apprehension break and play, then start again at an easier level.

Temperament Test

Before you start - Your dog should be very confident in you, and enjoy being on his lead and collar. He should have developed the 'Want'. Although the finished exercise is to be done in the stand, when you first start training, it does not matter which position the dog is in. The emphasis of this exercise is to teach the dog to enjoy being stroked by other people of all types, including strangers.

The use of your 'want' aid and/or titbits will be of paramount importance in teaching this test. The dog needs to associate people approaching him with something pleasant, but on the other hand it is not good policy to allow the dog to jump all over the prospective judge.

The UK exercise is not a stand stay, but ideally the dog should learn to stay in the stand position, preferably with all four feet on the ground, while he is being stroked by the judge. The judge is allowed to talk to the dog and will often ask its name before commencing. The judge should approach from the front and then stroke the dog gently down its back. Any resentment, cringing, signs of aggression such as snapping or snarling will be penalised.

In the UK the test is scheduled in the Novice class, there may be variations on the test in other countries for example some countries require the dog to allow its teeth to be shown.

Clicker Hints

The use of the clicker will help build the dog's confidence in this exercise and its associations. Click and reward the dog's good behaviour starting with the tiniest step in the right direction and then building up to more and more tolerance.

Step 1 - Teach the dog to enjoy being stroked by you his owner/handler. If he understands the stand then start with that position with the dog at your side if possible. *(See statics section - stand).* If you cannot manage the stand with any precision yet don't worry, the dog can still do the rest. Use a titbit or his toy in front of his nose to focus his attention.

Step 2 - The dog must learn that not everyone will have a sensible approach, sometimes they will make fast or sudden movements, or have things (like clipboards) in their hands. So you should teach him first by you taking this part before you expect him to accept these movements from others.

Have the dog in the stand and hold a titbit in your right hand. Allow the dog to nibble at your fingers, attempting to get at the titbit, then, bring your left hand a little faster than normal around to stroke the dog, and at the point where you come into contact with the dog's back, release the titbit into his mouth.

Your timing needs to be good, do not release the titbit and allow the dog to jump away as your hand approaches, he must associate the hand with reward. It may be beneficial to allow only a little of the titbit to be released, having more in reserve between your fingers.

Step 3 - When the dog is confident in step 2 you can increase the speed that your hand approaches the dog, and also the intensity, some judges will be quite rough, albeit unintentional, so vary the pressure and speed of stroking. Some judges will have a very light or dithering touch which may excite sensitive dogs so take this into consideration too.

A helpful social side to this exercise is to accustom the dog to the strange and sometimes unpredictable advances of young children, the awkwardness of some adolescents or the unusual movements of the mentally/physically disabled. You can advance to making mock grabs at your dog as a young child might, leaning on it or hugging it.

Also you need to accustom your dog to someone leaning over him on approach, a common mistake that even some experienced handlers/judges make is having an overbearing body posture. This can make some dogs defensive. Don't put too much emphasis on the dog staying in the stand position, it is more important that he is not worried by the experience. Practice leaning over the dog so that he comes to accept it as normal human behaviour and nothing to be worried about.

Step 4 - Once the dog is happy and confident with all of the above you can enlist the help of a friend to act as the first introduction to the dog. Instruct them on how to approach your dog, i.e. they should keep their body upright, and to start with simply walk past the dog, whilst you keep his attention on you with a treat. You can then gradually work through the stages starting with your friend lightly stroking the dog and then progressing as you did in the above steps. Make sure that the dog is confident before moving the steps on.

    Step 5 - Use many friends and associates to follow the steps as above. Make sure that they all build up the dog's confidence before being too presumptuous.

    Soon you will find that a dog is blasé to any situations like these, and if a judge is clumsy in their approach it will not cause you problems for the future.

Preparing for the Ring

Make sure that you and the dog are aware of the possible links between exercises, i.e. he must be able to follow from another exercise although judges often put this test at the start of the round.

    Go through the routine of setting up, likely verbal interaction between you and the judge/steward preceding the test and work towards being as quiet as possible during the test (although you are permitted to talk to the dog in the UK).

    If possible get someone the dog knows to steward you and to reward the dog through the process prior to competing and following any negative or bland experiences.

Trouble Shooting
Previous Bad Experience

If your dog does have a bad experience in the ring or other environment then to start at step one of this section will help enormously. However, you must take extra care to go slowly through the stages making sure that the dog's confidence builds all the time.

Careful choice of friends to help is also important. If someone specific frightened the dog, don't opt straight away for the type, sex or size of that person. These can be carefully and gently introduced much later when the dog has been flooded with good occurrences.

To introduce specifics that the dog is fearful of you can use a friend the dog prefers as a block, the more frightening person can start behind them and walk by as inconspicuously as possible, so that the dog hardly notices.

It may be beneficial to change your keyword for stand in the temperament test so that you eliminate any bad associations with your word usage.

Many repetitions of good motivational encounters will help enormously. A group of people all with your dog's favourite food will build confidence quickly.

Lack of (or Problems During) Socialisation

Many things can go wrong during the socialisation process. Some dogs are particularly sensitive to their developing senses and will react more than others. Breeds such as Border collies, German shepherd dogs, Belgian shepherd dogs, Pyrenean sheepdogs can all be ultra sensitive and reactive.

All dogs naturally go through development stages known as fear impact stages. One such stage occurs in the first few weeks of life (around 5-12 weeks of age) and then another stage occurs at around 5-14 months. During adolescence and puberty the dog will be extra sensitive as well as at the onset of adulthood. At these times they can be very sensitive to anything even mildly frightening, new or strange. How they come through this and how you react to them will affect their perception of life at a later stage. Therefore it is important to try to support them at these times and jolly them along when they seem concerned.

If they do have lasting affects of fear relating to these stages it takes a bit more work to create a bolder dog. Repetition and flooding of good occurrences with lots of reward related training will be the key.

Dog clubs can help by setting up a situation where the dog gets lots of treats from strangers. Also go up to everyone you know at a show and give them treats to give to your dog. With the right sort of high value reward the dog will soon be dragging you over to meet strangers!

The Recall
(To the Present Position)

The recall exercise is split into several parts. The dog is put into the static sit or down, he then must wait while the handler is instructed by the judge or steward to walk away, halt, turn to face the dog. Then on command and/or signal the dog must recall smartly to the handler and sit in front at the present position. He will then be required to go to the heel position before the exercise is finished.

Teaching the Keyword 'Come'

This is a keyword that can be taught from a very early stage, incorporating feeding time with training. Therefore once the dog develops a relationship with you and food you can start!

There are many times when you can incorporate the word 'come', and the training of it in your daily life:

1   Whenever the dog comes to you of its own accord, put the word in and enthusiastically encourage and reward the dog.

2   A perfect time for establishing good link with this word is at feeding time, prepare his food, and then go to where he is with the dish. Get him to come to you by showing him the food and encouraging him to you. As soon as he is coming, introduce the keyword 'come'. Back off a couple of paces, repeating the word 'come', and

then give him his dinner. As he becomes more confident you can back off longer distances.

3   When out for a walk on lead, pick times at random and simply back off, calling the dog's name and the word 'come'. Of course he will come, because he is on lead so you have full control, reel him in by progressively shortening the lead - still repeating his name and the word 'come'. As the dog gets the idea pick times when he is paying the least attention to you to work on an instant recall. If you have a longer lead, (an extending lead or a tracking line is good), this can be done from a distance with a positive result.

It should all be done with great enthusiasm and fun from you, but incorporating the control element.

4   To get a clear message to the dog that the come command connects with something good take a handful of titbits, give the dog one and at the same time say his name and keyword 'come'. Repeat this several times then move a few inches away and repeat allowing the dog to follow and reward each time he makes contact with your hand.

5   Get a member of the family or close friend to play at calling the dog between you. Use reward and to start with be close together, but once the dog has the idea extend the distance between the handlers, soon the dog will be running on command to each handler for his reward of treats, play and praise.

6   If the dog has a tendency to ignore your calls when he is running free, take him out on a long line until the habit is broken. Once the dog is giving better responses, you can gradually shorten the line so that the dog becomes progressively less aware of it. Young dogs that are starting to develop and grow up will go through this phase. As soon as you recognise it, start taking them out on a line to avoid this natural behaviour becoming a habit and a problem.

7   Some dogs are highly sensitive to natural posture. Turn away from the dog to encourage him to you. Turning is a natural way of telling the dog that you do not pose a threat. It will also encourage him to follow. Making high-pitched sounds to imitate a whimper will also help.

Clicker Tips

The clicker can be incorporated from a very early age. When feeding, click before putting down the pup's food, when the dog comes for a cuddle or a game. This will help to intensify the meaning of the clicker in the dog's mind and link it to all things good.

When using it within the training program make sure you don't fall into the trap of clicking for attention as this will teach the dog to look away or follow a different behaviour pattern in order to be clicked! Click when the dog has his full attention on you and is coming towards you. The exercise can be broken down and shaped in the normal way.

Linking the Recall to the Static

To provide the link between the static position that the dog is left in, (sit or down) and the recall, you must train the dog so that he understands the progression, but making sure that he does not start to control the exercise himself and come before he is called. Therefore, once the dog understands how to stay in a position, sit or down, you can formalise the exercise a little by putting him in position, leaving him a pace or two and then, backing off. Call him using his name and the keyword. You can also incorporate your 'watch' command to make sure you maintain your dog's attention as you leave him.

This is of course done on lead so that you can control the dog's behaviour all of the time. Build up and randomise the amount of time he is left in position and the distance he is left, in gentle stages. Never go too far

too soon, and never leave the dog if he is unsure, fidgety, tired or unsettled. Train for success every time then the dog will not learn bad habits. Also always consider the training environment – check for any potential disturbances or distractions.

If the dog does break the position this must be worked on first - going back and rewarding small improvements and not putting in the recall until the dog is confident and stable in the static position. Of course you can still work on the recall as above, so don't let this setback stop your training.

It is not necessary to put in the 'present' at this stage as we are teaching the 'come' rather than the 'present'. That can be trained separately and linked in when both parts of the exercise are stable.

As with all training it is very important that the dog learns in a good variety of circumstances so that he learns to generalise the behaviour to the commands in all situations.

Rewards should be varied and given in the right manner, *(see Rewards)*, in order for the dog to see a reason to work. If rewards are always there, no matter what, he will soon learn that he does not have to try. Aim to give big/high value rewards for extra good performance, minimal rewards for mediocre performance once the dog has the idea, but you may need to start with high value rewards to motivate the dog initially.

It must be remembered that the dog will not understand in all situations unless you train from the basic level many times, in a great variety of environments, and with many different distractions. For many dogs, other dogs are a great distraction, but you will find that once you have developed a good rapport with your dog, this will become less of a problem. Use your other trained exercises to help e.g. watch, leave. If you train with threat or in a negative manner you will find that your dog will find other dogs, and often even other people, much more interesting and attractive than you. So remember keep it fun, keep control, and enjoy yourself.

Trouble Shooting
Too Slow

1   A good way to work on speed for a
    recall is to get someone to hold the

dog for you, you then run a reasonable distance (10-20 paces) away. Position yourself sometimes in a formal stance, sometimes bobbed down in a more welcoming stance, sometimes holding a toy out for the dog to latch on too. Call the dog and give abundant praise/play/reward. If his static position is sound you can do this on your own, but be careful that you don't create the opposite problem and the dog starts to anticipate the recall.

2   Another way to speed up the recall is to call the dog and then, when he is nearing his approach, throw a ball, toy or titbit behind you so that he keeps going beyond you for his reward. You can send him between your legs if you are tall enough to do this safely. Dogs love this type of training it gets their heart rate up and creates a good desire to work.

3   An elastic rope, sometimes known as 'bungy rope' (available from DIY stores – you need approx. 10 meters or so) with a toy on the end will also help motivate your dog. Even though the dog is chasing after it (helps retrieve and sendaway too) he soon becomes keen to get back to you so that you can set it in motion again. To instigate this you can put your foot on the line and reel him in still playing with the toy. Dogs that are not particularly toy motivated can be converted because of the movement and chase element of this technique.

Be careful to set it up with a secure stake and with empty space beyond. When you pull the toy back and extend the elastic and then release, the momentum can take the toy a long way, and you don't want it to hit something or someone or fling back and hit the dog.

Anticipation of Recall

If your dog does anticipate the recall, i.e. come before he is called, you must go back to the basic training of the static position and then progress to the link between the sit/down and the 'come'. Be patient and pleasant in your training as we want the dog to be as happy at the static as he is on the move to be sure of a perfect recall. If he breaks, do not chastise the dog for coming to you, (but don't reward him either) after all this is what you want, it is just that the dog is doing it his way instead of yours! If the dog goes wrong simply start again and make sure you are in a position to guide him into the correct way.

Too Fast

Some dogs are so motivated that they come in too fast and are in danger of doing the handler an injury. (This is especially so with larger breeds). To slow down the approach walk steadily towards the dog. Use a keyword 'steady' as you approach. Once the dog is responding you can decrease the forward movement gradually until the keyword becomes enough on its own.

Lack of Attention

Dogs that do not pay attention to the handler and/or gaze around on the journey to the handler can be retrained to enjoy and become more focused by increasing the desire to get to the handler. When a dog lacks drive in this way the most common reasons are as follows:

A   He his not rewarded or motivated enough.

B   The reward is always there and lacks variation therefore he does not have to try hard.

C   He has done that many recalls in his time that he finds them boring.

D   He has been chastised, perhaps for a bad present, and now is reluctant to come and is adopting a displacement behaviour to put off the inevitable.

E   He thinks this is the way it should be done because this is what he always does.

Whatever the reason you must go back and make sure that your reward system is sound and then start from the beginning, training for success every time, never letting the dog lapse back to his old ways. On lead and close training is a must, as you cannot control at a distance or off lead.

Indirect Approach

Some dogs (particularly herding breeds) approach with a curve. While this is not a major problem it will normally lose points. Start with very short distances (a single pace away) and retrain the approach step by step. Work very hard at the stage just before the normal start of the bend. It is a good idea to get the dog to focus on a particular part of your body with his/her head quite high, as the lower head position is conducive to the natural curve. *(See Presents - targeting)*. It is also beneficial to use barriers to run the dog through e.g. a double row of poles, poles and a rope or a narrow corridor.

Over Shooting

A similar problem to the two above – you need to teach the dog to focus on the target i.e. the center of your body. *(See Target Training.)*

Presents

Before you start the dog should have achieved the 'want' and be comfortable in close proximity with the handler.

'Present', or a signal for this should mean to the dog that he comes and sits in a straight position, immediately in front of you, with his head held up, watching and waiting for the next signal. His spine should follow a straight line to the ground and he should sit reasonably close to you, although it is not imperative that he is in actual contact, many handlers like the dog to come in very close.

In the UK handlers are permitted to put their hands in front of the body to form a target for the dog. However, most other countries require the handler to keep their hands by their sides. Targeting and barriers are the best techniques to achieve the latter.

Around the shows and training halls we can hear a varied deluge of 'verbal diarrhoea' for this quite simple exercise; 'Come, straight, front, present, get in, oy, not there, here', and many, many more, together with the 'St Vitas Dance' style body language - no wonder dogs get so confused! It is better and far simpler for both dog and handler to use one simple keyword coupled with a hand positioning signal, to show the dog where you want him. The hand position is a useful signal because when you need to work without commands in the higher classes, the hand position will act as a trigger in the dog's brain to guide him correctly. When he looks at you he will have the conditioned response and will immediately know what to do next.

The simplest keyword is the dog's name and the word 'Come'. The hand position tells the dog whether to jump into your arms and have a cuddle and a game, (open and inviting arms), or to 'present' in front of you, (hands positioned in front of your body close to where you will want his head to be).

Clicker Hints - If using clicker training simply click on the part you are working on, you may wish to shape the behaviour for better and better presents, but with added guidance you should be able to speed up the procedure. Not all techniques lend themselves to clicker as you may have too much in your hands to be able to click – however you can use the same principle but condition in another signal such as a special word.

Target Training – If your dog is target trained you can place your target in a central point of your body and give your dog your target keyword 'touch'. Once he is readily doing this you can add the sit. You could also teach the dog to target to your hand instead of a target stick – this is great for larger dogs especially.

Lead and Hands on Guidance – This technique is best for dogs who enjoy being handled.

Step 1 - At the outset we play games during which the dog is called with open arms and given lots of cuddles and a rough and tumble play. As always the game is on lead, down at dog level and the 'want' aid is used. The dog starts to associate the keyword 'Come', with lots of fuss and open arms, and will soon be hurtling to you when he hears the word. *(See also The Recall - to the Present Position).*

Step 2 - The next stage is to incorporate the above game with some guidance of the dog into the correct present position. So play with your dog and when you are ready and feel in control, gather up the lead, simultaneously giving his name and keyword. Bring your hands together, flat on your stomach, (or lower with a smaller dog), and then reach down with one hand to the dog's rump to make sure he sits squarely in the correct position. Bring your hands back together, guiding his head up as you go, all the time try to keep your body posture as up right as possible, (difficult I know, especially with a smaller dog, but keep it in mind).

Pretty soon you will be able to manoeuvre the dog so that he comes into the correct position without the need to reach over. Make sure you always place your hands clearly and in a central position on your body, so that the dog has something to aim for. You may find it easier to use your toy or a titbit to give him incentive to 'present' in the correct place.

Using the Collar to Guide - Another technique is to guide the dog in by slipping your hands through his collar at the front, and gently guiding him into place. The upward movement of your hands in the collar gently tilting him back into the sit position. Not all dogs respond quite so easily to this, particularly if they have been used to the pull of the collar meaning chastisement, but it is a very quick and accurate method if your dog is responsive and happy with it. Read Your Dog.

Steps 3 - Once your dog is happily coming into the 'present' position, with whichever technique you use, don't become totally formal. Keep the speed and 'Want' up by doing lots of play recalls with open arms.

Step 4 - You can now go on to teaching the dog to come into the 'present' from various angles. This reinforces the understanding of what is meant by the keyword 'Come', linked with the hand signal to 'present'. To start this, leave the dog in the sit position, stand slightly to the side, but facing your dog

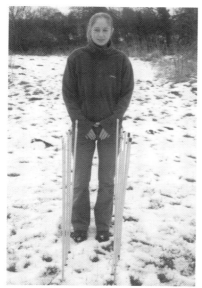 

Here we have used a number of sheep fencing posts to form a channel to aid the dog. The handler stands at the end with feet parallel and hands in a present position.

The dog is placed at the end of the line in the sit. (It is advisable to run the dog through the channel a few times without asking for anything to make him feel comfortable.)

at lead's length. Place the leg nearest to the dog out a little, so that the dog has to come around it to come in straight, this helps to bring him into the correct position. Call him in, gathering in the lead, and bringing your hands to the 'present' signal position. Be ready to help every step of the way. Remember that the training procedure should be carried out in an exuberant fashion just like the play. To attain good keen responses, your dog should not think there is a difference between work and play. When the dog completes the position, finish as usual with your release word and play.

Step 5 - As the dog grows more proficient, you can make the angles more acute, but remember start each training session with the basics, to make sure your dog is on the right wave length. Occasionally the dog will respond better starting at more acute angles, there being a much bigger difference for him to home in on. Experiment and see which works best for you.

Step 6 - This can only be achieved when you have taught the 'finish'. Once both the present and finish are taught it is good to link them together bringing the dog from one to the other, helping at first as you did in step 4

The dog is then called into the present position and encouraged as close as possible. The poles prevent a crooked present.

The handler encourages the dog to target the centre of the line and handler's body by enticing with the fingers.

with the angles. The dog will enjoy this exercise and you will have fun, plus a party trick to impress the neighbours! The dog can be sent for either a left or right handed finish if he knows both, but make sure he does not choose for himself - keep in control but have fun.

Barrier Control

To help the dog understand what is required you can use some form of barrier to help him get into the correct position. This technique is best used once the dog has some form of control, but before the straight present has been achieved. *(See illustrations).*

Seated Present

A good way to encourage a very close present is to sit on the edge of a seat with your legs parallel and encourage the dog into the present with a reward. The next step will need to be a half stand half sit in order for the dog to make the connection. If you go straight into the stand and ask for a present some dogs will not be able to make the connection.

With dogs that are highly food motivated you can throw a treat a little distance away onto the ground and then encourage the dog to come back to the present in order to gain another food reward. Release the food when the dog is in the perfect position.

Presenting with a Retrieve or Scent Article

Presenting with an article should not be a problem if you have taught the above with careful step by step patience, guidance and fun. The dog may not realise that you require the same thing, (i.e. the present to front) to start with, so it is best to go through the basics of the present, (once he has learnt to retrieve), allowing the dog to happily hold the article in his mouth. If you have done your job properly with his 'Want' toy, you may be able to show him what is required using this. Do not at any time put any mental or physical pressure on the dog that might result in him losing confidence in you or his toy and will lead to mouthing because an anxious dog will not be able to control his mouthing.

The dog needs to learn that the same exercise is required even with something in his mouth.

Finishes

Before you start - The dog should understand the keywords 'Sit', 'Close' and have 'The Want'.

The object of the exercise is to send the dog from the 'present' position, to the heel position, with the dog ending up in a neat sit by your side. It should be performed quickly, and the dog should not jump up or take a wide, erratic or distracted berth around the handler. In the UK the dog is permitted to go around to the left or to the right to achieve the finish.

Teaching finishes is generally either neglected or over done. Currently in the UK competition ring, the left-handed finish seems to be the preferred discipline. The usual reason given for this preference is that the dog can be seen all of the time, and the handler does not have to worry what is going on behind. The right handed finish, i.e. the dog going behind the handler to the heel position is often the preferred style of handlers with larger breeds - but not always. Many handlers like to teach the dog both, and then make their choice later.

Teaching is relatively simple if you follow the steps. Some of these steps will need to be progressed over several training sessions, unless the dog is already well versed and mature. Don't expect to get perfection in one go.

Clicker Hints – You have two main ways to use your clicker for this exercise, shape the behaviour a step at a time or guide the dog and click when he is in the finish (heel) position. The second way may be quicker to teach and remains quite stable. You can also combine the two, by guiding some of the way and then clicking. Then once this is sound, extend it with more guidance.

Teaching the Left-handed Finish
Step 1 - Get the dog in the correct frame of mind, i.e. create 'The

Want'. Put him in the sit position in front of you, tell him 'Sit'. Hold your lead and your toy in your right hand, and place your right hand in the present signal position, keep it there as much as possible *(see Presents.)* Use your left hand to run down the lead towards the dog's collar. Step back with your left leg, call the dog using his heelwork word - 'Close'. Continue walking backwards (if necessary) to create a good backwards flow, using your left hand to guide the dog back and round into the heel position. Your left hand will also prevent the dog from jumping by holding a little downward pressure. Guide him round until you have his head coming into your leg. Then take a few steps forward, just enough to bring the dog into the correct position. Stop and place him in the straight sit position. Reward him in the position and then release.

It may help to have a treat or favourite toy in your left hand to help guide the dog and give him incentive to go. If the dog prefers a hands off approach just use a food lure to guide him into position instead of the lead.

The whole procedure should have a smooth action to it, although this may take a little time for the handler to perfect.

Step 2 - When the dog is able to understand the above, and is performing with enthusiasm, you will gradually be able to take less steps back and forward. Work on this until the leg movement is limited to one step back, then forward to join your static right leg.

Step 3 - The step back can now be shortened to make it less obvious, but if the dog is unsure, lengthen your step when he needs it. Try to start off each time with both hands in the present position, because this is what the dog will eventually see.

Step 4 - The left hand going down the lead can now be less exaggerated, working towards a minimum, but continue to use it as the signal. This way the hand is always going in the right direction if the dog needs help. Again try to start off with both hands in the present position.

Step 5 - Vary your aids, sometimes step back, sometimes use your lead. Introduce turns following the finish, so that the dog does not start to assume that he will always be released at the end.

Trouble Shooting

Reluctance to go - Some dogs do not work well when you put tension into the lead. If this is the case you can guide the dog using a titbit only. It is a good idea to use a barrier such as a wall to ensure that he does not swing out too far.

Jumping – Although it can look cute, a jump into the heel position will lose you points. In training keep your hand low to ensure that the dog follows the lower position and does not jump around to heel. Transfer this hand signal to the ring.

Wide Circle – Again a barrier can help to keep the dog closer. Also make sure that your left hand is keeping close to your body when you guide the dog around, and draw him in from behind.

Too slow - Usually this is because of lack of enthusiasm. Do lots of training with food or toys as lure and reward. Link the exercise to a fun start and finish – don't get to formal.

Crooked Sit – Use a combination of placing and guidance on a regular basis (at every training session) do not rely on the dog to get it right without daily help and guidance. Do not test your end product very often, do more training than testing. When using a titbit lift it high and close into your left side to help lift the dog's body into the correct position. Cup your hand backwards, exposing the reward just ahead of where you want the dog's nose.

Anticipation – See below.

Teaching the Right Handed Finish

The Right handed finish is often favoured by handlers of larger more cumbersome breeds. It does not require such a tight turn, and the dog can whip around with ease and speed if sufficiently motivated.

Step 1 - Get the dog in working mode i.e. achieve 'The want'. Put him in the sit position in front of you. You can remain quite close, hold your lead in your right hand, fairly close to the dog's collar. Tell the dog 'Close', as you step back with your right leg, taking as many steps as necessary to get the dog on his feet, and on his way past you on your right. When the dog reaches your side, start walking forwards so that the natural momentum

makes the dog move around you, transfer the lead into the left hand and bring the dog around into the sit position beside you - his shoulder level with your left leg.

If you feel that you are getting in a taffle with your lead, you can pass it behind you and into your left hand before you start. Then just reel it in as the dog comes into position.

Step 2 - The obvious progression is to gradually take fewer steps, before bringing the dog around, and after he comes into position. The more you motivate him the quicker this will come. This can easily become a very boring exercise so make sure that you keep it exciting and light - do not repeat it many times in each training session. Make sure that the dog is remaining tight behind you, keep the lead tight so that there is no room for error.

Step 3 - As the movement on your part is reduced, your right hand going to the right can become the signal to the dog. It will therefore always be there to help if necessary.

Trouble Shooting

Slow - If the dog is slow coming around use your toy to motivate him, do not place him in the sit, instead just throw the toy as he comes around, and let him go forward for it. You can soon introduce the sit to a motivated dog, it is more difficult to speed up a switched off dog.

Anticipation - Once you have perfected the finish do not tag it on to every relevant exercise, if you do the dog will soon start to anticipate and/or lose the sparkle. Keep him guessing by being adaptable and not always doing that which will occur in the ring. If you have taught both left and right-handed finish, use both so the dog is not quite sure which way you are going to send him.

Wide Sit - Position yourself near a wall or in a corner, so that when he comes into the heel position, the wall prevents him from going wide. Or use a titbit or toy and move it quickly behind you to entice him to follow closely.

Recall to the Heel Position (Test 'A' Recall)

Before you start the dog should understand the 'Heel position', 'Sit or 'Down', 'Close, 'Watch', be well motivated and have the 'Want'.

In the UK, the recall to heel comes in two different exercises. The first is test 'A' as a test in its own right and the second is a recall following the sendaway (test 'B' and 'C').

Test 'A' - The dog is left in either the sit or the down position. The handler leaves the dog in the position of their choice and walks away at a normal pace as directed by the judge or steward, it may be in a straight line or there may be some turns. The handler will be instructed to call the dog and is allowed to use the dog's name and a command, signal or both whilst continuing to walk away from him. The dog is expected to join the handler in the heel position and continue walking to heel with him until the judge/steward instructs them to halt. The dog must then sit as in normal heelwork until the exercise is finished and the handler releases the dog.

Tests 'B' and 'C' - In the UK obedience tests 'B' and 'C', the recall will follow the sendaway exercise. The handler may be walking in any direction (as directed by the judge/steward) when the dog is called by command or signal, (but not both). In all cases the dog will be expected to join the handler quickly and smoothly, and work in the correct heel position, continuing as directed by the judge or steward until halted.

General Points - The exercise can be taught with the dog being left in the sit or the down position. (As required for test 'A'). The down position is most popular for a combination of reasons. Firstly, most dogs are more settled in the down, and secondly, the exercise will be done with the dog in a down following the sendaway exercise in test 'B' and 'C'. Also, starting this exercise in the down gives the dog a clear differentiation from the novice recall,

(recall the dog to the front present position), this is helpful when the dog and/or handler are new to training.

Before you start be sure that the dog is stable and confident in your chosen position, sit or down. If he shows any confusion or apprehension go back to the Teaching Statics section before moving on to teaching the recall.

For the purpose of this exercise it will be preferably that the dog should not be laid flat in the down. It is useful for him to be able to watch the handler's direction and be ready to go smartly to the handler when called and make a good pick up into the heel position.

Clicker Hints

Be sure that all of the elements needed are well trained and understood. When linking them together decide what you are working on and focus on it. It is a good idea to build up bit by bit in each training session – rewarding with your clicker each part of the exercise before trying to put it together.

Step 1 - As usual the training begins on lead. Put the dog in position. 'Sit' or 'Down'. (For the purpose of this explanation the down will be assumed, but the advice generally applies to both).

Take time to ensure that the dog is happy and confident before you start. Hold your lead in your right hand. Remind him calmly 'Down' before and as you take a forward step away from the dog, keeping your back to him. Run your left hand down the lead towards the collar ready to guide the dog. Then with friendly, positive encouragement turn you head to the dog, looking over your left shoulder, call the dog using his name and your keyword for heelwork, *'Freddie Close'*. Use your left hand on the lead to guide the dog into the correct position. Walk a few paces with the dog in the heelwork position remembering to keep your body posture upright, and your attitude friendly. Then break and play. If preferred us a titbit to lure the dog into position instead of the lead.

Do not be too formal at this stage. Repeat a couple of times at each training session, until the dog is confident and coming into position with accuracy and a minimum of help.

Step 2 - The next stage is to build up a little distance before calling the dog. Build up very gradually, literally a step at a time. As you build up the exercise you can join two leads together, use a longer line or extending lead, to give more distance and yet remain in control. Reel the lead in to help the dog to take up a good heel position. Make sure that the equipment you use is easily controlled, and that you are not struggling with too much length or bulk of lead. If you do get muddled, simply stop and play with the dog, and then start again, having gained control.

Step 3 - Once you have perfected a straight recall to the heel position (about two lead lengths), then introduce a turn so that the dog learns to come into the heel position whilst you are at an angle to him.

Go back to being only a pace away from the dog, and have just one lead again. Place him in position and then turn to your left, in front of the dog no more than a pace away. Call him using your keyword *'Freddie Close'*, and at the same time step back with your right leg, (or left if you lead with your right foot on left turns in heelwork. See left turns). Run your left hand down the lead towards the collar, and sweep the lead back, just as you would for a left turn in heelwork. Guide the dog into the heel position neatly. Take a few paces forwards with the dog in the heel position and then break and play. Don't be tempted to formalise and put in sits at the end, teach the sits later and separately *(See Heelwork sits)*. Don't lose sight of what you are teaching. Have patience perfecting this stage, keeping up the motivation level to be sure of a neat pick up. Don't be tempted to rush ahead just because you have had a successful straight recall. Good groundwork now will save heartache and confusion later.

Step 4 - This time take an extra step forward before turning to put in a little more distance. Then proceed as above. Once again, use your lead to sweep the dog back and then into the heel position to teach a neat, tight pickup. Build up to a lead's length or two, as before, making sure that you have control all the time, but do not progress at the expense of enthusiasm, keep it fun.

Step 5 - Next teach the right handed pickup, this is not quite so easy as the dog has to come around you to the heel position, but take your time and be positive in your actions.

Once again leave your dog in a confident down. This time you will leave the dog a couple of steps and turn right. Remind the dog 'Down' as you leave him. Hold your lead in your right hand and use your left hand, as before, to guide him in. Turn and show him your toy or titbit to encourage him around you. Run your left hand down the lead to the dog's collar, gathering the lead up as he comes towards you. Guide the dog close into the heel position, using the heelwork keyword, 'Freddie Close'. Take a few steps forward to keep the momentum and then finish the exercise.

Again build the exercise up slowly, taking time to make sure you have a good heel position, and a neat, tight pick up, without any surging or banging.

Teaching the turn is very similar to teaching the turns for heelwork, you will find that the training for one will aid the other. Use these starting blocks to gain the dog's confidence in the exercise. Keep it fun and light yet control for precision. If the dog anticipates do not chastise him. Simply call him into position, and then go back to the static position and train him in the down without calling him. If you chastise the dog, at best you are putting in anxiety and confusion and at worst, a reluctance to do the exercise. You must remember not to get cross when the dog is actually doing what you are trying to teach him, albeit a little too soon for your liking. It does not make sense to be angry, although we see people doing it all the time. Remember, you are too late if you give chastisement after the event, even fractions of a second after the start of the event which may be still in action. *(See Timing)*. If things go wrong simply go back and spend more time on the static part of the exercise. Put enthusiasm and enjoyment into the whole exercise and not threat. Reward the dog for the correct behaviour, ignore and restart when he goes wrong. Aim at making incorrect behaviour boring and meaningless by putting all of the emphasis and fun on the correct behaviour.

Step 6 - After you have mastered the basic control training, there are some exercises that will help build up confidence and style. Leave the dog in the down position go to the end of your longer lead and to the left a few paces, then simultaneously call the dog and start walking backwards. When the dog reaches your leg, start walking forward and guide him in. Once the dog is happy doing this pick up to the left, try turning to the right and repeating the process. This helps the dog to adjust his position on pickups, and can actually be used solely as the teaching method for the recall to the heel position.

Step 7 - Another useful exercise is to leave the dog in the down, still holding the lead and turn left, right etc. and say the commands as the steward would, for example, 'Right Turn, Left Turn, Halt, Call your dog'. This will help accustom the dog to you turning, as directed by the steward. Return to the dog and reward him whilst he stays in the static position. When you first start this you may need a friend or a tape recording to call whilst you reassure the dog of the down position. If you already have problems then you definitely need to concentrate on the dog, reassuring him all of the time.

Trouble Shooting

Anticipation - Don't repeat the exercise too much in one session, as the dog will start to anticipate and come before you call him. Ideally be unpredictable as to whether you call him or not. Set up the exercise and call him, and then repeat, but this time do not call him, reward him for staying down. Too much ring work, or mock ring work, and not enough training can also cause anticipation. The dog soon becomes conditioned to recall when he hears someone say, 'Call your dog'. If you do mock ring work, then make sure you train at the same time. If you set up a ring make it appear like a show, but train your dog.

Reluctance, Distraction or Hesitation on Recall - If your dog is reluctant to come, or is easily distracted, then you need to spend more time and enthusiasm in calling and rewarding. Be exciting, get out a toy or a titbit as the dog comes into position. Or, as the dog comes toward you, throw his favourite toy ahead and slightly to the right of you. Allow him to chase after the toy.

Wide or Inaccurate Pick Up - If the dog has a tendency to come in wide, set the dog up and then, as you call him to heel, throw a toy across yourself. Throw it well to the right hand side to encourage and motivate the dog in close to you, let him follow and collect the toy. This of course means the dog is not actually doing the exercise, but he is coming into the correct direction and learning that it is fun. Do not formalise the exercise. Alternate precision and play, so that one begins to be part of the other. Train all of the steps in a controlled manner to build up the correct association. Use your lead and/or titbits to guide the dog into the correct position, remembering to keep your hand in close to your body as the dog will follow the line drawn by your hand.

General Advice - It is not necessary indeed it is pointless, to repeat the finished exercise over and over once the dog can do it, save the masterpiece for the ring. Faults should not creep in unless you are doing more ring work than training, show off to often, or leave the dog to complete the exercise without the training aids and the dog will start to devise his own version of events.

Preparing for the Ring

To prepare the exercise for the ring, gradually alternate the use of commands, reward, incentive and encouragement *(as described in the section on eliminating commands)*. In the UK obedience ring you are allowed only one command and signal in test 'A', and a command or signal only in test 'B' and 'C', in all classes you may use the dog's name also. Your dog will have become accustomed to you turning your head in training to call him into position.

This head signal can be used, in conjunction with his name in the ring. The head signal is a great signal to use for both you and the dog because:

a) It means you can see that the dog has heard and responded.

b) It directs your voice towards the dog. (This is very important if you have a light voice, or the wind is strong and in the wrong direction).

c) It is a friendly invitation to the dog, he will respond to your expression and this will help him to get it right.

Work on the static down. Set up situations so that you can teach the dog that you may walk, around and stewards may call, but it is nothing to worry about or to respond to until he hears the keyword. Although we do not want the dog to fall asleep while he waits for you, he needs to be confident and unruffled by any external disturbances.

When any faults creep into the exercise, go back to the drawing board, i.e. start from the beginning. It won't take long, and will save a lot of anguish. Correctional training always shows itself in the ring, the dog that is taught by correction is normally disjointed and erratic in his work, and so will be marked down by the judge accordingly.

Stays

In the stay exercise the dog is required to remain in a static position for a set period of time (depending on the level). The handler leaves and returns as directed by a steward.

The teaching of the sit, down and stand needed for stays is covered in the Static Positions section. Once each position required is stable, you can then go on to the applications – in this case for stays. *(See also Progressing the Positions in the Static Positions section.)*

Clicker Tips

You can incorporate the clicker with all of the techniques explained. You just need to be clear in your own mind, which bit you are working on and so clicking on.

One of your problems may be if the dog is used to the click ending the behaviour, at some point you will need to move on to the dog getting clicked for holding position, but being released on command or signal.

To extend time, simply withhold the click for progressively longer periods of time. To keep the dog in position instead of ending on the click, simply repeat the position command as you click, use a lead to aid control if you wish, dogs soon make the transition and the clicker becomes a confidence builder too. *(See Clicker Training)*

Building Time and Space

Once you have correctly taught the dog the three positions, you can then start to introduce a little time and distance. As usual, take a step at a time, building confidence all the way. Many occurrences of good controlled exercises will be far better than one long one that keeps going wrong. You can probably remember an instructor yelling, 'if your dog breaks, you've gone too far too fast'. How easy it is to ignore this advice, and to fall into the habit of continual correction. Remember, what the dog ends up doing is what he has learnt to be correct, irrespective of what you do to amend things afterwards. So it is imperative that your basics have sound foundations, and the dog has developed a confident attitude.

It is a good idea to start each session close by the dog, even when he is reasonably well trained. This way you are reminding him what it is that you want. For an example the sit will be discussed below, but the same procedure will apply to all three positions.

Step 1 Place the dog in the correct position, as his bottom comes to the floor give him the keyword 'Sit'. Reward this action and then, once you are happy that he is relaxed and confident, break the exercise and then set him up again.

Step 2 This time lean your body away from him, keeping your feet still to start with. As you begin to lean, repeat your keyword and be ready for any faltering on the dog's part. Lean back towards the dog and reward and then release, remember your timing, *(see Concepts section - Timing if in doubt).*

Be ready, as you move from the dog if he shows any signs of confusion or moving, you must help him to remain correct. Notice we are not preparing to correct him, correction teaches nothing except that 'if you move you will be put back again', some dogs grow to enjoy this game, others become confused and anxious as their handlers grow more frustrated.

Watch the dog's body movement, posture, facial expressions, ear carriage etc. and try to prevent movement by guidance and reassurance.

Step 3 The next stage is to take a step away from the dog. Again set him up carefully; make sure that he is fully aware of what you are trying to do. Give him the keyword 'Sit' and adjust the lead to the back of his neck, hold it up and away from the dog to give you good control. When you are sure that the dog is stable, take a slow, smooth step away to the right with your right foot followed by your left foot. Encourage and give confidence with your voice and firmly but gently guide with the lead holding it above and behind his head. The tautness of the lead will give him confidence so long as you have not been harsh with your lead in the past. However, as his confidence grows you should move to a slacker lead so that he does not learn to depend on the contact.

Step 4 When you are sure that the dog is stable with you taking one step away from him, you can build on to take another, and then another and so on. The secret with the build up of this exercise is to take things gradually and to instill confidence all of the way. Many short repetitions that can be rewarded will aid the learning process.

Avoid standing facing onto the dog, and watch that your hand position is not as it would be for the recall signal. It is easy for the dog to misconstrue your wishes reading your body stance. The dog watches body movement and gestures and interprets more from this than he does from our verbal language.

Step 5 It is also important that the dog starts to learn that you mean the same thing even if the circumstances differ. So, this means taking the exercise from the beginning in differing places, at differing times, and with different people, animals or objects around. You should also sometimes be a little different yourself, perhaps change your coat or your perfume, all of these things can come into the equation of a dog's understanding of any number of situations. The first time that you change the situation with any relevance the dog may be very confused, be patient. Treat it as a brand new exercise again, he will soon start to understand from your stability that things are meant to be the same, even when some of the variables differ. The section on understanding the dog's mind will help you to understand your dog's confusion. You must learn to think like a canine!

When your dog is confident in a given situation you can use this medium to build the exercise up and increase your time and space. Don't expect the dog to progress in leaps and bounds, take things a little at a time and get it right.

Step 6 The next thing to do is to vary the length of time the dog is kept in position. Counting to yourself is a great aid in self-discipline. For instance set the dog up in the sit position, count to three, then return, reward and release. Then repeat, counting to five, return, reward and release, then repeat counting to eight, return, reward and release, then repeat counting to two, return and release. Of course you must be flexible, if the dog shows any signs of confusion or movement abandon your count, assist the dog and start again, controlling the dog in the required position.

When you have managed a couple of paces away from the dog in many different situations, and for varying lengths of time, it is appropriate to take things a stage further on. Each time you want to progress, remember to start from the beginning as if the dog knows nothing. This will build his confidence, and help him to accept something new tagged onto the end of something he already knows.

Step 7 Once your are confident that the dog is stable and sure of himself, you can move on to off lead training. To start this you must remain by his side. Set him up as usual go through the routine for your normal procedure and then carefully unclip his lead. Keep the lead off for just a couple of seconds, then clip it back onto his collar. Reward and release. Do not release him from the exercise until his lead is re-connected to his collar, this will help to teach him not to move before the end of the exercise. The habit of re-connecting the lead will become part of the exercise and he is less likely to 'self release' when it matters, i.e. in the ring!

Building in Confidence

It is useful to be able to train your dog with other dogs around, especially if you can work towards the sort of line up of dogs that you will experience in the ring. Don't forget to train your routine in this situation as all others, don't expect too much too soon, and certainly don't attempt to do things that you are not sure will work, even if everyone else around you appears to be more advanced. One of the biggest mistakes in dog training is trying to keep up with others. People and dogs vary and everyone in your training group will have trained differently and for varying lengths of time. Your dog may be more immature, less confident, more easily confused, you may have done less training - who knows? Don't make errors because of other people's pressure, remember that what the dog is **doing** is what he is **learning**. You can't afford to get it wrong too many times otherwise your dog training sessions will become perpetual re-training sessions and you will find it difficult to progress further.

Remember you should go through the same dedication to the training procedure with all of the three stay positions, don't assume that if the dog can do a two minute sit he will be able to do a two minute down without adequate comparable training.

Preparing for Distractions

Now that your dog can master the positions, and is confidently working like a pro, introduce some of the sort of things that may go wrong in the ring. For instance consider how your dog would react if, as you left him, you sneezed, had a coughing fit or dropped your dog lead? To be sure he will remain in position, and that you are not going to blow your chances of winning the ticket just because pollen tickled your nose, train for it! Close on lead control to start with and then progressing to put in the distance. This means standing by him to start with, and then progressing to just as you leave him, and then at varying distances. Pretend to cough, sneeze, drop something, chat to someone, basically introduce any of the things to your training that may happen to you in the ring, whether they are intentional or not.

What would your dog do if another dog started to wander around? You can teach your dog to ignore this by training with other dogs loose in the room or training area, make sure that they are friendly and pose no threat of course. Your own dogs or those belonging to friends are good ones to start with. Also getting someone to weave their dog in and out will help to get your dog to be blasé about such things.

There are other things that may occur, such as children by the ring side, cycles or joggers going past, loud noises, dogs getting excited etc. Although show societies generally try to situate the stay ring in a quiet area, it is not always possible to do this or to predict the disturbances that may occur. For example at a show in a public area you could get an ice-cream or hot dog stand close by! There could be other events taking place that will distract your dog such as main ring or sporting events. At one show near my home we had a quiet morning but by 2.00 in the afternoon we were faced with cannons going off in a main arena, marching bands marching by, and hot air balloons overhead, a good few dogs broke the stays that day!

You should also train in all weathers (within reason). It is quite common for dogs to break stays because there has been a shower of rain, or a blustery wind has excited them.

Avoiding Sniffing - What would your dog do if the patch of ground chosen for him to stay on had a particularly tempting smell? You can train to avoid the inevitable interest that may lead to a roll or change of position in order to get a better sniff. Put him in one of the static positions, point to the floor and area around him and then use your keyword 'Leave'. (See leave on command.) Reward him for correct behaviour, but be ready to prevent him from getting things wrong by having him under control on lead.

Angled Leave or Return - What would your dog do if you left at an angle instead of straight? Train for it on lead. Give the keyword, leave him in your chosen position, (start with his favourite), and then move across him, slowly and smoothly twist and turn, stand sideways, walk around him, turn every conceivable way, (not all at once of course), and all the time keep control with the lead. Build the dog's confidence with your voice and positive handling, doing a little at a time.

Training for Fatigue/Boredom - What would your dog do if he became tired or bored with the position he was in? You can train for it. Have the dog on lead, standing by your side, put him in position, let us say the 'sit'. Give him the keyword 'sit ', hold the lead in your right hand and apply gentle pressure with your left hand on his shoulders, as if you wanted him in the down, but keep saying the keyword 'sit'. If the dog attempts to go down, and most will try, at least to start with, lift him up with your lead in your right hand and move your left hand to maintain the position of his rump, or raise your lure hand to signal the sit as you originally taught him. Repeat the keyword 'sit' as you help him to maintain the position, and praise the dog when he is holding it correctly. The dog will soon learn that in this situation, he must listen to the keywords and ignore variables. As soon as he starts to actively resist the position change he must be rewarded so that he knows he is correct. Watch your timing, the reward must come as he resists the break of position, in connection with your keyword, if you are a little late and he has relaxed he may take this further and misconstrue your reward as being for relaxing ready to change position.

Work your way through any other position changes that may occur in the same manner, tempting the dog to alter position, and then pleasantly reinforcing the keyword position with confident, positive handling. There will of course be more than one possible change from each position, and all of these should be covered. You will find that the most common changes are dropping from the sit to the down, and from the stand to the sit.

It must be emphasised that you are not trying to fool the dog, or catch him out, you are merely placing him in position, and making sure that

he understands the meaning of the keyword associated with that position. He will soon learn, and will enjoy pushing back against your hands in order to maintain the keyword position. If your timing is correct, he will know that reward and your appreciation come for the correct action, and incorrect actions will be guided away from, until they become extinct.

Training for the Ring

Most judges will ask for handlers to have their backs to the dog even in the lower classes. Some will say it is okay to stand side on, others will allow handlers to face the dogs. Facing directly is not really a good idea as the dog could misconstrue and think he is to be called as in a recall. Your training as above will naturally lead you to standing sideways so this should not pose a problem. To progress to standing with your back to the dog take it slowly turning for a few seconds to start with and then build up the time as you feel the dog gains in confidence. A mirror will help you to keep an eye on the dog and you can still talk to him to help him maintain the position.

Going Out of Sight

Going out of sight of the dog should never be rushed. When first attempted you should be out of your dog's sight for a very short time, seconds only. Leave the dog in his favourite position and in a very safe area where the dog feels confident.

The first stage is to turn your body sideways to the dog, and then progress to turning your back to him. You also need to build up periods of silence while the dog stays in position with you in sight. He will then get used to no comments from you before you desert him!

When you are very close to the dog you can feel any movement through the lead, but if you have done all of the above training correctly there should be no movement at all. If there is, go back to your basics.

A simple step in teaching the dog to accept you being out of his view is to pass behind an obstacle or person, and then immediately reappear. Your disappearance should be momentary only, and if you then return to the dog and reward him in his position no problems should occur. It is only when you try to disappear for too long or in stressful situations that the problems will start to creep in.

Make sure that once again the basics are covered well to avoid problems later. If the dog builds up oodles of confidence in training he will be able to cope with any minor disturbances or changes in the ring much more easily.

Another good training experience can be done in the home or specially set up in the training hall using mirrors. If correctly positioned, you can go out of sight, around a corner, or through a doorway, but still see your dog so that you can verbally give him help and encouragement when necessary. You can build in the silences that will occur when you are in the ring remotely, because you can see his reactions in the reflection on your mirror, without him seeing you. You are then able to return to him if he looks unsettled and certainly before anything goes wrong. Of course to do this effectively you should not actually be very far away, you can't allow it to take very long to get back to him, and you should only go on to this stage when you and the dog are ultra confident.

Training for the Time Span - When training 'stays' for competition, you should aim to build up to a longer time than is required, and then the dog will learn to be settled for suitable stretches of time. Build up gradually sometimes going back to shorter stays to help build confidence. Choose places that will sooth the dog to start with rather than opting for a distracting environment until you are sure of the dog. Try to train with other dogs too – in the show ring they will be in a line so recreate the scene and put your dog next to one that is stable when you first start.

General Preparation - As often as possible, you should train among other dogs, even if they are your own, but make an effort to get among other people's dogs as often as possible too. If the only place that your dog meets other dogs is at a show, all is not lost, you can always get together with a few

friends and enlist their help in a quiet corner of the show ground. But caution; be careful that the help you enlist doesn't interfere with your dog or show aggression, even towards their own dog, as this is not going to have the required effect for your type of training. You must look for a good, sound, friendly atmosphere for teaching your dog.

It sometimes helps to teach the dog to be tethered to a fence or a stake in the ground. This way he gets used to you being close by without having the opportunity to have contact. This can be built up over time to out of sight. Go slowly and to start with do not ask for any positions, let the dog choose. Just be content with him being tethered and away from you. Reward him for his good behaviour.

Trouble Shooting

Many handlers find stays a problem, and some of the keenest, stylish heelwork dogs blow a good round with poor stays. When a handler comes to me with problems, my advice is nearly always, as with most exercises, 'go right back to basics'. This should be done to the degree that you pretend that the dog knows nothing and retrain from the beginning. People find this difficult, but it really is the best way. It builds confidence, and teaches the dog just what it is that you are trying to achieve. Of course before doing this, you should consider the training methods used, if the dog is breaking stays, then you may have done something to confuse him at some point. This may not be the case, it may be that he has been frightened by some occurrence in the stay ring.

The dog is not deliberately disobedient, he will innocently react to a set of circumstances. Sometimes circumstances have made the aims become or seem to be distorted. When the dog becomes confused, he uses his memory bank of triggered reactions to deal with things by himself. This is not always how we would like it. A sound basis to training will make things work for you.

Breaking The Stay On Return – Many dogs break the stay as the handler returns, usually because they are anticipating the reward or fun that will follow. Occasionally it is because they feel uncomfortable due to chastisement on return on previous occasions.

When training all of the praise should come while the dog is holding position and not on release. Release from the position is reward enough without making it ultra exciting for the dog.

If the dog should break the stay, do not chastise it as this will cause more problems due to a break down in confidence or even fear. Simply and calmly take the dog back to the position if there is no real reason for the break, reposition the dog and calmly go into your training routine. Build up slowly again to put back the confidence and stability.

Only In the Ring - Sometimes there are faults that occur which only seem to arise in the ring. The reason that this happens normally is that the basis of the training has not been thorough enough. Occasionally something happens in the ring to frighten or confuse the dog, for instance a sudden thunderstorm, having to lie next to a dominant dog, or be disturbed by an aggressive handler, (even when the aggression is not directed at your dog.) In cases like these, we still go back to basics to give solid grounding for the dog, but we may have to recreate the point at which the dog becomes confused, and help him through. For example, a friend's dog only broke the stays within seconds of her leaving the dog with other handlers leaving at the same time. He had become spooked when another dog did this in the ring once. So along with sound basics, we set this situation up and helped the dog to overcome his confusion by on lead reward based training amongst other handlers who were calling their dogs.

Retrieve

The minimum that your dog should understand before you start: The 'Want', 'Play', the keyword 'Come'. A good play retrieve is also useful. The minimum you should understand before you start: Timing, bonding, the dog's mind, and the objective of the exercise.

The essence of what we require from the retrieve exercise is; the dog is to remain sitting in the heel position. He should be still and quiet but alert. He should respond instantly when, on the command or signal of the handler, he is sent for the article. The dog must make a natural, positive, and direct out run and a neat clean pick up of the article. He should return in a brisk, unhesitant, straight run and present the article to the centre front of the handler. He should sit squarely in a neat, centrally accurate position, in perfect line with the handler. The dog should hold the article until the handler (on instruction from the judge/steward) reaches forward to take it. The dog must then wait until given a command or signal to go to the heel position. The retrieve article must at all times, during the period that it is held by the dog, be carried in a positive manner, without chewing, rolling or otherwise mouthing. The dog should perform this task, as all others in a 'happy natural manner'.

In the UK there is no retrieve in

Pre Beginners. In beginners the handler can use any article. In Novice and test 'A' it must be a dumbbell and in test 'B' and 'C' the article will be supplied by the judge. In other countries there will be variations on this for example for FCI the dog is required to collect one of 3 wooden dumbbells and also retrieve a metal dumbbell over a hurdle.

Retrieve is one of the major stumbling blocks for handlers in competitive obedience. Such a natural instinctive exercise should really pose very few problems, but it does. Most puppies quite naturally retrieve; the problems normally start to creep in when any form of precision is introduced by the handler/trainer.

From studying the chapter within the concept section, covering the understanding of the dog's mind, you will appreciate that this is in fact a very complex task. Such precision and accuracy can only be achieved and maintained, if the dog understands, and is motivated to enjoy every tiny component of the exercise. To achieve this we must break down the task into fragments.

Most handlers will have achieved some form of play retrieve. If your dog does not like to play, this is dealt with in the concept section under *'play training'*. The play retrieve is a very useful motivator to use in conjunction with teaching a more formalised retrieve. It also serves to help the dog differentiate between the two.

Word Usage - The handler should use a different keyword for each style of retrieve i.e. play and formal. For example, *'hold'* or *'carry'* for the formal retrieve, and *'fetch it'* or *'get it'* for play retrieve. The actual words that you choose don't matter, use whatever you feel most comfortable with, but be consistent and think about what you are saying and doing. Make sure the words that you use cannot be confused with any others and that the keyword that you will use in the ring is just one word not two. (You could be penalised for using an extra command if you used *'fetch it'* as your ring command).

It will be of great benefit if you have effectively taught your dog the meaning of the keyword *'come'*. If the dog is instantly and happily able to respond to this word, then it will avoid any pressure or jerking on the lead to ensure the dog returns. Lead use when the dog has an article in his mouth can cause him to drop the article.

If your dog has not learnt the controlled *'sit'* don't worry, you don't need it to start with. You can introduce the control and sit part of the exercise, when it has been successfully taught, as a separate exercise. Likewise the *'present'* and *'finish'*. Don't lose sight of what you are teaching at each stage, in this instance the retrieve, be sure that the dog has had a thorough grounding in each component before attempting to put things together.

Article Choice - Once you have decided on the keywords that you intend to use. Find a suitable article for the dog to learn the exercise on, and have a clear mental picture of the exercise. The article that you choose should be comfortable for the dog. If you decide that you would like to start with a dumbbell, then it is a good idea to wrap some thick, soft cloth around it, toweling is ideal. This is particularly important if you are training a puppy, a soft mouthed dog, or if you have a dog which has had bad experiences in the past.

A wider diameter mouthpiece is less likely to be moved around in the dog's mouth than a thin one, and so it will be easier for you to prevent the mistakes of mouthing, chewing etc.

A snug fit will help prevent the dog moving the dumbbell from side to side. The length of the mouthpiece should allow no more than a small finger's width either side. The sides of the bell should allow good clearance from the floor so that the dog does not scrape its mouth, while being small enough so that they do not cover the dog's eyes.

It is not important to start with a dumbbell, you could use any easy to hold article. A favourite of many handlers is to take the inside tube of a toilet roll and stuff it with newspaper and then seal it with tape. Or choose anything that is non-injurious and that you feel the dog will be happy to hold.

Retrieve for Puppies - With puppies it is best to wait until they are through the teething stage, before you put in any serious work, but informal preparation is covered in the section on *Starting with a puppy* and *the 'want'*. Play retrieves can continue as long as the dog is not teething too painfully. Avoid too much tugging during teething. Painful early experiences can make teaching retrieve very difficult.

If your pup likes to carry things around, encourage it to you with the article, sometimes taking it then rewarding with another throw of the article or with a treat and sometimes just rewarding by stroking and praising in a fun manner and leaving the dog to claim the article. If you take the article every time, the dog may be less likely to want to bring it to you.

It is a good idea to have a variety of articles in your pup's toy box so that he can get used to the feel of different substances in a relaxed environment. Include any safe item made of metal for example a large spoon, a check chain or bunch of disused keys. Also include items such as a rolled up magazine, plastic tubes and some items that will dangle when carried. All of this light hearted fun will build confidence for later when more formal retrieve items are introduced.

General Points - Timing *(see Concepts Section)*, is a crucial element in teaching a good and reliable retrieve. If your timing is not 'spot on', you could end up achieving the opposite to your wishes! It is a good idea to practice timing without the dog, just as you might perfect footwork for heelwork on your own. Pretend your left hand is the dog's mouth, open it, place your article, tell it 'Hold, good boy', take it and keep quiet. Get used to placing, taking, praising, and using keywords at the correct time, before you go on to the real thing - the dog!

Most dogs prefer to retrieve a moving target. Being of a predatory nature, it is in their basic make up to hunt. In the absence of hunger to drive them, they will enjoy practicing the skill of the chase. This is the part of their instinctive behaviour that we are about to modify, in some dogs, the 'prey drive' instinct will be stronger than it is in others.

Clicker Tips

Retrieve can be taught very successfully using the clicker to mark the hold. You can start off with a targeted touch *(see Target Training)*, and then move this to a more adventurous hold, gradually shaping the behaviour a step at a time. Blend in the recall commands to get the dog back to you. It can take time for the dog to make the connection that it should come to you with the article still in its mouth, especially if your click terminates the behaviour. Therefore, click on any good clean hold or carry behaviours until they become stable and then work on length of time in the mouth.

Teaching the Hold

This is a more formalised technique for training. It is most effective if the dog is happy and confident with close handling. It is important for the handler to be patient and remain motivational and positive throughout.

Step 1 - Have your dog on lead, and a comfortable non-restrictive collar. Start with your dog on your left if you can, although this is not crucial. Take your article in your right hand, entice the dog to take hold of it by waving it around along the floor, or in front of him just beyond his reach. Once he is stimulated by it, allow him to go forward to take it, praise him, *'Good boy'*, and then take the article, before he has time to move it around in his mouth, or wonder what he is supposed to do next. Repeat this a couple of times, and then go on to another exercise at this first training session. To start with it is best to say

nothing to the dog, except maybe to make a few exciting sounds to motivate him to make a move toward the article - *'Ready, steady!'*

Step 2 - Repeat as step one. When the dog is confident in taking the article, introduce the turn towards you by calling him. Using your keyword 'Come', gently guide him with the lead, collecting it up as he comes towards you, then take the article from his mouth. Don't yank the lead as the dog may think that you want him to drop the article. The amount of time that the article is in the dog's mouth should be minimal, seconds only, not allowing time for the dog to start any chewing.

Step 3 - Once step 1 and 2 become stable and you have got used to the speed and movement of your dog, you can introduce the keyword *'hold'* as he goes towards and takes the article.

Remember that this is the first stage of what you are trying to achieve, i.e. *'hold'* means go out, pick up and bring back. Your voice should not sound threatening at any time, *'hold'* should be fun, and it should sound the same as it will in the ring when the masterpiece is complete. You should be very appreciative and encouraging to the dog at the time that he is doing what you want, that is, going forward and taking the article.

Once the article has been taken from the dog's mouth, immediate calm and quiet is necessary. Do not carry on praising, remember the dog cannot associate praise for a job which has been done, only to what is happening at the time of the reward. If you carry on praising after you have taken the article, the dog will start to throw the article at you, or even refuse to pick articles up in the future, associating praise at the end of the exercise as the thing that he is rewarded for. It is human nature to praise after the event, in a *'Good dog - well done'* manner, but we must learn to think like a dog if we want to be successful at training.

Step 4 - So now you have the dog happily going towards the article, collecting it from your extended hand, and returning to you. Once you have perfected the above stages you can start to work on other components of the exercise to introduce the precision. Depending on the type of dog, it is sometimes appropriate to now introduce the control element, i.e. the sit prior to going out. This is normally the next stage for a very attentive and keen dog. Sometimes it is better to begin, progressively, to get the article nearer and nearer to the ground, no more than a few inches at a time, and going only as fast as the dog remains confident. Sometimes it is a good idea to combine the control and the progression. You must read your dog and aim to achieve success all the time.

When you do get to the stage where you have the article to the floor, keep your hand underneath it to give the dog confidence, and help to make the progression more positive. The next stage is to have your hand just by the article as the dog goes down to pick it up. Don't jump the stages from holding it near the floor to standing back and sending the dog because, either he won't understand what you mean, or you will be allowing the dog too many chances to go wrong. Either way problems will occur.

Step 5 - When you feel the dog is very confident in picking up the article and coming back, and having taught the present as a separate exercise, *(see Present)*, you can begin to introduce the present into the retrieve exercise, linking the two components together.

It is a good idea to start with the dog holding and put yourself into the present position and take the article so

that he can make that connection. Next set him up with the article in his mouth just a pace away from you. Collect up the lead, bring your hands together into the present position signal as the dog comes towards you. Guide him with your lead, keeping it under his chin. To start with, you may not be able to get a perfect present, do not lose the retrieve in favour of the present, simply guide the dog and step by step get nearer to what you want. Reward when the dog is correct, ignore when wrong. Keep your reward, toy or titbit high and central on your body to help the dog to aim for a good present, if he looks up to you as he approaches, his

body will flow naturally straight. Sometimes you can hold the reward under your chin. This leaves your hands free, and also means that the reward is in full view, and central for the dog to aim at. Be careful, if you have a very lively dog, this might prove a little hazardous for you, i.e. the dog may catch your face if he jumps towards his toy in excitement, so only do it if your are sure of your dog.

Step 6 - When the dog is happily collecting the article from your outstretched hand, the ground etc., then you can work on getting him to take it bringing your hand progressively closer to the dog, so that eventually it is immediately in front of him. Working back to this stage will help him to understand more fully the concept of the keyword *'Hold'*. By the time you are at this stage the dog should be automatically turning and coming into the present position, with only a modicum of help and guidance. Remember to keep the time that he has the article in his mouth to an absolute minimum and not to put the dog under pressure.

Step 7 - Start to increase the time that the dog has the article in his mouth only when he displays a confident and accurate attitude to the job in hand. Then, the time should be extended by only fractions of seconds each time, sometimes going back to shorter times to give a random effect. Never put any pressure on the dog, an anxious dog will be the first to mouth. Think about yourself, if you are nervous, anxious, or simply excited, your mouth goes dry and you lick your lips, if you have something in your mouth this is not so easy, so you try to adjust the thing in your mouth to make yourself more comfortable. In obedience dogs we call this *'mouthing'*. From an animal's point of view, it is very difficult to control, particularly when you do not possess the brainpower to understand the reason or cause. So, we humans must use our brainpower to achieve the results that we want, and realise that what is going on within the dog's body is beyond his control.

Step 8 - Now the dog is beginning to be competent, it is time to introduce other exercises which will have a beneficial effect on the end product. Teaching the dog to go around the article to collect it can be a good idea to employ, particularly with a fast dog, because it avoids a pounce prior to the pick up. This exercise is accomplished by, holding your hand over the article, guiding the dog from your left hand side with the lead around the article which is placed a few feet away on the floor. The dog is guided and blocked by your leg and body, so that he has to collect the article from behind when he is facing you. This is then progressed by placing your foot to the left of the article and guiding the dog around to pick up from the back. As the dog gets the idea, you progressively pull back your foot, so that it is not quite in contact with the article as you send the dog. The dog will continue to work as if your foot was there, and of course, you are ready to move in if the dog should show any signs of going wrong. Your movement can become progressively less, but don't forget to do the basic exercise at each session so that the dog does not start to introduce his own variations on the theme!

Step 9 - Once the dog is confident, introduce many variations into training so as not to become predictable, and to keep the dog attentive and interested. If you continually throw the article and send your dog, (a trap that many fall into once the dog has mastered the basic exercise), the dog will become either bored or over keen and difficult to handle, and certainly mistakes will creep in all too quickly. Training should be controlled, varied and fun. Build up routines, always going through basic control steps at each training session and prior to going into the ring. Save the masterpiece for the very odd occasion to convince yourself that the training is working and, of course, for the ring.

Teaching the Dog to Pick up Different Articles

The same principles of retrieve training apply to the dog learning how to pick up different articles and different textures. Everything should be taken step by step. Introduce one new thing at a time and get the dog confident before introducing another.

Good preparation helps, allow and encourage the dog to play with a variety of toys and items made of varying materials, so that when formalising to different articles the concept is not unique.

Train the dog a good variety of items include different materials such as metal, plastics, cloth, cardboard, sponge etc. Also train to items that have more than one part. If you train from step one on each item you are far less likely to get the dog making up his own way of carrying the item.

Trouble Shooting

Dislike of Certain or Specific Articles - Sometimes new items are not desirable for the dog and so they may need to be masked, and introduced gradually, in order for the dog to accept them. To give you an example of this, I had a dog that did not like to pick up cloth, in fact he positively hated it. He did however love his squeaky ball. So we decided that the best way to tackle the problem was to make a hole in the ball and stuff the cloth inside. At first the dog was not convinced, as he could associate the smell of the cloth, although he could not see or feel it. So, then we acquired another ball, identical to the first, and got him motivated on this. While he was keen, we swapped the toys over and he came in with the cloth stuffed ball, mildly puzzled, but happy enough. Immediately, we reverted to the other ball, and built his confidence back up, and then once again, when he was ultra confident, threw the stuffed ball. Each time he was sent for the stuffed ball he grew more and more confident. After several separate sessions, built up over a few days, we decided that the time was right and pulled a tiny corner of the cloth out from the ball. Again at first he was a little puzzled, but such was his confidence now that we were able to progressively pull out more and more, until eventually he would retrieve the cloth and then the ball alternately, learning that the cloth was not so bad after all. Once he was confident we carefully introduced the precision, a tiny step at a time. Always having the ball at hand to encourage and motivate him. Of course, he understood the concept of the precision, because we had done our groundwork correctly in the first place, and so therefore he progressed in leaps and bounds.

You can use this technique in a variety of ways with other articles, wrapping or tying articles with something more acceptable to the dog. Alternating confident articles with not so confident articles, building on confidence all of the time and then bringing in precision later.

Lack of Confidence at a Distance - Some dogs become excellent retrieve dogs, but lack the courage or confidence to work away from the handler, the technique of throwing toys alternated with retrieve articles will build up confidence for distance. Only do this once you know that the dog is accurate, or as a play exercise, not expecting precision, because when the dog is at a distance you are leaving him to his own devices. Do it too often, and he will devise his own version of retrieve!

Anticipation – Retrieve is one of the most common exercises for anticipation as many dogs love the thrill of the chase and find it hard to contain themselves. Work hard on the statics rewarding with something the dog really wants so that waiting becomes an exciting part of the exercise too. Vary the time that the dog is expected to wait before being allowed to get the article. Throw in differing directions so that he has to concentrate on where the article is going.

Use a fine lead, pretend to take if off, and then throw the article while holding onto a short (but not tight) lead. Try to prevent the anticipation by repeating the sit command and pulling back just enough for the dog to realise he is attached. Bring the dog back into the sit if he does anticipate. Do not do this on a long lead because if the dog lunges forward and is then stopped you may damage his vertebrae. Build this up until the dog is never really sure if he is on lead or off. In the ring this can translate to a slight pull back on the collar in the set up.

Apprehension/Reluctance to Go – Usually caused by too much formality, lack of confidence in the handler or the article or chastisement for anticipation. Build up confidence with lots of play retrieves gently interspersed with just a few more formal retrieves. Don't ask the dog to wait for very long (if at all) to start with. Go through the formal set up, but then send the dog straight away. Don't always ask for a present, just take the article and throw it again. Keep the exercise light and fun.

General Advice - It is always a matter of striking the balance and reading your dog, confidence without assumption, accuracy and precision without boredom. If things keep going wrong don't sit back and watch, while the dog repeats the mistake time and time again, gradually losing your temper or worse still becoming annoyed with the dog. Step in and alter the situation to guide the dog into the correct actions. Don't be frightened of mistakes we all make them.

A toy such as a kong or tug of some description on the end of about 10-15 meters of bungy rope (available from DIY stores) can act as a great incentive to turn reluctant dogs into keen retrievers. Stake the elasticated rope out so that the it can be pulled back and then released with the dog being allowed to follow it out. Don't put it against a solid barrier as the momentum of the rope may make the toy hit the surface and fling back. Make sure there is clearance behind. This game, that can be moved into more formal training later, can have a very positive effect on many dogs. It can also aid sendaway and general confidence. When starting out with the rope play around with the toy on the end of the rope moving it quickly to spark off interest using the dog's prey drive.

Technique 2 - Incentive Retrieve

Many handlers will make mistakes along the way, often resulting in the dog not wanting to participate in the retrieve exercise at all. Sometimes dogs are just not that interested, even though they will quite readily play. This is where one of the most important things in a dog's life comes into play, 'FOOD'. Play is a building block in the natural process of learning how to get your food if you are a dog, *(see Play training)*. So therefore food is a primary motivation. If your dog is food motivated, then you can use this to teach him to retrieve. The same procedures can be followed, as above, but substitute the article for something that the dog can smell has food in it, but will not be easily broken by the dog. For a soft-mouthed dog a cardboard sweet tube, or bag tightly wrapped and enclosing treats will be suitable. If you have a dog with a harder bite then you may have to use a more solid tube or packet. The dog does not necessarily have to get his reward directly from the packet although, if this can be arranged, it works very well. As long as the dog can't take the food himself it will work. You will need to keep some of the same food in a container that is easy to open, to reward the dog.

The stumbling block with this method comes if your timing, which is even more crucial here, goes wrong. You must aim to reward the dog very quickly as he brings in the article, but he must learn that *you* take the article and *then* he gets the reward. If you don't he will soon get into the habit of spitting it out at you, in order to eat his treat. It is crucial that he soon starts to associate the keyword *'Hold'* with reward. If he does drop the article before you can take it, do not give him his reward, instead make a point of returning the reward to its pot, and then start again. It is useful to have a pot of treats on a chair or table by your side, the dog can then see the reward, and can also see when he is not rewarded as this becomes far more obvious to him if the treats are out in the open. Here we are using the shaping technique, ignoring incorrect behaviour and rewarding correct behaviour, building up his retrieve, by incentive, a second at a time. As the dog progresses the rewards are given for that little bit more effort, to encourage when the dog is unsure, or even for a small step forward. The dog soon starts to eliminate the behaviours that do not get the reward. Once the dog is confident, transferring to other articles is the same as above. Take your time be patient and you will be rewarded.

Retrieve Over a Hurdle

A retrieve over a hurdle is required in many countries and is part of the FCI competition.

Jumping a hurdle is a relatively easy task to teach a dog. Obviously we must wait until he is old enough and strong enough to take a full size hurdle, but even as a young dog, we can be introducing him to a keyword for jumping. For instance, each time he takes a jump over a small log in the park, introduce a keyword *'over'*. Be observant use the environment and day to day life to aid your training.

Step 1 - When the dog is old enough, and well developed physically, more formal training can start. Begin with a very low hurdle, say 15cm/6" from the ground and jump over with your dog. Keep him on lead of course, just walk briskly towards the jump and over. Throwing his toy over and allowing him to run forward will also help him to be enthusiastic and will aid your retrieve.

Step 2 - Once you and the dog are happily going over, introduce your keyword for jump, e.g. *'Over'*, the word should come in just as he is about to lift into the jump.

Step 3 - When the dog is happily doing this with you, you can try sending him. Don't just send the dog on his own, first stand between the dog and the jump, to the side, and encourage him over. Increase the distance, a little at a time, until you can stand at the side of the jump with your head looking at the dog from the other side. Guide him with the lead, so the options to do anything other than jump are minimal. This normally sparks off a keen reaction. If your dog already knows the static sit position you can leave him in the sit, go over the jump yourself, and then call him over. You will have a hold of his lead to guide him and prevent him from going in the wrong direction. Remember praise and the keyword must be given at the correct time. Praise him as he lifts and comes over, not when he is over and by your side and the exercise is all but finished. The sequence should go like this: 'Freddie - Ready Ready, Over - Good boy'. Work on this until the dog is confidently going over the jump and collecting his toy, on and off lead.

Step 4 - Now the dog is confident, we must introduce the return. This should come relatively easy. Simply position yourself at the right hand side of the jump. Put the dog in the sit position, (on lead) facing the jump, and to your left. Throw the dog's toy over the jump, send him over to collect his toy, as he goes over the jump, reposition yourself to the front of the jump, ready to call the dog as he turns with his toy. Use your lead to guide him back, over the jump, to you. You may find it advantageous to have another toy to encourage the dog back.

A short cut to this is to teach the dog in an area where the only option to get back is over the jump - in a corridor for instance, or over a fence. This works very well as the basic teaching principle, but you will need to use your lead to guide the dog the first time that you introduce any new hurdle to make sure that he understands what you want.

Step 5 - Once the dog is doing the jump, retrieve and return, introduce the present. Again, the dog should be on lead so that you can guide him into the correct position. Don't expect that he will automatically know, just because you may have taught it as a separate exercise. As soon as you introduce a variable like this the dog is likely to be confused. Follow the principle as for teaching presents, guiding him into the correct position with your lead, and position your hands for the signal *(See Presents).*

Step 6 - All this time you have been using a toy as the retrieve article, this is to give confidence. Now you can change to your dumbbell or other article. Start on lead as you did when you commenced the teaching. Help the dog all of the way, never expect too much, and work through all of the stages. By now the dog should be very confident, and if your normal retrieve training has been implanted correctly, the dog will have no problem transferring to any article.

For FCI the dog will be required to retrieve a metal dumbbell supplied by the judge and this is likely to be quite weighty so get the dog used to both of these aspects.

Directional Retrieve

For FCI and in some countries the dog is required to collect a wooden dumbbell from 3 that are placed out at a distance. He is first sent to a marker and must stand awaiting the command to go to the left or right for the dumbbell. (He is never expected to collect the centre bell it is there solely as a decoy.) The first part of this can be taught as a sendaway or better still with targeting to a marker.

To teach the dog to go in the direction you point get the dog used to retrieving toys from the direction that you point – throw the toy point and send - this will help to get his motivation level high. Then progress to placing the toy – first to one side then to the other allowing him to watch. Once he is competent with this, place the toy without him seeing. Keep the same enthusiasm in yourself to ensure he remains motivated. Once all of this is achieved allow the dog to stand forward of you at a marker before he is sent – gradually increase this distance, before you start sending him to the marker and linking the two sections together. When all of this is competently performed introduce from the beginning with the dumbbell.

Trouble Shooting

Reluctance to Jump - If the dog shows any apprehension, go over with him again and encourage him to collect his toy.

Deviate Around the Hurdle On The Out Run - If the dog tries to go around the hurdle to collect his toy, throw the toy over and go with him a few times to eliminate that behaviour, again and encourage him to collect his toy.

Deviate Around the Hurdle On Return – As the dog goes over the hurdle and picks up the article go forward to the centre of the jump and call him back over. Do short ones on lead to give even better guidance or have another reward such as another toy or titbit and show this to the dog as he turns towards the hurdle, move back out of his way as he comes across and draw him towards you with the treat.

Knocking the Hurdle Down – Consider your starting distance, are you allowing the dog enough space to take off and clear the jump. Make the dog aware of the jump by pointing to the cross bar, some dogs get fixated on the retrieve and don't see the jump. Make sure that you are not over stretching the dog, start with very low jumps and build up gradually. Use other poles to create a barrier so that the dog can see a block rather than just one pole at the top.

Important – make sure the dog is physically fit enough to do the exercise. Hereditary problems such as hip dysplasia or injuries will inhibit the dog's jumping style or cause him pain and thus reluctance to perform. If in any doubt get your dog checked out by your veterinary surgeon.

Sendaway

Before you start - The dog should be confident with you and you should have achieved 'the want'. Basic steps can then be started but before you can proceed to the formal part of the exercise, the dog should also understand the basic static sit and down positions.

The sendaway should be great fun for both dog and handler. The object of the exercise is for the dog to go, in a fast straight line, to a specific place or distance. In the UK, the handler can handle the dog and physically, (but not harshly), direct its head in the required direction, as part of the set up. Normally the handler indicates to the judge his/her readiness by standing up straight. The dog is then given a command and/or signal to go. Another command/signal is allowed to stop and down the dog. The dog will then be expected to stay still until recalled from the area. When recalled he will join the handler in heelwork until the handler is told to stop. The distance of the sendaway, how the area is marked, the movement of the handler before recall, and the length heelwork following will be at the desecration of the judge.

For the FCI competition the dog is required to sendaway to a marker (usually a cone) and then stand. He is then redirected to a marked sendaway area (usually a box). Other countries have variations on this theme. A combination of the two techniques for the UK described below will help to achieve the FCI version.

Fast, keen sendaways are achieved by creating a great desire in the dog to arrive at the given point. As with other exercises, there are several methods of teaching, but the incentive methods are the most reliable.

You need to find a toy or titbit that the dog really likes. If using a toy, it should of course be safe, and preferably not too big. An article that can be made smaller as time goes by is ideal, a piece of carpet or toweling material for instance, but this is not essential. It is more important that the dog loves his motivator. If using titbits, you must obtain a pocket size tin that can be put down on the ground when you are training, this will prevent the dog being able to help himself and discourage sniffing on the ground!

All of the following procedures are done with the dog on lead and with the handler instigating great excitement. Try to be quick in your actions and create a good momentum.

Clicker Hints

Using the technique below it can be quite difficult to introduce your clicker because you will have your hands full controlling the lead, dog, toy and getting the dog into the positions that you want. It will require you to break the exercise down carefully but it can be done. You may prefer to use a targeting technique. Teach the dog to target to an item that you can stand on or in the ground and then gradually build up the distance until the dog is running a ring's length to his target. Of course he will be touching and standing by the target at this stage and while this is okay in training (and for the first stage of the FCI sendaway) we then need to introduce a down. This should be done as a separate exercise. Work on the speed of the down by clicking on progressively faster downs and ignoring slow ones as you build on the exercise.

Step 1 - Play with your dog and get him really motivated onto the article or titbit box.

Step 2 - Hold the dog's lead in your left hand, and your motivator in your right. Stand sideways on to the dog and show him the article in your outstretched hand, then move, fanning backwards in a circular movement, enticing the dog to run around, forward and towards the toy/tin. The object of the exercise is to get the dog following the direction of your out-stretched arm. At this stage the dog will actually be going around in a circle, but this doesn't matter. The important factor is that he is enjoying going towards the motivator. Let him move a few steps at a time and then reward him with his toy or titbit by holding your right arm still and letting him come onto the reward. If you are using the tin of titbits, it is a good idea to have some in the tin and some in your hand. You need to get to them quickly in order to keep up the momentum, the dog must think that they came from the tin in order for there to be sufficient motivation involved, but sometimes it is easier to cheat a bit. So as long as the dog knows (thinks) that treats come out of the tin, and that he gets one when the tin is in your hand then the method will work.

Step 3 - Once you have the dog looking intently, in the direction that you are pointing, just prior to the movement, introduce the keyword that you want to use for the dog to look towards a sendaway, for example *'Look'*. When you have completed this stage you have him looking in the direction that you are pointing on the keyword *'Look'*. It is quite a difficult concept for the dog to grasp as dogs do not naturally look to where you are pointing, they are more likely to look at your finger. So take your time and make the incentive good.

Step 4 – Next you need to introduce the sendaway command. Examples of this are *'Away'* or *'Go'*. Hold the dog back with his lead using your left hand. Stand forward of, and sideways to, the dog with your toy in your outstretched right hand. Excite the dog into looking at his toy, when he is looking give the keyword *'Look'*, and then when the dog is raring to go introduce your keyword *'Go'* and let him run towards, and be rewarded with the article. You can still use the circular movement to keep up the momentum.

Step 5 - Now we must introduce a fast down. To get a good down in the ring the dog must understand that, in order to get his reward, he must go down immediately that he hears the keyword *'Down'*. To ensure this, the training is quite specific. We will progress as step 2, but then as the dog is going around at a decent speed we introduce the *'down'*. To do this, you bring

the motivator to the floor, in front of the dog. The action should be carried out with urgency and excitement. Try to keep the toy covered by your hand. Stop the dog in his tracks by halting your left hand and dropping it to the floor. Then swiftly move your left hand to the dog's back just at the base of his shoulders to help push him into the down. You may then have to run your hand down to his backside to push it over because some dogs halt in the play mode, i.e. bum in the air. Follow this up by releasing the reward between the dog's two front feet whilst he stays in the down. Be careful to ensure that the reward is well within his reach, we do not want him to get into the habit of crawling forward or sniffing to find his reward, it must always be immediate. Allowing this very fault to creep in has lost many a ticket. At this stage of the training procedure it is quite easily avoided.

Once you are confident of your handling of this stage, introduce the keyword for dropping the dog. *'Down'* or *'Flat'*.

Do not over do the instant down training for the first few sessions as you may find in your dog, a reluctance to go if he thinks that the only way to get his reward is to be in the down position. So split your training sessions into work on the down and work on the outrun at different times before combining all of the above.

Step 6 - When you and the dog are confident in all of the above, and have trained in varying situations and environments, you can introduce the next stage, which is to put in some distance. It is useful at this stage, if you can get the dog to stay in a position when you leave him a few paces, although it is not imperative. If you are unsure of his stability, tie him up or have a friend hold him, rather than have him ignoring your keywords.

The first stage is to place your motivator just a few feet away, and then follow steps 3 and 4. Go with the dog, still on lead of course, and make sure he goes into a fast down **before** he gets the reward. On lead it is easy to control this, and the lead can be used to stop the dog, just before he reaches his quest. If your initial training is thorough, the dog will be very keen by this stage, therefore your timing will be put to the test. Allow yourself more space than you would expect to need, in order to get the dog down. You will be surprised how fast he will approach to get to the toy. The timing of your keyword *'Down'* is crucial, the word must leave your mouth momentarily before the tension goes on the lead to stop the dog. If the dog shows any reluctance to go, or starts to decrease his speed, go back to the relevant training steps to ensure that your dog is confident.

Gradually you can increase the distance a step at a time. The further the distance, the more the chance of things going wrong, so be very careful and sure that the dog is confident before progressing. Be sure that the dog is

going into the down when you say the
keyword, and prior to getting the reward,
before you allow so much distance that
you cannot control it.

It will be beneficial to set up
some sessions where the dog is encouraged to go for the reward without the
down command being introduced. This
will help keep his speed and confidence.
Make sure when you do this that you give
him specific instructions using a fun
retrieve command such as *'get it'*.

Step 7 - If your dog is good and
stable in the static sit or down, leave him
in position, (if he is unstable have
someone hold him), place your motivator
article about 2 metres away, and then stand with the toy, but to the side,
facing the toy. Give the dog his *'Look'* word to get his attention onto the area,
followed by his sendaway word e.g. *'Go'*, and encourage him towards the
area, patting the floor or waving the toy to motivate him. You are then there,
in position to make sure he goes into an instant down, before he is rewarded.
Thus, he is now going to the designated area, on his own.

Step 8 - Train your dog in an area that will make his motivator less
easy to see, train from stage 1, don't miss
any stages, to avoid confusion and build
up gradually. Keep the motivation level
high all of the time. This is a vital stage
in teaching the dog to always expect to
be rewarded, even if at first, he cannot
see his reward. If you have a green toy
for instance, train on grass, if you have a
dark toy, choose a dark surface e.g.
tarmac or concrete. If you have a toy that
is hard to disguise try training on longer
grass. Be careful that you do not always
choose the same surface as the dog may
start an association with surface to
exercise. You may therefore have to
introduce more than one motivator. *(See
Play training)*

Step 9 - Follow step 6 but this time stand at the side, between the article and the dog, keep just a couple of steps away from the article to start with, as you are going to follow the dog up, to make sure he goes down before getting his reward. When you are sure of this you can progress the distance, back towards the dog, step by step, until eventually you can stand with the dog and send him. The progression must be gradual and the dog must be kept well motivated all of the time. Do not try to build all of these steps in one lesson, a few feet per session is more reliable. Always go back to the beginning, i.e. step 1, and work quickly yet purposefully through, at the start of each session. If the dog shows any signs of apprehension or confusion you are going too far too fast.

Step 10 - We are now going to introduce differing articles and obstacles for the dog to either go to, or ignore. At a show the scene may be very complicated and the dog should learn to go to, through, onto, or wherever he is told. Start by introducing markers or obstacles scattered, ad lib, around your training area. Train from stage 1 to avoid any confusion. Train for the dog to ignore the articles completely to start with, your initial training will have taught him to look only for his toy.

An easy marker to teach the dog to recognise as a starting point is a mat. It is beneficial to get him to lay on the mat while by your side or when relaxing so that he builds up an acceptance and even a like for the mat.

Set him up as you would for step 6, but with the toy placed to the back of the mat. You will be using his keywords, *'Look'* and *'Go'*, and now introducing the new keyword, *'Mat'*. Position yourself to ensure that you are able to drop the dog on the mat, and then follow up with his reward. Tell him *'Look - Mat'*, and then an excited *'Go'*. Race with him to the mat, help him into the down, and reward. Whilst he is still on the mat point, at it, and say, *'Look - Mat, Good boy Mat'*. The emphasis being on the keywords, any *'good boys'* or *'brilliants'* should be less obvious to the dog and the keywords should come out very clearly. Remember what you are trying to achieve, this is not the meaning of *'Good boy'*, but the meaning of the new keywords. Once again, build this up as if it were a new exercise, because to the dog, it is quite different, it may take a while for the new word to register a meaning. If there is any apprehension regarding lying on the mat, put it in his bed for a few days.

Once he has mastered the above try another piece of common ring furniture, for instance a pole. Exactly the same procedure applies, the toy is placed just behind the pole, set him up, say *'Look - Pole'*, and then *'Go'*, and follow it through.

Next try introducing marker cones *'Cone'*, sending to one cone, and 'Box', sending to the centre of a box made up of any four markers, are two more useful associations for the competitive obedience ring.

Step 11 - The dog can be taught to go into a box which you point to, and ignore others. This will help him in ignoring other obstacles and ring furniture. Set up a box of cones or other articles in a large enough square for the dog to comfortably turn and drop at speed, without knocking any. Place his toy in the centre or towards the back if he is very fast. Then call him into the area. Make sure you are in full control, don't allow mistakes. Once he has successfully done this, set it up again but start at the opposite side, put him in the sit, show him the centre of the box with his toy and call him to it. When he has confidently done this a couple of times try if from the side, repeat, and then the other side. To build the distance, introduce a gradual progression following all of the steps.

A similar procedure can then be followed setting up markers in the four corners of a ring, sending the dog alternately to each of the areas. All this good positive training will help the dog to deal with ring situations. If you are not thorough like this, he will, when confronted with distractions, try to come to his own conclusions, normally homing in on the first thing he sees.

The dog is capable of learning many different associations. In order to avoid confusion think clearly about what you are trying to achieve, bob down to dog's eye level before making any assumptions. Don't just look at your objective, look beyond and consider all of the possibilities of the dog's eye view.

How Does it Work in the Ring?

In training never get to the stage where the motivator is taken away completely. As the dog progresses and becomes ultra confident, the article is placed so that it is not so easy to see, in fact sometimes it is hidden altogether, under a cone perhaps or behind a log. When it is hidden and the dog has done a successful sendaway, run out to the dog and reveal the toy and have a game. Sometimes you can throw another toy to the dog from a short distance away. If you stick to the rule that the dog is always rewarded somehow, then the very few times that this is impossible, i.e. in the ring, the dog will not realise that it has happened. Also the method of training will have made the dog so keen to do the exercise that it will become self-motivating.

When you are competing at a show give yourself and your dog every opportunity of getting it right. Check out the ring and the sendaway that you will have to do. If it is at all possible train your dog at the show to something as similar as possible, choose to train in a similar sort of area. Don't forget that the sendaway set up in the car park may look totally different when set up out on the field. Look at the whole aspect of the area, any markers or ring poles used, the background, and beyond. Then, having gone to all of this trouble, train - don't just practice the end result.

Other Training Aids

Bungy Rope - The use of a length of bungy rope has become very popular and is a very effective way of motivating many dogs. The rope can be obtained from DIY stores and needs to be anchored to the ground at one end while the other end has a favourite toy attached. The elasticated rope is then pulled back and released and the dog allowed to follow it. Make sure the ground behind the anchor is clear as the rope will progress past that point. It is easy to bring the dog back in, even if your recall is not brilliant, as you can use the rope to continue playing with the dog.

Once the dog is really keen to run out after the rope, you can cease to pull it back so far. Eventually just lay it down on the ground or in a marked sendaway area and the dog will run out to it in a highly motivated way, as long as you include some moving bungy sessions too.

Get the dog interested in a toy on the end of a bungy rope.

Make sure the excitement is well established before progressing.

Favourite Sendaway Spot – It is a good idea to have a special place on a walk where you send your dog each time. This will help to build confidence and distance.

Trouble Shooting

Over Keen on the Toy - With a very 'toy mad' dog, sometimes it is necessary to hide the toy most of the time, just as the food for a titbit dog is concealed in a tin.

Occasionally it is necessary to use a toy for the motivation to go out to an area, calling the dog to it, and then, as the progression takes place, the toy is thrown out to or beyond the dog when he reaches the correct position, and is down. This method is only for dogs that are so hooked on toys that they cannot concentrate on anything else. You may

Pull back the bungy, hold on to the dog and then let the bungy go, quickly followed by the dog.

find it better to choose a less motivating motivator if this is possible! You must be very careful using this technique that the dog does not try to come forward or hover waiting for the toy to be thrown. If he should do this, withdraw the reward, put it in your pocket and start the exercise again. You may also find that the introduction of a secondary motivator will help to keep the dog under control, *(see Reward Training)*.

Lack of Confidence/Hesitation/ Dropping Short - If a dog is unsure, and/or has a tendency to drop short or the required area, do not chastise him as this will make his apprehension worse. It is better, and more productive, to reward the dog for the part that he gets correct. For instance, having sent the dog he starts to hesitate, the second you identify this call out your keyword for *'down'*, and run out and reward him for getting that far. Then start him off again, but from where he is, show him where you want him, call him to the spot and reward him again. Set up the exercise again, this time starting the dog just a few feet before the position that he first dropped, put his motivator in the correct position, and send him. He will get nearer, even if he does not get it right first time. The abundance of praise and reward comes, of course, when the dog is correct, but you should at first reward quite lavishly even when you have had to drop the dog incorrectly. This reward gives him confidence to go on, and you can adjust the level of reward to be a little less each time as he gets progressively nearer to the correct place, and the abundance of reward is then transferred to the correct place.

This method of training is called shaping, (successive approximation), getting the dog nearer and nearer to what you are trying to achieve, and is the method employed to train dolphins to perform incredible feats on the blow of a whistle.

Too Slow – Often this is caused by lack of confidence (see above). It can also be the result of too many downs and not enough out runs. Work on getting the dog to enjoy the out run without expecting to be told to go down. Also the bungy rope will help to build speed and confidence.

Sendaway Block - Sometimes dogs get, what handlers call, a block. The dog may have been doing sendaways for years, and then suddenly, he/she can't get it right any more. This may have been caused by external interference, a stray dog in a ring, an aggressive judge, a freak storm, there are many possibilities, and nine times out of ten the handler will have no idea why the dog is reacting so. If this happens you must simply retrain, and set up situations similar to those that frighten or confuse the dog and train through them, using high motivation techniques. You may simply have to do a lot of playing in certain situations, you may have to enlist the help of people who can act as judge or steward etc. Suffice to say that the problem won't just go away, you will need to set it up and train through it.

Sometimes the block is less easy to identify, but if you think it through, look at the point at which the dog starts to go wrong, and identify what is happening momentarily before that. In most cases, if the dog performs correctly in training then the linking or set up of the exercise is not the same in training as it is in the ring. You need an exact ring mock up, judges, stewards, ropes, furniture, procedure, warm up outside the ring, exercise linking the lot and then **train** through. *(See Linking).*

Deviation – It is quite common for herding breeds to have a curve to the outrun. This is because they have been bred to round up sheep and the curved outrun is important when going out to lift a herd of sheep. However in obedience it will lose marks. This normally occurs due to lack of consistency of training in the initial stages, so the answer is to go back to square one and work on short, motivated outruns. If necessary use barriers to keep the dog in line. A hallway in the house, or a line of closely positioned poles will help teach the dog to run straight. Just have fun running the dog up and down so that a straight run becomes the norm. This technique is also useful when teaching straight presents from a distance.

Anticipation – This can be solved in a similar way to the retrieve anticipation. Work on the dog enjoying the whole experience, not just the outrun. *(See Retrieve anticipation).*

The Recall

The recall from the box is not really anything to do with teaching the sendaway, and certainly should only very rarely linked together with the sendaway in training, if you wish to avoid anticipation or fidgeting in the sendaway area. The training of the recall to the heel position is covered in the recall to heel ('A' recall) section.

It is necessary to build up the time that the dog is kept in the down position, prior to a recall command. Once the dog is doing very good confident sendaways you can introduce some walking around before going back to reward him, keeping your eye on him and remind him *'Down'* whilst you walk around. It is also useful to throw in the odd *'Call your dog'*, as the steward would say in the ring, to accustom the dog to hearing this phrase, but learning to ignore it. If you don't work against things like this they can become a stimulus to the dog to perform the next part of the exercise, and therefore, in ring terms, we have anticipation. The dog is not being naughty, but merely acting on learnt stimulus, really he is just being a dog. With the very keen, actively competing dog the words *'Call your dog'* should be followed by your *'Down'* word, to ensure the dog realises that he must listen to your words only and not the steward or judge.

Redirection

This is not needed for the normal UK obedience competition but it is needed for FCI.

Start by getting a strong sendaway. Once this is achieved set up another marked area a few metres away from the first one, place a favourite toy in the area but don't make it too obvious to see from the starting point. Make sure it is not too close to cause confusion when you do a short sendaway to the first area. Then leave the dog in the first area and call him over to the second one. Reward him with his motivator.

Once the dog has achieved this progression over a period of repetitions you can start to step back from the second box as you did when training the straight sendaway. Do this at first in line with the area, but as the dog gains confidence you can start to come away in the triangle between the two sendaway areas.

Introduce a hand signal to point in the direction that you need the dog to go. Soon the dog will be looking towards the new area. Don't progress too fast as the dog may start to anticipate to the second area. Keep breaking it down to short runs.

Next set up a sendaway in the opposite direction and start from the beginning again.

It can help to set the second sendaway up behind a fence so that the dog runs along the fence line to the new area, but doesn't see it on the first sendaway.

Simply placing out toys a good distance apart and teaching the dog to go to the right or left toy will also help him to understand about going where directed.

Scent Discrimination

Before you start the dog must be confident in you and have achieved the 'want'. As you progress he will need to understand how to hold, come, present and finish.

Scent Discrimination is a test to determine the dog's ability to find and retrieve a specific scent. In obedience in the UK, all scent tests are done on cloth, (although this was not always the case). In other countries it can be differing materials, wood, metal, plastic. For FCI it is wood.

In the first stages of UK scent the dog will be expected to find the handler's own scent, but later he will have to find a stranger's (the judge's) scent by matching it to an identical one that he is given. Decoy scents, i.e. scents from other people, are also used, and the dog must learn to ignore these as well as neutral cloths. It is best to read the guidelines for this test, as set down by your governing body or Kennel Club.

In the UK the tests vary a little over the 3 levels (test 'A', test 'B' and test 'C'). There is no scent discrimination in the lower classes (pre beginner, beginner or novice). In all classes the size of the cloths is the same. They will be no smaller than 15cms x 15cms (6" x 6") and no larger than 25.4cms x 25.4cms (10" x 10"). Also in competition the cloths will be placed at least 1metre (3 feet) and no more than 1.6m (5feet) apart. In test 'A' there are 6 clothes whereas in test 'B' and 'C' there can be up to 10 (minimum 6). In test 'A' the cloths will be placed in a straight line in any direction. Decoy scents are introduced in the two higher classes only one in test 'B' and more at the discretion of the judge in test 'C'.

It is thought that dogs have around 220 million scent receptors in their noses (although the figure differs depending on the research studied). Balanced against our mere 5 million, this is pretty impressive. The dog can identify scents that are so dilute, that we do not have instruments to measure them.

The odours that the dog comes into contact with have an effect on his behaviour, indeed odours have an extremely powerful influence on the whole of the dog's life.

When a dog sniffs and takes a scent, he takes the odour over a bony structure called the subethmoidal shelf (humans don't have one of these), and onto the lining of the nasal membranes. When the dog breathes normally, the scent molecules remain in nasal chambers and accumulate in nasal mucus; the chemical odour then sticks to receptor cells. These receptor cells convert the chemical odour into electrical signals that send messages to the various parts of the brain that are responsible for dealing with the particular message or emotion.

Julie Strickleton (now Garnett) and Obedience Champion Shucks its Mine (Dusty) about to take part in Scent discrimination at the Crufts Obedience Championships.

The dog is much more of an expert than we at the art of taking scent, so it is important to work with his natural ability rather than fighting it. Although we can influence some of the odours that he takes, if the dog experiences a bad association, we must be very patient and sympathetic in our training. Although we talk about 'teaching scent', we are really channeling the dog's natural instinct and showing him how we would like him to use it to discriminate between differing scents and choose to bring us the scent that we require.

Teaching scent discrimination is an exciting experience for both dog and handler. The basis of the scent exercises can be taught in the early days, even whilst the puppy is still restricted to safe areas like the house and garden due to inoculation incubation. You can be kept busy and your dog will be 'learning to learn' in the process.

Avoid wearing perfumes or scented hand creams while teaching scent, these are very strong with false smells, and will not help the dog to learn the exercise that we need him to achieve.

If you are just starting scent training with an adult dog, don't be afraid to treat him like a pup and follow these first stages of training. Even adult dogs need to learn how we want them to discriminate, and what procedure we would like them to follow.

Early scent training should be achieved using a familiar article, a knotted sock or favourite toy. This can later be progressed to a variety of familiar articles that the dog can enjoy relating to and will want to find. The use of a fabric article for training is a good idea particularly for UK handlers, as all scent discrimination in Kennel Club obedience competition in the UK is done on cloth, (at the time of this book going to press). Having said that it is advisable to have a few differing textures and materials, and include a variety of substances e.g. plastic, nylon, card, wood and even metal in your training bag to add interest and awareness as the dog progresses.

There is nothing more natural for very young pups, than to follow scent trails, they are genetically programmed to do so from before they leave the nest and onwards. This is a defense mechanism to prevent them from straying too far from the nest. It develops as a hunting and social skill later on. It is a simple task for we humans to elaborate on this superb doggy skill, but yet a task that often goes badly wrong because we try to apply human emotions and characteristics to canine behaviour and this canine super power. In essence we must, once again, try to think like a dog.

Clicker Hints

If using a clicker for scent remember which bit you are working on and click for good responses to each stage of the training. Initially you may be clicking on the dog's recognition of or movement towards the scent, even if he has not picked it up. This is then progressed as in retrieve.

Step 1 - Choose a favourite toy or rag, bring yourself to dog level, sit on the floor with a smaller dog or puppy, a low non restrictive chair may be useful with a larger dog, and play. Have the dog on a lead so that you can reel him in to you, and have a food or toy treat to encourage him just as in the first stage of retrieve. When he takes the article, if he knows them, use your keywords 'Hold' and 'Come'. Help him all the way to make sure he comes back, with the article, produce your food as he comes towards you, but try to avoid him dropping the article to take the food. If he does not yet understand 'Hold' and 'Come' this is covered in the retrieve section, (incentive retrieve). You can do the first few stages without the dog having an understanding of hold and come, simply by taking the article from the dog's mouth. If your basic 'Want' training is good, the dog will be happy to come back to you for a cuddle and the continuance of the hide and seek game will be motivation enough i.e. he is rewarded by you for not stopping the game. If you can manage without the food lure at this stage, you will find that the pup is less distracted, but if you need to use it do so.

Step 2 - Teach your dog to take scent from your hand or from an article. We will start with your hand. Most dogs will reach forward to their handler's hand if it is held in front of them. Try this and link your scent word to the behaviour as it occurs *'Smell'* or *'Find'*.

If your dog is not interested you can use an incentive. Food is always a good incentive so, to start with, handle some smelly titbits like liver. Let the dog approach your hand, hold the titbit in your fingers and let him take it. Next take a titbit, and hold it between your finger and palm, hold out your forefinger and thumb as if the titbit were there, and let

This step can be taught from a young age.

the dog sniff, as he does this introduce the new keyword, *'Smell'*. Once he is doing this, transfer the titbit to the other hand for rewarding. Still use your right hand offered to the dog in the same gesture for him to take scent, but as soon as he smells your hand bring out the reward from the other hand. Increase the time that he is sniffing slightly, and then reward.

Step 3 - Next, introduce a toy or rag that you will be using for scent, and repeat the above procedure, using the food or his favourite toy as reward when he sniffs. Next let him sniff his favourite toy and reward him with it. Soon he will be sniffing anything you ask him to.

Step 4 - Once you have the dog interested and stimulated, allow him to watch you put the scent toy under your hand, and then, encourage him to try to get it. As soon as he acknowledges that he knows where the article is, reward him with it. Repeat the exercise, over several sessions until the dog becomes confident.

Step 5 - Once the dog is confidently acknowledging, and actively seeking out the article, introduce your keyword for 'go and search', e.g. *'Find'*. Let the dog sniff the article, try to hold your hand open, in a signal that will be used later when he takes scent without an article there. Hold him back for a few seconds whilst he watches you put the article out of sight, somewhere in close proximity, under your leg for instance, and then release him on the keyword *'Find'*. Encourage him to seek out the article, help him if necessary by indicating in the general direction of the hiding place. Call him so that he knows to come to you when he has the article. Reward him as above and repeat the exercise.

Once he is keen, and finding the article easily, restrict the prize for a few moments. Holding down your leg, for seconds only easily does this, just long enough for him to really use his nose and acknowledge the scent.

Step 6 - When you are happy that the dog is stimulated to confidently find on the keyword, change the hiding place to perhaps under your other leg, behind your back etc., still let him see where the toy went. The more confident he gets the more hiding places you can try, but remember, make it easy, train for success. You will enjoy progressing this to hiding the toy behind furniture, under a rug and so on. Keep introducing the 'Smell' word, and encouraging the dog to take the scent of what he is going for, before he goes, sometimes directly from the article, sometimes from your hand.

Step 7 - Now we have the dog taking scent, searching, and finding his article, so at this point it is a good time to try a different article, thus he learns to enjoy the exercise with a different motivation. You should choose a familiar and fun article, and the dog should enjoy holding it.

Start at step 1 again. It is very tempting to start where you left off with the first article, but this is a dangerous thing to do. The dog has to learn that you mean the same thing again, and to be sure that he knows, give him all the help you can by starting from the beginning. It won't take very long, and the more times you are successful, the more chance you have of succeeding in the long run.

When he is happy with this, try an article belonging to someone else, so that the introduction of a foreign smell is not alien to him, and he will happily adjust if, to start with at least, the article is fun.

Step 8 - Apply all of the above training stages in varying environments and terrain, i.e. halls, fields, gardens friend's houses, etc. Also with differing textures and other people's articles. With each new environment or article, start at step 1. Have the dog on lead so that you can guide and control his actions.

Step 9 - Take your dog into an area of long grass and play with him with his toy. Drop the article into the grass and let him retrieve it. Hold him back by his collar and throw the toy a metre or so away, when he is raring to go release the hold on his collar and let him find the toy. Of course, it is best to still have hold of the end of the lead to avoid any problems of the dog wandering off and being distracted, it is unlikely that this would happen if the dog is sufficiently motivated, but it is better to be safe than sorry.

If, for any reason, he doesn't acknowledge the article, (he should start searching straight away), call him back and go back as per steps 1, 2, 3 etc. until he gets the hang of it. Repeat this stage several times making sure that the dog becomes confident. Sometimes letting him take scent from your hand sometimes from the article. Taking scent is now becoming part of the game.

Step 10 - Walk with your dog in the grass, do heelwork if you wish or just play, drop the article behind you as you go. Take the dog to a point that is just within a few feet of where you dropped the article, turn him towards where it has fallen, point to it and send him using his keyword *'find'*. Keep your voice exciting and motivational. Remember this is supposed to be fun so enjoy it.

Don't leave the dog on his own if he looks apprehensive or stops working, go out to him get involved and help. Call the dog to you when he has the article and make a great fuss of him. We are teaching scent so it is not necessary to put in a present and finish, simply call and praise him. Take the article from him and repeat or go on to something else.

At this stage you can start to introduce some off lead work, try just dropping the lead to start with, and then, if you are sure that the dog is not distracted by anything else, you can try some short, off lead search backs. If you do not find that the dog is ready for this don't worry you can proceed on lead all the way through the training. In each section you will be doing some on and some off lead, building confidence in freedom, but making sure that accuracy and concentration is not sacrificed for freedom. In other words make sure that every stage is good on lead before releasing the dog to do it lead free.

Just because the dog is released this doesn't mean you should let him work on his own, still help him, go out into the scent area with him, and generally make sure that all goes according to plan.

Step 11 - Follow step 10 and increase the distance of search back, change the article, and generally vary the area that you drop the article. Don't do all this at once. Choose one of the above, let us say that you decide on this occasion to change the article. Just do a short search

The dog needs to be taught how to hold the scent cloth in the same way as he was taught to retrieve and to present just as in the Novice recall. (See Retrieve and Presents).

and make it really easy for the dog to find it to start with. Once the dog is confident on his article gradually increase the distance of search by half a metre at a time. Do not train on one item for too long, it is better to do a short session, and then change to something else, and then come back and pick up a step or two back from where you left off.

Step 12 - Find, in the environment, out on a walk, or in the garden, some obstacles e.g. stones, boulders, hay bales, etc. and hide your article behind these. Have fun with your dog, sending him to find it. This valuable step need never be forgotten and any time that you are out walking your dog, whether he works the beginner class or the top class you can enjoy this game in the knowledge that it is giving your dog confidence for scent.

Caution - Try to avoid sending the dog over areas where the article has been dropped previously. The reason for this is that the dog will be able to smell the scent, still lingering on the ground, from where the article lay before and he may become confused. The more experienced he becomes, the more confused he will be if you make this error, because he becomes accustomed to picking up the scent rather than a specific article. We could, through training, teach him to ignore the scent unless the article is obviously there, but then this may result in the dog not attempting to pick up less obvious articles. Cloth that is the same colour as the ground, or laid very flat on concrete, will tend to be ignored by dogs taught to ignore lingering scents left by articles. So it is better to avoid the problem than to create one.

So far so good, you have taught the dog to find a variety of known and unknown articles in differing environments, ignoring other obstacles, and scents. Now to bring things out in the open a little more, and to start to simulate ring conditions.

Introducing formality is where things normally start to go wrong. This is because handlers want to go too far too fast. It is possible to teach an adult dog to perform a good basic scent discrimination fairly quickly if you don't miss out any stages. With the older dog that already understands some basic keywords like sit, hold, come etc., and is easily motivated, the exercise can be ring worthy within a week. However, if any stages are missed the dog may lack confidence and enthusiasm or may be confused.

Step 13 - Select some objects to use as neutral articles,(i.e. articles that are not to be selected by the dog as correct). These should be things that are not easy or attractive for the dog to pick up, we do not want him to touch them. Wall or floor tiles, preferably light colour, are ideal because they are square like a cloth. If you are handy at woodwork, (or know someone who is), you can make, (or have made) some scent boards. These are wooden boards, the size of a scent cloth, and onto them you pin scent cloths. This is an ideal training aid, it looks like the real thing, but it is not easy for the dog to pick them up. To make this even more authentic, you need one board without a cloth, and this one will be used to place your own scent on. If you use this system, you should keep your board for your own scent separate from the others.

It doesn't matter if you handle your own scent board, but you must not handle the neutral articles or boards. If you do handle them, you must protect them from your scent by using high-density rubber gloves or better still metal tongs. If you use tongs don't be fooled into thinking that metal doesn't carry scent, because it most certainly does. Don't touch the end of the tongs that you are going to handle the articles with, and don't handle with them, any items that you have handled previously, as this will transfer your scent.

If you can imagine putting your fingers into a pot of paint, and then handling various items, you finger prints would show up on everything that you touch and the traces of paint would be passed onto any article that came into contact with those that you had touched. Also, the fumes from the paint can linger on items that have not even been touched, but have been in the vicinity. Scent transfers in a similar way, except that unfortunately, we can't see it, so we must be ultra careful so as not to inadvertently confuse the dog and spoil all of our hard work.

To give you an example of how scent can transfer; a drug detector dog in Florida identified a drugs haul by finding the scent of cocaine on money that had at some time, been hidden behind the dashboard of a car. The money was no longer there when the police brought the car and driver in on another offence. Such was the trust in the dog's ability that although nothing was found behind the dashboard when the dog identified that something was there, the prisoner was interrogated and eventually the truth came out. The money had been handled by drug dealers, and hidden there the previous week.

When you have selected the necessary training paraphernalia you are ready to start the next stage.

Introducing the Formal Exercise

Step 14 - Place one neutral article or scent board on the ground, and let the dog see you throw his favourite scent article out. Go out with the dog, and encourage him to pick up the correct article, using the appropriate keywords. We are not asking for formality at this stage, only success. So make sure you are with the dog, helping all of the way. Allow him to sniff the neutral article if he wants, if he lingers too long, encourage him to identify and pick up his own article. Once he has satisfied himself that the other articles are boring, and not suitable for picking up, he will learn to ignore them just as he did the boulders etc. in your environment training sessions.

This is a very important lesson for the future. To learn to check and ignore incorrect articles. It is not imperative that the dog checks every article, some dogs always take scent on the air, and don't seem to need to get their nose down. It makes sense to not get too strung up over this and to leave the actual physical technique of scenting to the expert with the 220 million scent receptors!

Step 15 - Place on the ground two neutral articles or boards. Once again throw the dog's article in amongst or beyond them. Send him out and proceed as above, aiding him in every way to guarantee success.

Step 16 - When he is confidently bringing in the article in step 14 & 15, try walking with him past the neutrals, dropping the article, and sending him back as in steps 9 and then 10.

Step 17 - It is still best to use your scent boards. Place your own board, i.e. the plain board that you will use for your own scent, in-between the other two, each approximately a metre (3feet) apart. Choose one of your dog's knotted cloth articles and place it on the centre board. Distract him from the situation for a few moments with a little game, and then set him up very close to the boards. Point to the area, let him sniff your hand, and then send him out, go with him to give him confidence.

Step 18 - When the dog is confident in step 17, untie the cloth, and try the exercise again, it will look slightly

different to the dog, so he may be a little apprehensive to start with. Help him by doing a play retrieve on the open cloth in the opposite direction, aim for success.

Step 19 - Add another board to the neutrals, and repeat as above. You can now start to build up to a maximum of ten boards. Don't do this all in one session, and at each new training session start with the basic search back and fun scent training before going on to this more formal side.

Introducing Patterns

Using scent boards means that you can introduce formality without the dog having the opportunity to go wrong.

Step 20 - The boards need not necessarily be laid in a straight line, some times just put them out ad-lib, sometimes put out in a pattern, a 'T' shape for instance or a circle. Sometimes standing away from the articles a little, other times standing in the middle of them. Sometimes point the dog directly at the articles, other times face away or at an angle to them. A good exercise is to stand in the centre of a circle of cloths, and keep send the dog from different directions. The cloth will remain in the same place each time, but it will be difficult at first, for the dog to know exactly where the correct cloth is, (especially if you do a few double about turns on the spot). He will get used to working around the circle until he finds the article. The dog can become very clever and work this out after a while, so don't repeat it too much and it will be a useful training exercise.

If the dog shows any apprehension or confusion, take him back a few stages, to the start if necessary.

Don't be afraid of repeating the early stages at any time, you are not going backwards, but you are helping the dog to understand and be confident.

Step 21 - Once the dog is ultra confident at all of the above, try repeating with a cloth which is not so well scented, i.e. get a new cloth. Start at the beginning of step 19 and work through again. Rub the cloth well making sure that it has plenty of your scent on both sides. Remember although the dog is able to detect small traces of scent, he is used to having lots on his articles, so we must help him by making sure as much as possible is on the new cloth.

When you are at the stage where the dog is extremely confident and is working various patterns of cloths, finding and bringing out your scent cloth without a problem, it is time to formalise the introduction of decoy scents. The dog, of course, is used to ignoring all sorts of scents, but the introduction of 'hot' human scents to his articles may cause problems if you do not follow a training procedure carefully.

Introducing Decoy Scents

Step 22 - Now we will go back to 2 scent boards only, to make the first introduction to a decoy scent. A decoy is a strange scent on one of the cloths that we do not want the dog to pick up. In actual fact it is even better if you can take a friend for a walk with you, to find the boulders that you used in the early stages, and ask her/him to touch the boulder to put on it their scent. Then you repeat the early stages, sending the dog in for your cloth. The new scent introduced is best to be someone that the dog knows and is not afraid of. Thus he will acknowledge the scent, be aware of it, but will not have the opportunity to pick it up. Don't be afraid to tell the dog what you want, help him at any stage. Do not allow yourself to fall into the struck dumb stage, if the dog needs help give it.

This is then progressed to your scent boards. Keep a few boards that are specifically for decoy scents so that the other boards are kept fairly neutral. This is not imperative for training as the dog is learning to find your scent only at this stage, but to simulate ring conditions as much as possible, the cloths that are neutral must remain that way, and fresh decoy scents should be used each time where possible. If you do not have someone with you while you are training then a good substitute will be to use an old decoy, but obviously one that neither you or the dog has touched. As the dog becomes more competent, you will need to ask friends and neighbours for their help. You can ask people to decoy cloths and put them in plastic bags for you to use later, but keep them well away from the other boards and cloths. It is important, to avoid mistakes. The decoy should not available to be picked up by the dog, so it must be attached to your decoy board, but remember you must not touch it!

Step 23 - Once the dog is working confidently over the decoy board, more neutrals can be introduced. Build up again as in step 20.

Step 24 - When the dog is confidently ignoring your friend's scents, both male and female, try introducing a stranger's scent, again starting with only one or two neutrals plus your scent and the decoy. The only scent being available to pick up is of course the correct one, yours. It is also worth considering the actual odour of the person in comparison to you. For instance, are you a non-smoker or a smoker, does your decoy wear perfume or work in a fish factory?

Step 25 - You will have spent much time and effort training all of the above stages, once they are competently carried out you will introduce the present and finish, starting with very short recalls, from the scent area on lead to show the dog what is wanted.

However, it is important that before you get to this stage, you have been training the retrieve and present of various articles, including cloth in preparation for this exercise. It is not a good idea to try to perfect presents and finishes when you are concentrating on scent work, keep them separate and put them together only when they are good and stable individually.

Preparation for the Ring

Get the dog used to the articles being set up without him seeing you do it. Train towards being able to stand up straight before you send the dog. Any help that is given should be minimised and the dog should get used over time to you being quiet while he works as any commands over the scent area will result in total loss of marks. However, if you stop speaking without a gradual reduction your dog may wonder what he has done wrong. Accustom the dog to the links of walking to the area, the exercise, the present and finish.

Preparing for Test 'C' - (Finding a Stranger's Scent)

If you are a dedicated trainer, and get to enough shows, it won't be very long before you need to teach, what is called in the UK, test 'C' scent, i.e. finding the scent of a stranger (the judge) from a matching scent.

Many handlers leave this to the dog, and only ever go as far as the above steps, even when the dog is competing in test 'C', they leave the exercise to the dog to work out. The handler is working on the assumption that they are teaching the dog to match scents. In training the dog is offered a cloth to take scent, from which has the handler's own scent on and then he is sent out to match it. This system does work, as has been proved by many handlers. Obedience champions have been created using this technique. However, following the experiences of many who have left it to the dog in this way, it has been noted that, once the dog becomes very competent, and has reached the stage where he is no longer learning new things, this

matching technique becomes a little too hit and miss. Whilst doing the handler's scent is very confidence building, if the dog is never, in a controlled training situation, sent for anything but the handler's scent, he may reach a stage where he will start to look for handler scent only. You cannot prevent the dog from taking your scent as well as the judge's in the ring as you have to give the scent to the dog to take from the judge's cloth, and so the confusion creeps in. We therefore need to teach the dog to discriminate in a more exact manner.

Step 26 - A good place to start teaching the dog to go for a scent other than yours is to let a knowledgeable obedience friend or relative do the standard scent with your dog. Only do this if your dog is very happy and used to being handled and played with by the other person. Take the exercise to the basic level, i.e. only the right cloth and a couple of immovable neutrals. Most dogs that have been carefully trained in the basics will have no trouble in adjusting to this.

If you are training on your own, or don't feel that your dog would take to this then simply ask someone that the dog knows to put their scent on a couple of cloths for you. Handle them carefully so as not to put your own scent on the cloths, and place one out on a board. Place out a couple of neutral boards, and then hold the cloth in front of the dog and encourage him to smell it. He should by now be very happy 'Smelling' when told.

Way back in the early stages, you will have started to introduce other people's articles, so this will not come as a completely new thing, and of course as you progressed to ring work, the cloths were always someone else's property. You don't need to wrap the cloth around the dog's muzzle, or pump his stomach, as some people tend to do. You have trained your dog, in a very natural manner so far, there is no need to change just because you are hitting the big time! When the dog takes his nose away and is happy with the amount of scent that he has taken, send him out and go with him. He may well go straight to the right one, but help him to make sure, by taking out the matching cloth, letting him have another smell if necessary, and encouraging him to collect the right one. Use your keywords *'Smell'*, *'Find'*, *'Hold'*, *'Come'*, *'Good boy'*, in the relevant places and order. Encourage and reward with your voice, make sure the dog knows that he is correct. Repeat using the same person's scent but on fresh cloths until the dog becomes confident.

Step 27 - Once the dog understands stage 26, you can go one of two ways; either you introduce another, different friend's scent for the dog, or you use the same scent and introduce a friendly decoy. The training is exactly the same each time you change something. That is, take it from the beginning, help the dog, aim for success.

Step 28 - Now the art of discrimination is really starting to show. The dog can now identify an odour that he knows, ignoring a familiar decoy to bring in the correct scent. Then, on another day the scent roles can be reversed, and the dog will competently identify the matching cloth in the scent area. When you reach this stage you are really seeing the dog's nose in action. Eventually you could have all the cloths decoyed, plus the right one and the dog will discriminate.

Take it slowly, continue to use the boards to avoid error, and don't confuse the scents by fouling or cross scenting them. If you make a mistake go back to the early stages of training and carefully work back up to this stage. You must think about what you are doing. The dog's nose is superb and your job is to educate the dog into how you would like him to use it.

Step 29 - It is a simple step now, to introduce scents that the dog is less familiar with, by allowing the dog to meet someone new for a few moments, and then using their scent. Still as a training exercise, just use two or three cloths on boards to start with, using all of your aids where necessary; voice, lead, etc. It is unlikely, by this stage, that the dog will have any hesitation, but be ready to help, go out with him, allowing him another sniff of your cloth and encouraging the correct behaviour.

The dog is now able to discriminate between scents. Still take time to do basics, search backs, finding your own scent, informally finding things belonging to other people in the field or garden. Always give him the scent from your hand, an article, cloth, or garment belonging to someone else. Do not be indoctrinated into formality, enjoy your dog's skill.

Trouble Shooting

Standing Over the Scent Area - One of the major stumbling blocks in teaching scent discrimination is the 'struck dumb' approach! Many handlers perfect the early stages of training, but then, once any formal training starts to take place they seem unable to move from the spot or speak! Scent is like any other exercise; the dog needs to learn what we want from him. Yes, he has a more superior nose than we do, but this does not mean that he automatically knows what we want him to do with it! He can probably run faster and better than us too, but we still continue to teach him and perfect how we want fast pace to be developed, even after he has started to use it in the ring. So don't be afraid of communicating with the dog, be with him, help him, and show him what you want. Don't leave him hovering over a scent pattern getting more and more confused.

Mouthing the Cloth - This is a common problem, and one that has its root in either anxiety or excitement. Either way it should be approached in the same manner as it is in retrieve - as a separate exercise. It is not a scent problem, it is a retrieving problem.

Snatching or Mouthing Incorrect Cloths - Snatching or touching incorrect cloths is a behaviour that often creeps in as the dog becomes more confident. It is normally a behaviour with its roots in excitement, but sometimes apprehension. You need to spend much time on immovable objects and scent boards to break the habit - in other words back to basics.

Failing Scent - The most common problem relating to failure to find the correct cloth is confusion in the dog. Handlers become frustrated, especially if the dog once did good scent and suddenly he fails - usually when it matters! When dogs go wrong in this way, handlers tend to try to correct the dog, but it is better to start at step one, and run through the basics, to put the dog back on the right track giving him confidence as you go.

Sometimes the dog finds it hard to discriminate due to health problems. It is not unknown for dogs to have hay fever, tonsillitis, and other ailments that will affect their ability. It is even possible for a dog to lose its sense of smell. If there is a sudden change, it is best to check with the vet.

Bringing in the Decoy - Dogs often bring in the decoy due to confusion, i.e. they bring in the first hot scent. Go back to the stage where you are working with a decoy and your own scent only to build up the confidence. Make sure the decoy is pinned down to a board so the dog can't go wrong.

General Advice - Whatever the problem, it is always best to go back to the early stages of training and build back up, rather than trying to correct the dog. This way the dog will develop confidence and you will both continue to enjoy the experience.

Distance Control (DC)

Before you start the dog should enjoy and be well motivated by his toy or a titbit. He should have acquired 'The Want'. You should decide on the words that you will use, the tones of voice that those words will be spoken, and you should practice saying the words and throwing your voice over a distance. When you train the dog the same tones should be used at close quarters as you will use in the ring.

What is Distance Control?

Distance control, often referred to as DC, occurs in test 'C' in UK obedience. It is also an FCI exercise and occurs in many countries at various levels, sometimes in its entirety and sometimes in parts.

The ultimate goal of the exercise is to leave the dog in a position, (sit, down or stand), as indicated by the judge. Go a minimum of 10 paces (more, at the discretion of the judge), and then on the instructions of the judge or steward, tell the dog to change position six times in sequence. Each judge that you work under will decide what the sequence will be that day. The dog should not move more than a body length in any direction. This always seems a little unfair on the small breeds, but then their stride is arguably shorter, so quid pro quo. Each change of position should be clean and smart. The handler is then instructed to return to the dog's side. For each change of position the handler is allowed only one command or signal, together with the dog's name. Some handlers opt to use variations in the tone of the dog's name, either with the command or signal, or on its own.

For a beginner the exercise sounds complicated, but if you start early you will enjoy teaching this fun exercise. By the time you need it (test 'C' in the UK), you will feel confident and so will the dog. Even if you don't see yourself hitting these dizzy heights DC is always an impressive party piece and it is a great exercise to train for in the house when the weather outside puts you off going out for a training session!

All of the DC positions can be taught by physically manipulating the dog, or by using a toy or titbit to motivate and direct the dog into position. The latter is more fun and is, in most cases, much easier for both dog and handler. A ball is the easiest motivator to use, because you can throw the ball for the dog to catch, and it will be an instant reward when he goes into the correct position. A squeaky ball is even better, because it works two-fold; obviously it can be thrown but also, the squeak can be used to maintain attention when necessary. Other toys will work equally well, so long as the dog is sufficiently motivated by them. Make sure that your toy is safe. *(See Toys and Play Training before you start).*

Be very careful with your body posture, tiny signals, and even your intake of breath, the dog will learn to read your every move. Teach him to move when you give a clear keyword or signal, and not before. It looks really cute when the dog takes up position as soon as you take a preparatory breath ready to say the next position, but it is difficult for the judge to decide whether the dog has anticipated or not. Leave no room for doubt, because doubt means points lost.

Clicker Hints

Some handlers who do not normally use clickers for their obedience training have been known to use them to perfect DC. This is because with the dog working in front of the handler it is an ideal set up for this exercise. Of course you can use the clicker in conjunction with teaching the positions, but it is also extremely beneficial for tidying up or speeding up the action and response.

Step 1 - Start on lead, although you will soon find that you can dispense with the lead as the dog starts to enjoy this exercise. Hold your lead in your left hand and your toy in your right. Excite the dog with your 'Switch on' words, *('Ready, steady')*, and with the toy, get him playing. Keep your lead fairly short. When you are confident that the dog is happy, manipulate him so that he is playing in front of you. Step forward into the dog. At the same time raise your right hand and toy up above his head, aiming backwards to take him back into a natural sit. The lead in your left hand will come up, to help the dog into a sit position. You may have to adjust your hand and lead positioning until you get this right. The dog should automatically and happily go back into the sit position. The movement that must be achieved is a backward movement. The dog's front feet should sweep back to meet his back feet. He may even jump back into the sit if he is the excitable type - this is fine. Immediately he is in position give your command *'Sit'*, and throw the ball into his mouth for him to catch. As he catches say *'Catch'*. If he misses, go with him and encourage him to get the toy, say *'Get it'*. Don't let him run off to get it on his own, remember - 'team work'. As soon as he has the toy, put your right hand to his mouth, and take, or prise the toy out, by doing this you are entering into the game and the dog doesn't feel threatened. You are not giving commands to release, you are creating team spirit, and avoiding a stand off situation. If the dog holds on too hard, is very keen, or has a particularly hard grip, then you can use your keyword *'Leave'*, but remember to keep it light and fun.

Repeat this a couple of times at each training session, or whenever you have the opportunity at home, until it starts to become automatic. Play, play, play. Step towards him. Raise your right hand above him. Say *'Sit'* as he comes into position. Throw the ball say *'Catch'* as he catches it. Take the ball from his mouth and carry on playing. Try to keep up the momentum. Make your actions swift, clear and fun.

Step 2 - Now we will introduce the stand position. Sometimes it is easier to put the dog in the sit as above first, and then to bring him into the stand. This step deals with getting the stand straight from play, step 3 explains how to do it from a sit, train whichever you find easiest as the next step. The suggested keyword to use for stand is *'Back'*. The reason for this is that most people find it easier to say with any volume, and so the dog will be able to hear at the distance required in the ring, also it cannot be anticipated on the 'S' part of the word and misconstrued as 'Sit'.

Get the dog in 'play mode' with his toy. Manipulate the play until he is in front of you. Have your lead in your left hand and your toy in your right. Position your toy at dog nose height. Take a step or two towards the dog so that he steps back away from you. Push the toy forward so that the dog moves backward to maintain contact with it. Keep the toy at nose height then hold it still. As the dog becomes stationary say *'Back'*. Throw him the toy, say *'Catch'*. Play. Take the toy from the dog and repeat several times.

The dog may take several steps back before becoming stationary; this doesn't matter in fact it has positive benefits. It means that he is taking an active measure towards backward movement. In the ring tendencies are for the dog to come forward towards the handler at each change in position, this is because the dog is isolated and wants to be with the handler. If the dog is trained to go back into each position this tends to compensate. As part of your training you can extend this movement, and keep walking toward the dog so that he walks backwards. Repeat your keyword *'Back'*. Take this a few steps at a time and always reward and play as part of the exercise.

Step 3 - Teaching the stand from the sit. Play the dog into the sit position as step 1. Next, with excitable dogs simply step forwards into the dog. Push the toy forwards in line with the dog's nose, and make the action appear as though you are going to go right through the dog. Normally the dog will spring back up into the stand position. As soon as the dog is in the stand tell him 'Back' and reward him. With some dogs you may need to place your left foot in between the front and hind legs to gently push the dog's hind legs back into the stand position to start. This should not be a kick, but merely a gentle prise to manipulate the dog's back legs back into the stand. As soon as the dog is in position say *'Back'*, and reward him with his toy.

Soon he will start to come up into the stand as soon as your leg starts to move. Repeat at each training session until the dog becomes confident, later if you wish you could use this leg movement as the signal instead of a command.

Step 4 - Teaching the down from the stand. This is an easy move, play the dog into the stand position. Hold your lead in your left hand and your toy in your right. When the dog is settled in the stand sweep your hand forward bringing your toy swiftly down between his two front paws as near to his chest as possible. The dog should hinge back into the down position. As soon as he is down say the keyword *'Down'*, and release his toy. He may flop his body over as if doing a down for stays, although this is not the posture that you want it is best to ignore it. If you start handling him too much he may become apprehensive and feel pressured. We can alter this body position and get him into the correct 'sphinx' style down by using the reward and sit position in the next step.

Repeat until the dog is happy going down, whatever his position, as long as he does not come forward into it, and then go onto the next step.

Step 5 - Teaching the sit from the down. The dog has already learnt the signal for the sit position in step 1. To get him from the down to the sit is a very similar procedure. Use your toy in your right hand to lift up and over his head sweeping him back and up into the sit. Use your lead to help him in the right direction if necessary, and you may find it useful, particularly with the heavier dogs to push back with the inside of your right foot across the dog's front feet. The aim is for his front feet go back to meet his back feet, and not visa versa. Some dogs get very excited when training and the fault that may creep in here is that the dog lifts his bottom and has a tendency to stand before sitting. This is not acceptable so make sure that you control it with your lead to avoid the problem. Taking it more slowly with excitable dogs will also help keep the dog on the ground.

Step 6 - The sit from the down once perfected will help teach the dog to do the sphinx down. Once the dog is confident doing the down in any style he likes, withhold the reward following the down, and bring him immediately into the sit, using the upward sit signal, with hand and toy, and then reward. Repeat this several times and the dog will start to work out for himself that it is easier to come into the sit and gain the reward from the sphinx than it is from the rolled over or flat down position when the action is fast.

Step 7 - Teaching the down from the sit. Play the dog into the sit, when he is confident and attentive, bring the toy down between his two front feet as in step 4. Again the main problem will be if the dog lifts into the stand first, so to avoid this, have your left hand ready to aid him into the down by pushing back and down on his shoulders. Watch the positioning of your hands, the dog will tend to follow them, so make sure they are low and giving a backward movement.

Step 8 - Teaching the stand from the down. This is probably the most difficult to perfect, as there is no straight forward natural movement that will easily show the dog what is wanted, it must therefore be a combination of moves. It is important to avoid forward movement in all position changes, but this is the combination that will bring the dog forward if anything does. To avoid forward movement, it is usually a good idea to over exaggerate the backward movement in training.

Play the dog into the down, have your toy in your right hand, lead in your left. When the dog is keen but settled, walk forwards into him, holding your right hand at standing nose height, bring your lead low and back over the dog's back, and be ready if necessary to sweep his back legs back with your left foot. This should all flow together, and should be approached with a pleasant, well-motivated attitude as usual. Once the dog is in the stand continue to walk him a few steps backwards, with your toy still at nose height.

Repeat a few times at each session, and the dog will soon be trotting backwards quite enthusiastically. If the dog tends to go sideways, work against a wall or other barrier to help him to learn to go straight.

Step 9 - Now we have covered all the combinations, and the dog is confident and enthusiastically going into them, it is time to introduce a few link ups. This is done with exactly the same attitude as before, making it all fun, and following the procedures as above. Do not be tempted to run more than one extra move at a time. If you link too soon, the dog may lose confidence. An example of a starting combination could be, sit-stand-sit. This is relatively easy and a good place to start. When the dog has perfected this, try down-sit-down, then stand-sit-stand, and so on, (not all in the same training session). Always aiming to make it easy for the dog. Choose the combinations of positions that the dog and you find enjoyable first. Don't fall into the trap of getting carried away sequencing, remember to make a point of throwing in some positions on their own and reward them.

If the dog does a position and it is not 100% correct go back and put in every aid to get it right, and don't forget to reward the dog. If the dog shows any apprehension or anticipation use your reward to get the dog into the correct mode, e.g. if he starts springing into the stand before you tell him, put in a sit with immediate reward.

Step 10 - When the dog has perfected these combinations, then you can try combinations with three different positions, stand-sit-down, and so on. Don't forget to keep on throwing in easy ones, like a simple sit on its own to give the dog confidence.

Step 11 - Now the dog is able to do all of the above it is time to teach him about distance. This should be done very gradually, starting from the beginning, one position at a time. He must learn that it is OK to do it at a distance. He will not understand what is wanted unless you apply the distance teaching principle to all positions and combinations. Building up distance is very simple, but you must be patient and refrain from racing on too fast.

Start with your dog's favourite position. Put him into it, give him his keyword take a couple of steps away from him, repeating the keyword, throw him his reward, *'Catch'*. Try this on all three single positions.

Step 12 - This time decide on the dog's favourite combination. Leave him in a position and from just a couple of paces away give him his keyword for the change of position. Use your body posture as in the initial training, making as if you were going towards him, and following it through to help him if necessary. As he goes into position, throw his ball to reward him, *'Catch'*. This can then be progressed to all of the combinations.

Step 13 - When the dog is confidently doing the combinations with you just a couple of paces away, you can start to gradually reduce the amount of extra body movement and signals that you give. Make smaller movements, and stop as soon as the dog is in position, but follow up with immediate reward. Sometimes your reward can be the toy; at other times just show the toy and reward with your voice. The toy can start to go in and out of sight, and be used when it is needed to give confidence. *(See Eliminating Aids)*.

Step 14 - At this point we have not yet taught the dog that we will be starting the exercise from the heel position. If we don't spend a little time on this, it will come as a shock when we need to set the dog up in the ring.

The dog by now should be very confident, practice playing him into position at your side. Play with him on lead get him motivated and then manoeuvre through your play until he is by your side. Use your hand signal with your toy; aid him manually with your lead, hand or foot if necessary, into the position. Choose his favourite position first, place him and reward. Keep it light and fun.

Introduce a keyword for DC that tells the dog that, although he is wanted in the heel position, he is not about to do heelwork. Most people use the word *'Control'*.

Step 15 - Now the dog is at the stage where he can be left from the heel position, and you can work a couple of paces away, with a minimal amount of help. Therefore it is time to start, very gradually, increasing the distance. This must be done gradually and the exercise should be split, repeatedly returning to the dog to reward him, and/or throwing the toy from the distance. This should be progressed, building up a pace at a time, for each position and combination of positions. Start with a single position, leave the dog a couple of metres, and then return. Next leave a couple of metres and give a change of position being ready to help with all of your signals and walk back towards the dog if necessary. The signals from your body and voice should be sufficient for the dog to understand if your basics have been taught thoroughly.

After each position or short combination, return to the dog talking in a soothing way, quietly helping him to stay put. If he moves, stand still and talk to him, when he is still reward him immediately from the distance. Think about what you are trying to achieve if the dog starts to do something wrong, just stop put it right, and reward it immediately.

The dog must be given confidence, and the precision will be kept up by continuing to break the exercise down to the basic level in training.

Trouble Shooting

Missed positions, forward movement, and breaking on return are the most common faults. Minor faults include lifting into the wrong position first, before taking up the right one. All of these faults are usually the result of insufficient basic and thorough training. If any faults creep in - go back to basics and retrain following the steps above.

There is also the chance that something happens in the ring to worry or confuse the dog, but again, go back to the training to give confidence, and to take away the emphasis of any problems.

Eliminating Aids

Before aids are eliminated the dog should be confident and keen in the relevant exercise.

One of the most common excuses handlers give, for not wanting to use motivational aids such as toys, titbits or clickers in training, is that you cannot take them into the ring. This is not a valid reason as you can't use any of the other aids for training in the ring either! You can't use lead control in any class, voice and signal control are limited to the start of each exercise in the higher classes. Nevertheless, handlers still, quite rightly, use leads, hands, voice and other things for teaching their dogs the various exercises. All training aids are much more effective when coupled with the right kind and sufficient motivation.

Everyone has to learn how to eliminate aids, whatever method of teaching they might use. Aids should be gradually reduced and substituted, in such a way that the dog does not miss them, in fact he should expect that they might appear at any moment. It is better that these aids are 'friendly', if we wish to remain friends with the dog. In the case of body and verbal signals, it is best to train with a minimal amount; thus there are less to eliminate and it does not pose such a complete change to the dog. The keywords and aids that you use should be clear, simple and effective.

Each training procedure, covered in the techniques section, will be made up of many aids to assist you and the dog to get it right. These aids should never be dropped all at once.

The biggest mistakes come when handlers win out of the UK Beginner and Novice class and decide to work test 'A'. That is, from a class where commands and signals are allowed throughout all tests barring the stays, to a class where only one command and simultaneous signal are allowed at the start of each exercise. Many handlers seem to make the mistake of going immediately dumb, poker stiff, unable to aid their dog and bad tempered! The temper is lost through frustration; the sudden inability to do well is most embarrassing and takes some living down, particularly if the handler has really shone in the lower classes. From the dog's point of view the world has become very puzzling. Once he had verbal help and encouragement galore, all of a sudden his time within the ring ropes has become akin to entering a different world.

The dog does not have to go through this, nor does the handler, if training and motivation are approached in a straightforward and honest manner.

Eliminating Clickers

Clickers are very much a training tool. Ideally the clicker is used in the teaching and perfecting of exercises, it is not necessary to keep using it on every exercise that you work through at your regular training sessions. You will be able to reduce the use of the clicker, as the dog becomes more and more motivated to do as you ask. Because of the nature of clicker training the dog will soon become keen to work, once you are happy with the result you can drop the clicker to occasional use and substitute with verbal praise where and when appropriate.

Reintroduce the clicker when you are teaching something new, when you want to give the dog an extra boost, or when you want to put the polish on an exercise. Hence the clicker will be unnecessary for general work by the time you come to working in the ring.

Targeting

If you are using targets such as your hand as a target in heelwork, it is a simple matter of gradually moving the target until it is beyond the dog's reach, or putting in commands to make him stop short of the target. The trained behaviour soon takes the place of touching the target.

Body Posture and Footwork

When teaching the dog, we should aim, where possible, to make sure that the first thing the dog sees is the natural body posture which will be allowable in the ring. This helps the dog to read you, and also helps him to adjust himself ready for the next action. To give you an example; when training the left turn in heelwork, and progressing to putting things together on the move, the first thing the dog should see and feel is your body posture altering. This is followed by your leading foot, (normally your left foot), going into the turn. This is then followed up, in training, by your hand going down the lead towards the collar, and a step back on your right foot, which over exaggerates the body posture in the ring. *(See Heelwork - left turns section for more details of this turn).* This principle is followed in all exercises, and the aids gradually dropped, but never all at once.

When an aid is dropped it is put back into the routine before another is dropped. There is a gentle and careful progression working towards the dropping of aids, but they are regularly there in training sessions.

Each basic training procedure will always be started with the only signal that will be left for the dog to see in the ring, when the aids are

dropped. This is normally a signal coming from the handler's body posture. Therefore in training it is of paramount importance that you pay attention to your body posture.

Having a training routine that can be utilised prior to an exercise in the ring will also help the dog to understand what is going to happen and what is expected of him. For example naming the exercise, dealing with any ring furniture or articles in the same way each time and assuming the same starting posture. When training the exercise, consider what you are allowed to do in the setting up of each exercise in the ring, and incorporate this into your training routine.

Verbal Commands

The section on Voice - Tones and Usage will help you greatly in understanding how to use words. Understanding how to get the best use of what you are allowed is an important factor in learning how to eliminate those extra words that mean the loss of points in the ring.

The dog's concentration span must be gradually worked upon. Most people who read this section of the book will be at least aiming beyond the beginner level, so it is best to start off as you mean to go on. You cannot simply become quiet, and go marching off into the distance, expecting the dog, who is used to a fairly constant banter from you, to stay accurately by your side in the heel position.

Your first task is to make sure that the dog understands the keywords, and has learnt to perform the exercises on the utterance of just the one word, with a little extra help and encouragement where necessary.

Once we are sure that the dog understands, we can then use the reward training, be it toy or food, to gradually extend the length of time that the dog works without the handler having to say anything. This must be done, just as all of your training, in stages. The keywords should not be repeated once the dog is performing correctly, the keywords are tools that tell the dog what to do next. To repeat them really serves very little purpose. The dog will need encouragement only, if your training is thorough.

If at any time the dog looks confused or worried, you should go back to your game and basic training to regain his confidence, and then the next time, don't try to keep going for so long.

Each individual exercise gives you suggestions of what words to use, and word usage is dealt with in the exercise training sections. The main criteria for eliminating commands is to make sure that your dog is taught to perform the task on one simple keyword. He will be aided with your routine, consistent body posture, pleasant, confident attitude and tone of voice. Eliminating word usage need not be a major stumbling block for you and your dog.

Toys and Titbits

The use of motivational aids, such as toys and titbits is a crucial element in all of the concepts and training methods in this book, and indeed of most modern training techniques. The sections on *Timing and Rewards* will have given you the information that you need on how to use them. To get rid of them is a gradual process. As far as the dog is concerned they will never go completely, he will merely learn to expect them less often and if this is implemented in the correct manner, he will work even harder to gain them.

It is scientific fact that, if you teach an animal to expect to be rewarded, and then withhold that reward, as long as he is aware and has been programmed to know that the reward will come, he will work faster and harder to get to the next reward. This is the principle behind limiting, randomising and spacing out your rewards.

Step 1 - Let's say for instance that you have been teaching heelwork with a toy lure/reward. The dog has reached the point where he is happy trotting along in the heel position, with his eyes fixed firmly on his toy. The first stage to elimination would be to enclose your hand around the toy to hide it from view. The dog obviously knows that it is still there. Take a few paces like this and then reveal it to the dog, and then reward with the toy and release.

Step 2 - Get the dog back into heelwork mode with your toy, when he is well motivated, move it behind your back for a few seconds only, and then reveal again while the dog is still working, then reward and release.

Step 3 - Get the dog in heelwork mode with your toy, then casually put the toy in your pocket for a few seconds. No more than a few seconds should elapse before you bring the toy back out, still with the dog working, then reward as before.

Step 4 - Repeat the above three stages, increasing gradually, the time that the toy is out of sight and at random, do short and longer spells with the toy hidden, trying not to become predictable.

Do not progress too quickly, as we do not want to bore the dog, or make him lose interest. Be ready at any time to bring the toy back if necessary. Keep it exciting and do not be tempted to change your attitude. Everything should remain the same, you voice, your body stance, etc. The only thing that differs is that the toy is not always in sight, but it soon reappears.

If the dog is distracted at anytime, don't yell, shout, check or drag him about, simply get out your toy and turn in the opposite direction to the distraction, taking the dog enthusiastically with you. Your attitude should be one of sheer amazement that the dog could possibly find anything more riveting than you. Turn on the charm! If the dog works particularly well, reward lavishly and quickly - if he is not so good, reward to a minimum and start again trying to help induce a better reaction.

Step 5 - Soon the dog will be able to work for longer stretches with a minimum of input from your toy. When you are sure he is becoming confident, try putting the toy on a table, without the dog seeing to start with. Do a little heelwork and then work in the direction of the table, collecting the toy, reward him. If he loses concentration or is distracted at this point then you should consider that you have not spent long enough on the above stages.

Don't ever get to the stage where you eliminate the reward completely, the dog should always assume that there is one just around the corner.

Step 6 – Work at varying distances from the table where the reward is. At the end of the exercise go quickly to the table and reward the dog.

This gradual weaning technique can be applied to all of the exercises, and the toy then becomes the reward for correct behaviour instead of merely a lure.

Trouble Shooting

Loss of Interest – Dogs usually lose interest because the rewards are taken away before the dog has learnt that the exercise itself is fun. It takes a lot of work and training to get to that point. It is also possible that you have dropped the rewards down to a level whereby the dog thinks he has little chance of getting one.

He may not realise that it is behaviour in relation to your keywords that gets him the reward – you may have to go back to some very basic training. If you haven't already tried it, have a go at clicker training. The concept behind clicker training is that the dog learns that it is his own actions that gain the reward, it is much less reliant on the handler's manipulation of the dog.

Only Works When Reward is in the Pocket – This is a very common problem. The dog knows when the reward is not there and is therefore less motivated. Sometimes he declines to work at all, at other times the sparkle has gone. As above you need to work on your rapport with the dog and build in an enjoyment for work. When moving to the table training take this stage very slowly, asking for simple behaviours in front of the table to start with so that the dog can see that the reward does not always come from you or your pocket.

Short Attention Span – Again very common once rewards are reduced. Build the attention span by breaking down the exercises and rewarding regularly from a table rather than your pocket/hand. Work on attention exercises and give lavish rewards for good attention. When the dog learns to look at you and not the reward in order to get it, you are naturally training in attention.

Section Three
Obedience Training
and Ring Craft

This section covers a variety of other areas of interest that will help your obedience work as well as how to motivate your dog using clicker and target training, to avoid and correct mistakes, work on problems that occur in the ring and generally prepare you for competing.

Heelwork to Music/Freestyle is also covered in this section.

Photo by J. Midgley

Circuit Training

Before You Start - You need to have achieved some basic heelwork training, and have a good bond with your dog.

Circuit training sounds rather tiring! But in fact it is designed to prevent you and your dog from getting bored - not particularly to keep you 100% fit, although it will help! The idea of circuit training is to set out as many obstacles as you can at your training session. These need not be heavy cumbersome obstacles, you could use bollards, markers, hoops, tapes on the ground, mini hurdles (e.g. a piece of dowel or cane between two bollards). Obviously if you are lucky enough to have a large garden or training area of your own, then you can be more adventurous. You also need four or six ring posts and some cord to set up a ring. The ring posts do not need to be heavy duty; they can be the plastic poles that many handlers use for sendaways, weaving or tracking markers (sheep fencing posts).

Construct a ring, and then place the obstacles, in any order, around the ring. Leave some areas clear and others with a number of distractions. Then commence working your dog around the obstacles. Start with some attention exercises and then progress to exercises that your dog likes the most.

When doing heelwork in the circuit, the object of the exercise is not to take a predictable course every time, but rather to twist and turn, working on keeping your complete concentration on the dog and his on you. You can use the cones to weave, the hoops to circle, etc. Basically you can do anything you like, but the important thing to remember is to keep the dog's complete and utter attention. Use your toy or 'want' aid to make sure that the dog really wants to be with you.

Don't become predictable. For instance, in the middle of a weave you can turn out and go in a different direction, or you could circle one of the bollards instead of weaving. The hurdle can be used whether you need jumps for your particular kind of obedience or not. It is there to give variety and help you to practice your control. The secret is to be inventive.

This type of training is not just for the more advanced dogs, it can be introduced at any time. Obviously, with a relatively untrained dog, you will not be able to do any precision work, but you can play and work on 'the want' amongst distractions and all of this will help you to keep your dog's full attention in all circumstances.

The circuit also serves to prevent you from becoming staid or boring in your training. It stops you from marching up and down in a set pattern displaying to your dog just how boring heelwork can be. Another benefit is that you must look where you are going. A common fault, as your training begins to progress, is that of looking at the dog all of the time, and not where you are going. This leads to an inability to walk in a straight line, or to take an acute turn. The obstacles make you pay attention to your route. Have fun.

Don't forget that in this, as in all training, the most important thing is to read your dog. Don't carry on too long so that he becomes tired or bored. Do use your 'want' aids, i.e. toy, ball, titbits and play. Use them in the same way that you would use them in teaching any other exercise, by giving and taking and keeping control of the game.

During the course of the circuit you can go through all of your set exercises, (in a training manner of course, not as the finished article). Variety is the name of the game, keeping a 'high interest level' for both you and your dog.

If you are training with other people, you can use each other to get the dogs used to working in close proximity, just as they might have to in the ring. A particularly good idea is to have one dog and handler working on either side of the ring ropes, this often happens in competition, but is rarely trained for. Another favourite with judges (or perhaps a failing of some ring stewards) is to work you right up to the ring ropes, to an obstacle, table or the like and then give you a halt or turn. Use your circuit to prepare for this.

Remember the first rule; 'You must be the most interesting person to the dog'. Do not threaten or chastise your dog into watching or paying attention, this will only serve to make him more anxious to look away, or in fact get away, from this horrible person! You must teach the dog that you are nice, and singularly the most interesting person he knows, even if this means abandoning your more formal training and having a good rough and tumble or game of catch with him. Remember that your fun and games must be kept in close proximity to you. Don't get into the habit of letting the dog hurtle half way down the field after his ball. If you allow this, all it tells the dog is that pleasure comes when he's away from you, all he gets when he's with you is boring repetition.

Once you have the dog's full attention, and have achieved 'the want', then you can go back into a few steps of heelwork whilst you have his full attention, thus getting perfection and full attention even with distractions. Even if you consider that what you get from your dog at this stage is far from perfection, if you have full 'wanting' attention then perfection is just around the corner.

To recap - Circuit training is not about a set routine. It is devised to keep you and your dog interested and keen, and to prevent you from becoming boring and repetitive. It also helps you to look where you are going! You might consider that you could do all of these variations, without going to the trouble of carting obstacles and markers to the training area. When it comes to a real show you are rarely isolated with no distractions. You certainly cannot decide for yourself what comes next! The obstacles will serve to help you to teach the dog that you are more interesting than anything around him, and also that obstacles, which may be used as ring furniture, are not frightening, nor something to be sniffed at or for leg cocking!

Routines

To help you as a dog trainer, to be consistent and positive, it is important that you have some set ideas or routines, to get you and your dog into the swing of things at each training session, and before you go into the ring. An Olympic sprinter would not be expected to go straight out onto the track and do a 500 metre sprint, without first warming up. Nor would we expect a college graduate to go in for an exam, without first doing some revision, no matter how clever he was. So why should we expect our dogs to go straight into a full advanced or even beginner round, without some form of warm up session that gets both his mind and body into gear?

To some handlers, this might mean marching up and down doing heelwork, and anything else that might be a particular problem at the time, practicing the faults as they go! But for the more discerning handler, a routine of tightening up and warming up exercises, that will not allow faults, but will re-confirm the precision required, with lots of incentive and motivation, has to be a better idea. Obviously, with a dog that is just starting to learn the exercise, then you can only go as far as you have taught, and then possibly, push on a little further if the dog is confident and happy. But with an older, and reasonably well trained dog, you can have quite a comprehensive warming up and training routine.

Start from the beginning each time with a little play. Your training routine, all conducted with the dog on lead, could go something like this:

1) The Want - Play with your dog, get him into play mode, and make sure you have the 'Want'.

2) Attention (the watch) - Guide your dog into the heel position with the 'Watch' keyword. Get half a second of perfect watch - then play. Build up your time as you did when teaching the exercise, but in this warm

up moving quickly yet progressively onto the next step with each success, praising and playing after each break.

3) Heelwork - Guide your dog into the heel position, give the 'Watch' keyword, and then 'Close', take one step forward with the dog in perfect position, and paying attention to you - then break and play. Just one step of perfect heelwork, then start again and the next time go for two. Build like this keeping everything fun and keeping up the want all of the time. The next time go for three steps of perfection, then four and so on but not going further than the dog is capable of maintaining full attention and the 'Want'. If at any time he loses concentration, you are going on too far, or the motivation is not good enough. Start again and set your sights a little lower.

4) Turns - Go through all of your training techniques for turn. Start by guiding the dog at a lead's length, and then gradually closing in.

5) Present and finish - Train all combinations without linking them to the relevant exercises.

6) Recalls - Work on the dog's want to come to you both to the front and to heel. Work on the statics and finishes seperately.

7) Retrieve - Starting with the hold, and then moving on through the progression of segments, don't miss anything and keep up the momentum of motivation.

8) Sendaway - Start with the instant down close to you on lead of course, controlled and using your 'Want' aids to keep up the excitement. Having previously set up an area to send your dog place his toy to the back of the area and then, from a few feet away, send him and follow up, putting him in the down, and then allow him his toy. Build up your distance, but only going as far as the dog is ultra-confident, and maintain the 'want'.

9) Scent - Take a cloth or similar article, allow the dog to hold as in the first stage of retrieve. Next, take a few steps of heelwork, drop the cloth and let the dog search back to find it. Next, move to a different area and do the search back with some other immovable objects around, improvise if you are out in a field by using stones, etc.

10) Distance Control - Go through each position in a fun manner, playing between every one, and going through the training procedure in quick progression to your best standard, but without doing the finished article as if in the ring.

11) Stays - Place your dog in each of the positions in turn, going through the training procedure, testing with the lead and calmly rewarding good stable positions.

12) Linking - Link some parts of exercises together keeping the flow going all of the time.

11) Circuit training - Keep the dog's interest high by being varied in your routines.

Remember allow your dog time to do some 'doggy things', release him and let him sniff around and relax if he wants to. Call him to you only when you are sure of getting a perfect and positive response. His reaction to you must be positive 100% in the ring, therefore outside of the ring, we must learn how to engineer the situation if necessary, to maintain a positive response. If when your dog is released he turns a 'deaf ear' then you must learn how to be the most interesting thing around by finding the way to his heart.

Remember in all things you must make the decisions, or at least the dog must think you did!

Linking

It is important to teach yourself to link things together, and to look at things from a dog's point of view. By breaking exercises into segments for teaching, we are making sure that the dog understands every part of the set piece. But then, if the exercises are to be performed with enthusiasm and to maintain 'the want', the dog needs to see each section of an exercise as a catalyst. One step leading to the conditioned response of the next step that we need. The ability to link without causing anticipation is the sign of a good dog trainer. Toys, play, and the techniques that we have dealt with to achieve 'the want', will help you to learn how to link.

Keeping the enthusiasm bubbling, and the dog's full attention on you, will help to make sure that the dog puts things together in the way that you want him to. If you do not maintain full attention then he will miss the next signal, and therefore the link. If you wish to keep your dog's full attention you must learn to give him yours. This is often difficult if you are receiving instruction, but if you watch the best handlers, they never ignore their dog at any point, even at the end of an exercise. If they are demonstrating with a dog they will give him his release command before turning to the audience. Therefore the dog learns that, unless told to finish, there is always something interesting about to happen, and he is motivated to keep his attention on the handler. If you are distracted it is not unreasonable to expect the dog to be distracted to. The more this is allowed to happen, the less likely you are able to maintain a link between exercises or even segments of exercises.

As your dog progresses and becomes confident in what you are trying to achieve, it is important to link exercises together as you will be expected to in the ring, often going from one to another, but remembering to keep up the 'Want' with a toy, play, titbit or praise. To give you an example - try breaking in the middle of some heelwork and have a good play session, then using your 'Want' aids, go back into heelwork for a few yards and link into retrieve, after which play again. This teaches the dog that you don't always finish something in the same place every time and that there is always some more fun to come. You could start with the dog in a present position, send him around to heel, finish and then walk straight away into another exercise such as a sendaway. Think of all the variations of links that could occur in a normal round of obedience and train for them a little at a time.

Linking is also about joining parts of exercises, and incorporating static basic routines into on the move action. For instance, take a static taught left turn and put it into fluid heelwork in such away that the dog can understand, then execute the turn with precision, and confidence. This again can be taught with your 'training aids, guiding and linking each part together, over-emphasising moves to make it obvious to the dog. Always leaving the dog yearning for more, not switched off or lethargic with boredom or confusion.

Avoiding Mistakes

Mistakes in the ring mainly occur because of nerves. Due to nerves, the handler does not perform in exactly the same manner as they do in training. Sometimes the handler is not nervous, but still performs differently in the ring, aware of the formality, but failing to train in the same way. Sometimes the dog makes mistakes because of changes or even fears that develop or occur due to circumstances beyond your control.

When teaching your dog you must be very careful to ensure that your voice, your body posture, your deportment, and your attitude are the same as they will be in the ring. This means careful choice and use of voice and commands/signals. It means learning to remain upright as much as possible when teaching the dog. Obviously sometimes you have to be down at dog level to start with, but you should progressively straighten, and aim at the end of the teaching of that exercise, to be in a good natural upright position, to mirror your posture in the ring. The dog cannot be expected to perceive that their handler, waving his body all over the place in training, means the same as their handler who stands rigid in the ring!

Many handlers make the mistake of not teaching the dog that the exercises are linked, one after another, when performed in the ring. *(See Linking).* Some may have made the start of an exercise in training, different to the start in the ring. This occurs particularly in exercises like sendaway, where the handler never goes through the rigmarole of preparing for the start of the exercise (as it will occur in the ring.)

On the other hand, only in the ring will the handler fiddle about with the lead, answer or ask questions, keeping the dog waiting to begin. Only in the ring will the handler send the dog straight to a sendaway following heelwork or other such exercise. Working like this is bound to create errors, the dog cannot be blamed for you not preparing him correctly for the ring procedure. *(See Only in the Ring!)*

As you will of course realise, if you have worked through the various sections of the book, we cannot become regimented and perform the exercises as per ring standard and expect the dog to carry on being accurate and precise. This is where the sections on Linking and Routines will help you and your dog to get into the right frame of mind, and avoid those ring situations that result in the loss of points.

Mistakes in training often occur because the handler does not fully understand what they are trying to achieve. They may not have thought out the exercise fully, or may have failed to break it down into segments that the dog is capable of comprehending. So obviously a complete understanding of the exercise and your teaching procedure is of paramount importance, before you begin to train the dog train yourself.

Incorrect Timing is also a major stumbling block, developing perfect timing takes time and patience, you must learn to think like a dog to get it right. In section 1, the chapter, *Understanding the Dog's Mind*, explains in a very simplistic way, how the dog relates to things. Once you understand this, you can then guide, reward, and control situations at the correct time, this transforms dog training from a task to a joy.

Take time out to read these sections and understand them and then you will look upon dog training in a new light.

Correcting Mistakes

It is very difficult for the dog to understand that, having being taught something, we then want to change part of it, or that's how it seems to him.

On heelwork for instance there are many faults that handlers allow to occur, wide working, wide about turns, inaccurate or inconsistent heel position, crooked sits, forward working - of course there are many more. Simply correcting the faults when they occur teaches nothing more than the fact that the dog should continually correct himself. This is no good for the ring. Although it might feel to you as though the dog knows where he should be, a dog that has been trained by correction of faults stands out a mile when you are a judge. The dog will be forever weaving his body around, some will be quite wound up over the fact that they must wiggle about until the handler is pleased. Most will assume, (quite correctly), that this is what they have been taught - to take up one position and then change it to another. Of course we see this as an error, justifying ourselves by saying that he knew he was wrong because he corrected himself! Of course we know that if the dog is not in the correct position at any time during the round then this is a markable offence. The fact that he might have corrected himself is quite irrelevant from a judging point of view. Admittedly there might be less points lost than for the dog who does not get into the correct position at all, but never the less there are too many points lost to win the class in most instances.

So where you have faults look at the problem objectively, teach to make sure that the dog understands every part of every exercise. Try to analyse at what point things start to go wrong and retrain the exercise, giving all the help you can to make sure the dog performs in the way that is correct for the ring. Also try to analyse the reason for the mistake as this may alter your training process or set up. Make sure you think carefully about your training, and pay attention, not only to the part of the exercise that was at fault, but to the whole thing, most particularly to the segment immediately preceding the fault as this will act as a catalyst to trigger the next move.

Also check health issues – could it be that your dog is feeling unwell, in pain, tired, hormonal etc., any of these could affect performance.

Consider development stage – if the dog is still growing up he will hit a variety of stages that will affect his view on life. Help him work through these.

Only in the Ring - Never in Training!

One of the most common pleas for help in the world of obedience training stems from the handler getting exactly what they want from the dog in training, but not in the ring - why does this happen?

The problems come in varying degrees. Sometimes the team have a problem with a particular exercise, but more often than not the handler's problems start, and refer to everything, from the minute that they walk into the ring, or even before that in the warm up session outside of the ring. This is such a common problem that the whole of the next chapter has been dedicated to it!

One or Two Specific Things Go Wrong on a Regular Basis.

Years ago a friend confided in me that she felt that, if only she could get the superb sendaway in the ring that she was getting in training, she could have easily won the championship class. Having come out of the ring twice on the trot, with the points lost on sendaway being the difference between winning and not even featuring in the line up it seemed that she could be right. A most infuriating case of the 'If Onlys!'

Obviously her training technique was good because the dog was super confident in training, and even when the dog was trained in new surroundings, and in a situation that looked, for all intents and purposes, like a ring, she never failed to do a perfect exercise. Obviously, the dog did not understand something when it came into the show ring, so something was different between the training sessions and the real McCoy!

The handler, although she had achieved this very high standard of obedience, was convinced that her dog was being naughty. Of course if you read the section on understanding the dog' mind you will know that the dog does not possess the ability to decide to be naughty or vindictive. He certainly is not able to single out one particular thing to keep on getting wrong, to prove a point to this human on the other end of the lead! Actions and thoughts like these are human vices and we should honour our four-footed friend with more respect.

So, having convinced the handler of the dog's integrity, we set about the task of finding out what the difference was that was confusing the dog. I watched them perform in the ring and then watched them in a training session, and indeed the dog performed as predicted. Then we talked through a typical training session when the handler was away from a show. Obviously the rules were being followed and her training was very thorough. When it came to sendaway she said that they realised the dog should not see the sendaway markers being set up every time, so they were set up at the beginning of most sessions, even before the dog was out of the car.

The handler trained with a friend of a similar level. They regularly stewarded each other to make sure that they were used to turning, stopping etc. when told, and also they were able to train against this to make sure that the dogs did not learn to work to the ring stewards commands. They obviously were taking things very seriously.

On sendaway the handler said that they called out the steward's commands for each other, and throughout the session, took it in turns so that the dogs didn't get bored. I asked the handler to talk me through her sendaway procedure, not just from the set up, but what were you doing before that. It transpired that the handlers were putting the dogs in the car having a coffee and a rest before going onto sendaway, scent and stays. This had become their natural breaking point. So the dog had become to learn that the sendaway came after she had enjoyed a snooze in the car, and that it was never linked to other exercises. *(See Linking)*.

Although we know that the dog does not think backwards and forwards, we also know that the dog's reactions are triggered by each other. In order to perform in a very specific way, he needs to learn how to sequence and link in the way that we need it. Once the handler learned how to teach the dog to link exercises together in training, she then went out the following week and won the championship class. All her other training had obviously been very sound, and it was just a simple chink in the armour that had prevented success previously. It is hard to believe that such a tiny error can cost so much.

When Everything Goes Wrong!

What do you do when just everything goes wrong in the ring? The dog is totally switched off, and even though he goes through the motions of doing some of the exercises, he is no where near as good as he can be in training.

Most handlers will have been told that it is themselves that are at fault. But what use is that for an answer? It just makes you feel totally inadequate, you feel like giving up. What you must do is look at yourself carefully, and try to examine what it is that is different about you and the way that you handle the dog. This might not just be one thing, there may be several answers to the puzzle. At the extreme, handlers have a fit of nerves, or fear of being shown up, and give all the wrong signals to the dog. So then we have to look at ways of controlling the handler, before we can move on to examining the ways in which the dog might perceive the actual situation. Firstly be aware that a judge, in most cases, is just another dog handler taking a day off from competing and doing their bit for the show society.

Every judge is a different person, and of course they will all react to their day of judgement in differing ways, but on the whole they are 'human', and most will be able to recall being in a similar position to you. So go in and relax! Easier said then done I can hear you say, but think of the pressure on the other end of the scale when top handlers go into the ring with an audience of people. Some of the audience wanting and expecting them to do well, and some of their fellow competitors hoping that they don't! (Are people really like that? Surely not!) So clearly everyone has a certain amount of pressure, it is learning to deal with it that is the important thing. Many handlers find relaxation techniques and yoga very useful and others have turned to herbal remedies to help.

Then you must make sure that all of the exercises taught to the dog are progressed to the point that will make sense to the dog in the ring. You must make sure that your voice sounds the same, your posture is correct and your footwork is accurate. Many handlers will teach excellent static exercises to the dog and then fail to combine those with the footwork and correct signals in the ring, and so the dog cannot understand what the handler wants. As you know from personal experience, anything that is too complicated for you to understand soon becomes boring, or is dismissed as beyond you, unless the goal is extremely rewarding. Even then, the goal sometimes seems so inaccessible that after a few enthusiastic attempts, your tendency, as an intelligent human, is to switch off, or change to something that you can do successfully. So who can blame the dog? He is trying to understand a different species from himself, a foreign language, a different culture, a different life style, a different recreation, and 'someone' keeps moving the goal posts!

To make sure that you are getting it right for your dog, read the sections on *understanding, linking, routines, timing*, and make sure that you are following all of the *technique* procedures accurately. Create ring like situations, not just for the dog but for you, get a friend to steward you from scratch, event to the point of asking what ring number you have, and the name and breed of your dog, 'are you ready', adding anything that a steward might say. That little bit of preparation will make both you and the dog more accustomed to the ring situation, and more relaxed when you enter the ropes.

Only in the Ring!

Many handlers suffer from 'only in the ring' syndrome! This tends to mean that the dog is fine in training but when he gets within the ring ropes he is a different dog. Mostly the answer lies within the handler. They tend to be, to all intents and purposes, a different person when faced with the stress of the competition. Many handlers get within the ring ropes and race around like a bat out of hell, or try so hard to be controlled that their pace is unnaturally slow or stilted. Not keeping calm, not handling as you have trained, even something simple like not smiling as you normally do in training will throw some dogs.

Many handlers are not sufficiently rehearsed in ring technique, and so the dog as well as the handler is confused by what is going on around him. Handlers will find it difficult to keep the dog, (and themselves) in the right mode when they are not used to being kept waiting by stewards. The concentration level necessary to keep the dog ready to work must be well schooled and the handler must, as part of the training procedure, teach the dog to switch on and off when and as required.

All of the above are a very necessary part of Obedience ring craft. You need help from like-minded people to condition yourself into the procedures. It is simple to learn to turn when you are ready, not so simple to turn as told under pressure. You need someone to talk to you at the beginning of an exercise, just as a steward would. Set up role-play exercises, pretending that you are at a show. This is beneficial for both you and the dog.

Spooks In The Ring

Sometimes things have happened that are beyond your control. The dog may spook at certain instances, objects, or particular types of people in the ring. Maybe a judge inadvertently frightened your dog. Noisy wet weather outfits are one of the main culprits for this.

To work on building your dog's confidence you need to use a counter conditioning technique, with distraction training. Find a situation that the dog is ultra confident in and introduce gently and from a distance the

object or person that the dog is spooked by. Use your special toy or an especially tasty titbit to teach the dog to play or accept being with the problem, and then gradually bring the problem nearer to the dog. There is no easy answer only patient training to teach a good association with good occurrences. Try to get the dog in the right frame of mind before he becomes frightened. Avoid the fear being brought on by surprise by choosing the situations in which to train. Fear is far more difficult to deal with for you the handler if you had not anticipated the fear response in your dog. Anticipating a problem means that you can start to steer the dog away, even before the fear has had time to get a hold.

Keeping Your Cool!

How easy to say, and how hard for some to do. It is probably equally difficult to keep calm if your are doing a run off for first place in your first beginners, as it is to run off for first place at Crufts. Keeping your composure is so important, because if this goes so does your deportment, your footwork, and your rhythm. Your voice turns to a squeak, and even your body gives off a different odour.

Some handlers find that Yoga and or homeopathic remedies help control and calm the nerves.

Preparation is the Best Tool

Before the show you should have got yourself into the habit of turning on a steward's commands. Even if this has to be a tape recording, it is better than not practicing at all.

You should make sure that you have covered in training all the exercises needed for the test, and all the various pointers covered in linking so that the dog does not get confused when you go from one exercise to the next. Make sure that you have good deportment and that your feet automatically go into a set pattern when you hear the turns called. The more you have practiced the less of this you have to concentrate on in the ring, and so it will be easier to keep calm.

Before entering the ring make sure that you know exactly what you will be expected to do. Watch the test before you go in. You should not try to memorise the round, but you should be aware what direction you will be starting in. You should know if there are any specific twists or turns that you should be aware of, or is there an unexpected halt somewhere. In the higher classes what pace will be first, where the first position comes, where the dog is meant to be landing in the sendaway, where the correct scent cloth will be. You should accustom yourself to the steward's voice, and keep an eye on the ring running order so that you are not called from the furthest corner of the show ground because you are wanted to work your dog.

Think Positive

Before it is your turn spend some time getting yourself and the dog in the correct frame of mind for working, by going through some training routines.

Don't be tempted to go through finished exercises, save the masterpiece for the unveiling in the ring. Olympic sprinters don't keep testing the finished article, they prepare and train prior to the event and warm up just before the start!

Think positive and do some breathing exercises to calm your nervous system down before you start. Keep taking deep breaths as you go in to the ring, and concentrate on your dog and what is being said. Block out everything else, and pretend that you are training with a friend, force yourself to be as normal as possible. If you feel that you prefer to work without a crowd, keep your eye on the ring and when the judge looks as if he is not busy, go over and ask if he would like you to work. Even if it is not your turn, it is quite possible he/she will say yes when there is no strict running order.

Don't try too hard, some handlers get so strung up in the fact that they have not got that illusive win that they wanted. At the end of the day there is always another dog show, you chose the sport as your hobby, relax and enjoy it.

Show Etiquette

The judge, steward and show officials have given up their day to help you to enjoy yours. They do it for various reasons. Some feel that, as competitors, they are giving something back when they forgo a day's competing to judge or help out. Some want to remain involved in the sport, in-between dogs, or after retiring from competition, and most I hope, do it because they enjoy it.

It is enjoyable to see lots of different dogs performing a test that you as a judge have set. It is a great learning ground, you can certainly see where a lot of handlers make mistakes. You observe the silly mistakes that handlers make, that can waste the whole round. At one show when I was judging, two handlers in my ring threw things out of their pockets whilst working, presumably because they had become loose or irritating, unfortunately and by coincidence I think, both handlers had thrown the articles to one side of the sendaway box. Guess where their dogs went on the sendaway exercise!

In entering under a judge, or finding yourself in their class when you get to the show, you have agreed to accept their decision, (providing it is within the rules set down by the Kennel Club or governing body). It pays in life to be pleasant, 'smile and the world smiles with you', as the old saying goes. Your judge is human too. Even if you find the judge's decision hard to take, so long as the rules are followed, he/she is entitled to their opinion, so you might as well grin and bear it. You can always avoid entering under that judge again. If you are really sore, send a polite note to the show secretary after the show. If he is a bad judge over all, show societies need to know, and will learn not to invite them again when people continually ask not to go into their class.

If you feel that the judge has acted outside of the rules, then ask for a quiet word with him at the end of your round, or when he has a minute. Give him chance to explain, you may have misunderstood. If you are still not happy then the next step is to have a word with the chief steward of the show. He/she may be able to help you to iron out any problems, but don't expect him to side with you if yours is a borderline case, he will almost always give the judge the final decision.

In all situations it pays to keep your cool and be sure of your facts. Always carry an up to date copy of the rules so that you can check your facts, before you open your mouth and look a fool. Refer directly to the rules that you feel are not being adhered to in any discussion or complaint with the judge or management. In extreme cases of misconduct, you can make an official complaint to the Kennel Club or governing body. In the UK, the procedure for doing this can be found in the KC Year Book, available from the Kennel Club, other countries will have a similar system.

Going into the Ring

When it is approaching the time for your turn, wait near the ring entrance. Make sure the score steward knows, in plenty of time, that you are available and waiting to work. Sometimes handlers will try to jump the queue by asking the score steward if they may work. If you see a lot of people around, you may need to point out to the score steward that your number is next on the scoreboard and that you wish to work. Sometimes the judge overrules the running order. Usually this happens because he has been kept waiting earlier, or because of bad weather etc., if this is the case you may have to have your name added to the list with the score steward. Be patient. If you feel that your running order is going to clash with your stay exercise or with your running order in another ring, have a word with the judge or score steward. Stays will take priority because they cannot hold up 60 handlers for the sake of one. A running order in the first ten, or in the championship class will take precedence, after that, but the judge must be informed and the score board marked with your reasons for not attending on time to be on the safe side.

When eventually you are invited into the ring, smile and say hello. Be attentive to anything that the judge or steward has to say. Try as hard as you can, to follow the instructions immediately they are given, and be as helpful as you can. Politely ask any questions if you are not clear on some point, and thank the judge/steward for their help. At the end of the round, thank the judge for the nice round, and the steward for his assistance. If your dog has not faired so well, or you have had to help him, thank both the judge and steward for their time.

At the end of your round, check the scoreboard and raise any queries first with the score steward, and then if necessary with the judge. In the lower classes you are almost always told (while you are still in the ring) how many points you have lost and on what. In the higher classes this is not the case, so it is worth looking at the judge's score sheet if this is made available to you, and check the master score sheet to make sure that they tally. Even judges make addition mistakes, take it from one who has made a few!

Sometimes, if you have not done so well, you may not wish to complete the scent or stay exercises, if this is the case you should inform the score steward that you wish to withdraw and ask them to mark the scoreboard accordingly. There is nothing so infuriating for a judge than to have to wait around at the end of the day for someone who has gone home. But, the decision to not continue should not be taken lightly, it is never over until the end, and you may have done better than you think. Not all judges mark in the same manner and a high score under an attentive judge may not be as high as you think!

Stay Tests

In preparation for the stay exercise, make sure that you are at the stay ring or appointed area, at least five minutes before the set time. Most stay stewards will want to position you and take your ring number so that they can be ready to start the test on time. It is in your own interests to be there in plenty of time, because then the dog has time to acclimatise to the situation. With a bit of luck you can choose a good spot to leave your dog, although at some shows you will be told where to stand, this may be in numerical or running order, or just for the stewards convenience.

Be aware that the rules on extra commands and signals apply equally in the stay exercises, and even in the lower classes you will lose your points if you talk to your dog after you have been told 'last command.' At the end of the stay tests check what the steward has written against your ring number - if you do not agree with his comments, now is the time to object, it will be too late at the end of the day. Sometimes stewards are inexperienced helpers, and of course innocent mistakes can be made - so don't just ask if your dog was okay, they may have marked movement against the wrong dog - check what is written there and then.

Scent Discrimination

The same applies in scent as stays, in that you must be at the ringside in plenty of time to do the exercise. In the UK scent is conducted after all handlers have worked. As soon as it looks like scent is about to start, go to the ring and find out what the plan is. Sometimes the judge will opt to stick to the running order, and therefore you will work in the same order as you did in the main round - this is especially so in the higher classes, but can apply at any level. More often scent it taken in any order, but be careful, not all handlers will do the test, so if you don't want to miss out, be aware of where they are up to, and get in line - often handlers will form a queue, but it can go down quickly.

At the End of The Day

Always check the score board at the end of the day, you may have done better than you thought. Every judge will mark faults a little differently. Some will mark every little thing, whilst others will mark only major faults. Under some judges for instance, the loss of seven points will mean you may as well go home. Under other more critical judges you may end up winning. Judges will be anxious to make sure that anyone in the top six or so receives their prize, make sure that you are there, or that the score steward knows where you are if it is possible that you might be included.

If you can stick around for the prize giving, even if you are not included this time, it is good to congratulate your fellow competitors. If you are lucky enough to be placed or even win, remember to shake hands and thank all concerned.

Etiquette at the show is all about following the rules, being polite, and treating others as you would expect them to treat you, basic 'life' etiquette really. Remember most people go to a show for a day out away from their usual lifestyle, for only a very small minority, will it ever be anything more. Most are in the sport for recreation, whatever your dreams, intentions or ambitions, try to avoid spoiling some one's day!

When you get home, and have time to reflect on the day, why not drop a line to the show secretary and thank the committee for a good show, they don't get a lot of recognition, but they work really hard so that you can enjoy your day.

Diversification

Mixing the Disciplines

Many handlers seem to have a fear of mixing the types of training with the same dog. Particular common phobias are those of mixing conformation showing with competitive obedience, for fear that the dog will want to keep sitting in the show ring. Working trials and obedience are often avoided in case the dog will not be able to cope with scent discrimination in obedience, as well as the area search in working trials.

There are a few handlers who, over the years, have proved that, with careful and well thought out training procedures, the dog should not become confused.

British handlers seem to be the most fearful, with only a comparative handful of handlers currently mixing their sports, and even fewer who have taken their animals to championship or top level in more than one field. There are probably two main reasons for this, one the fear of confusion, but even more, the fact that competition is so fierce, that all of the handler's energy, money and available time are put into their favoured sport.

In recent times there has been more handlers making a link with

Heelwork to Music/Freestyle and competitive obedience, because the obedience exercises make a good basis for the HTM/Freestyle moves.

Outside of the UK, there is more emphasis on promoting the handler's breed as a good all rounder, so it is more common to see dogs enjoying a variety of disciplines.

In Britain some breeds are encouraged in this way, and this is particularly common in the rarer working type breeds which are imported and then bred in the UK.

Within Your Chosen Sport

By the fact that you are reading this book, I would naturally assume that one of your main interests is competitive obedience, either solely or with other sports. If you are a single tracker, and obedience is your only goal, do not be afraid to introduce your dog to different things by way of a little light relief. In the section on circuit training jumps and obstacles are introduced to keep things novel and interesting. If you become too single tracked the more laid back dog can become bored, and the very wound up dog can become even more so because of the predictability of life. Take the retrieve exercise and the Leonberger as an example, unless you are a very inventive trainer, you may well reach the stage where he looks at you as if to say 'If you wanted it why did you throw it away?' The Collie on the other hand becomes so hyped up, wanting to get on to the chasing part, that he finds it hard to control himself whilst the article is thrown. I am not trying to suggest that by introducing a jump or a tracking session, that you will solve your retrieve problems, far from it! But, if you refrain from becoming too intense on specific issues, training will become more natural and more of a pleasure for both sides of the team. Even if all you have time for is to teach a few tricks in the home, you will find that the lighter side of training has a good effect on the rest.

Diversification is particularly useful for dogs that have already been taught all of the obedience exercises. Handlers will find that the minute that they stop teaching new things, the dog starts to become very clever at racing ahead in the things that he knows, this is especially true of the very keen type dogs. If you never stop teaching, then it keeps you both on your toes, and neither dog nor handler becomes blasé.

Obviously, time has a bearing on how much you can dabble in, or even take seriously, the various sports and disciplines, but if you can, make the time to add spice to your dog's life. Understanding how to teach your dog other things will also help you to understand more about dogs. Choose an exercise that your dog may have a natural aptitude for, or that you find interesting, and have a go!

Clubs

The majority of people reading this book will be members of dog training clubs, many of which are very good and give a high standard of instruction based on behavioural knowledge and up to date methods of training. Others (although these are becoming less and less) promote a style of training, which leaves handlers who attend week after week, tramping around a hall going through the motions of exercises that, although they look fairly accurate, would never win any competitions. Then those handlers wonder why, when they get to a show they are not often in the top six. It is easy to fall into an egotistical trap. Inside all of us is a little bit of a show off, and most people who reach beginner competition standard, are at a very advanced level, in comparison to the rest of their club members and the general public. At this level you may even be invited to demonstrate or to instruct. But, this type of training does not usually help your competition standard, and certainly does not increase the dog's 'want'.

It should be emphasised at this point, that you should not read this and hang up your club subscription for good, far from it, we need good clubs, and handlers like you, to set an example of what can be attained. However, you should give serious thought to what you are doing out on the club floor. Analyse whether your efforts are doing any good from the point of view of stimulating high interest and the dog's 'want' to work with you.

Some clubs are very competitive, and offer a high standard of professional style tuition. If you are fortunate enough to join a club whose aims are set high, then you are very lucky - make the most of it. If your club is more akin to the former, then maybe you can work your way around the situation without upsetting some of our most dedicated trainers. If there are enough handlers - keen like you - you could ask the committee to consider starting a special class within your club, purely for competition work. Why not ask local competitive instructors, ticket or C handlers to guest instruct, it is even worth offering payment or expenses in order to get the right sort of person to help you. Failing that just have a working session helping each other when the pet classes have finished.

Try to avoid the situation where you feel you must break away from your KC registered club, because without clubs we have no shows. If clubs lose people like you, then what have new handlers and enthusiasts to look to and aim for? New handlers coming into dog training may never hear of competitive obedience without someone like you to show them the way.

If all else fails, you can always go along to socialise and make the tea, or join the committee and help to run things, perhaps this way you will get that special competitive class.

Instructing is another possibility, and there are various bodies who hold excellent courses to help you to learn more about teaching people to train their dogs. They also issue certificates at various levels to confirm your ability.

If you don't yet belong to a club, the best way of find one is to go to your local obedience show, check in the catalogue for local entrants, and then ask them for advice on the best place to train.

The internet is a good place to look for information too.

Heelwork to Music/Musical Freestyle

Heelwork to music (HTM) is a relatively new concept or discipline of training, which adds another dimension to the training of heelwork that can be enjoyable for both handler and dog.

There are various types of competition around the world, the rules varying according to taste and demand. In the UK for HTM the dog must be off lead in the heel position (on the left or right of the handler) for most of the time. Other moves are allowed, but must be linked with heelwork. Freestyle as the name suggests allows much more innovation and the dog is allowed to work at a distance from the handler for more time than he is in HTM, heelwork is allowed in Freestyle but should be kept to a minimum. Handlers strive to create interesting and novel routines and this is particularly apparent in Freestyle.

Freestyle is usually a blend of dog obedience, dance, tricks and sometimes elements of agility. The dog and handler perform dance-oriented footwork in time to the music, and are judged as a team. Both Freestyle and HTM require the handler to interpret the music and marks are gained for technical merit, accuracy, content and interpretation.

In the UK a number of handlers had dabbled with working their dog to music but 'Heelwork to Music' as we now know it was given its debut by top Obedience and Agility trainer Mary Ray. She gave some awe-inspiring performances at the Crufts dog show and around the UK. In the early days the events were limited to demonstrations, but now there are a number of competitions open to all around the country.

If you are new to HTM/Freestyle it is a good idea to go along and watch an event first to help you get a feel for the sport. It will also show you the levels and give you an idea of what you will need to achieve to put in a reasonable performance in the Starters class - then go for it - I'm sure you and your dog will have fun.

The competition is open to anyone at any level of obedience, you don't need to be working championship level, all that you need is a reasonable level of control and a feel for music, and you have the basis on which to build a routine. You don't need any formal dance training although watching dance performances might help you in your interpretation of the music.

The principles of training for competitive obedience are also suitable for this sport. The dog must have the want and enjoy heelwork to enable it to work in a relaxed manner, but all of the other exercises can be incorporated and/or adjusted to fit routines to music.

Clicker and Target Training

This is extremely popular for teaching HTM/freestyle as it allows the dog to work at a distance with no or little contact. It also promotes freethinking in the dog and often leads to innovation created by the dog in his enthusiasm to work for the clicker or target.

Other Moves

Some of the more common moves that you will find useful are briefly described below.

Weave Through Legs

Use treats to encourage the dog thorough one leg then the other. It is usually best to start at a static, but eventually the dog can be encouraged through while you move forwards.

Walk Backwards

Use a treat, toy or target at nose height and push back as the dog steps back reward. Once achieved extend.

Circle

Around a prop - Put a pole in the ground and encourage the dog around it with a treat or target stick. Around the handler, use a target stick, hold it out at arm's length and encourage the dog to follow.

Walk Ahead

The ideal method is a target stick. Make sure the dog is very keen for his stick and then hold it ahead of you and move forward. The dog will then automatically be walking away and ahead of you.

Reverse

Have the dog in a stand in front of you (facing away) and then with a titbit, toy or target on his nose push back so that he takes a step of two back. Work in this until he will walk several steps back and even try it though your legs. To get him through your legs and back into heel, use a reward in both hands, push back with the right and then encourage forward with your left (or visa versa).

Twizzle and Twist

Use a target stick or a titbit in your fingers. Turn it slowly to start with in a reasonably wide circle that the dog can follow. Once he has turned give him the treat. You may have to treat on a half turn to start with if the dog is confused. Try to the left and to the right and then link the twizzle and twist keywords.

Donelda Guy a popular HTM/Freestyle winner.

Paw Lifts

A variation on give a paw, many handlers now use a variety of paw lifts within their routines. Some dogs give this behaviour quite readily, use of clicker to mark the behaviour is the quickest way to get it under cue. If not the dog can be encouraged to lift with gentle handling under the leg, or by using a titbit on the nose and pulling to one side until the opposite paw automatically lifts.

These are just some of the more common moves as a taster to get you started, there are many more moves that you can create. To get a good start try to go on a course or watch a training video - once you have the basics you can become inventive on your own.

Clicker Training
What Is It All About?

The idea behind clicker training is to teach the dog that, when he hears the sound of the clicker, he knows that a reward, (usually food, but it could be anything the dog really values) is coming.

This then becomes a very clear, precise and stable signal to the dog, that the behaviour he has given has been the one required and it will be rewarded - he is then much more likely to try to repeat the good behaviour in order to gain the reward. The clicker becomes such a good signal to the dog that, as he develops the skills, it would seem that he works to hear the sound of the clicker alone. You will reach a stage when less reward is needed as the behaviours and the system of training becomes self-rewarding. This is because the dog is having so much fun working with you.

The system is based on the work of a number of behavioural scientists but in particular, on the theories of the scientist B. F. Skinner. It was developed for bird and animal training for the military during the Second World War. Later, in the 1960's it was used in dolphin training and was found to be a most

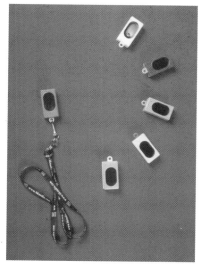

Clickers are now available from a number of sources including specialist pet shops, trade stands at shows, by mail (address at the back of this book). (Photo J Midgely)

effective 'hands off' style of training.

In more recent times animal trainers world-wide have found it to be an effective system for all manner of training. Its more scientific name is 'successive approximation', often referred to as 'shaping', because the art is in shaping, or progressing a behaviour, nearer and nearer to the required goal.

In 1984 Karen Pryor, a well-respected dolphin trainer, wrote a book that has since become one of the most popular books on operant conditioning. Despite its title, 'Don't Shoot The Dog!' it was not primarily written for dog trainers. However, dog trainers across the world took the book to their hearts because it provided a much-needed path to more humane motivational and enjoyable style of dog training.

The clicker is a small, plastic, rectangular box. It is fitted with a metal tongue that makes the characteristic 'click' sound when it is depressed.

What Does The Clicker Mean To The Dog?

At first, the sound of the clicker means nothing to the dog. He may have an interest in its sound, but once he is conditioned to understand what the sound implies, he will actively work towards discovering and performing the behaviours that produce the click and hence lead to a good reward.

He will learn that:

(1) The sound 'marks' the aspect of a behaviour that you require and therefore wish to reinforce by reward. It is rather like taking a photograph to catch the precise behaviour wanted. The clicker is sometimes referred to as a 'bridge', i.e. the clicker becomes the bridge between the action and the reward and allows the dog to understand the link between the two.

(2) The sound means that what he has just done is correct and will be rewarded.

(3) The click can mark the end of the behaviour, i.e. the dog learns to come for his reward when he hears the click. In this instance the clicker is known as a 'terminating bridge'.

(4) The click can also mean 'that's good, keep going'. This tends to become the case in more advanced training or when the clicker is used to reinforce, improve and encourage behaviours or exercises already taught. In this instance the clicker is known as an 'intermediate bridge'.

You will not have to continue clicking on every behaviour forever. The clicker is meant to be a training tool and so can be used less and less as the dog learns what is wanted and only introduced when teaching new behaviours, or when you wish to sharpen, re-establish or fine tune behaviours already taught.

Why Not Just Use Treats or Verbal/Physical Reward

In more traditional styles of training, before the use of conditioned reinforcers such as clickers, it was imperative that the reward came at the time the dog performed the correct act. Of course this is still the case unless you condition your dog.

With conditioned reinforcer training, e.g. clicker training, it does not matter what the dog is doing when he gets his treat, because the message that the dog was correct came with the click and, once conditioned correctly, he will connect good behaviour with the sound of the click. The click carries the message 'You are right' and it effectively buys you time.

You can give extra treats if you are especially pleased or if the dog has made a good progression, but one single click will get the message over, if it comes at the exact time of the correct act.

It is important with all training to keep it enjoyable for both you and the dog. Therefore, make sure that at every session, you put in some easy exercises to help give the dog confidence and keep his interest and motivation levels high.

The reason for using the clicker is that it takes away any need for compulsion in training, there is no need for physical manipulation of the dog. It motivates the animal to be responsive, keen and attentive. There is no place and no need for physical or verbal punishment, the behaviours are 'shaped' using positive reinforcement. You can even discipline an animal using this system (this will be explained later).

Implications For Competition

One of the misconceptions in obedience training is that handlers automatically assume that the clicker is an 'attention getter', but this is not what the system is all about. The clicker must be conditioned and trained to be affective. If used indiscriminately the dog will soon learn to ignore it.

Some handlers feel that the clicker is no good because it cannot be used in the ring, well of course not but, nor can any other training aid! You will

Clicking on near positions can shape a closer present. Ignoring or giving a 'try again' command for others will gradually extinguish the undesirable present positions like this one. (Photo M White)

also find that, because of the way the system works, it is easier to dispense with the clicker and its rewards for ring work, than it is the toy in your hand. This is because you can work with the food/reward off your person from the start.

The clicker can be used to shape new exercises or behaviours and to put the polish on exercises already taught. Of course once they have a good understanding of the system, clever trainers can think up their own conditioned reinforcers that are not visible or audible in the ring!

The Rewards (Primary Reinforcers)

Most trainers use food for clicker training. It is easy to dispense and the vast majority of dogs will respond to some kind of food reward. This is your 'primary reinforcer'. However, it is also possible to use other primary reinforcers such as toys, play or whatever the dog really likes

Caution is needed if the dog has a tendency to gain weight. The food should be added to the total food allowance for the day, therefore it might be necessary to feed less at meal times.

It is a good idea to have a selection of treats, so that some favourite treats can be reserved for extra effort. The titbits should be very small so that 20 or so repetitions will not leave your dog feeling full.

Where Do Commands Fit In?

Using a clicker helps you to get the behaviour you want, by allowing the dog to learn rather than being manipulated into the action. You should put the commands in, once the dog has learnt the action, then he will not get the incorrect association with the word. If you put in words before the behaviour is perfected, the dog may be learning a completely different association. For example if you continually say the word 'sit' but, achieve only a stand, he may think that sit means stand! (But then this applies whatever training method or principle you choose).

How To Use A Clicker

Getting to grips with a clicker is fun. It will not spoil any training you have already done, and will only take a few minutes of your time. Clickers are very inexpensive to buy, so it is worth giving them a try and it won't break the bank if you decide that you are not going to use it in the future.

Occasionally you will find a dog that is worried by the sound of the clicker. If you have a sound sensitive dog, muffle the sound of the clicker by cupping it in your hand, your pocket or holding it behind your back until the dog comes to realise that the sound has a good connection. You can get clickers with a variable level of sound. In extreme cases it may be necessary to sound the clicker well away from the dog while he is happily playing with you. You could even use a recording to desensitise very sensitive dogs. It is a good idea to sound the clicker every time you feed your dog but again, remember to muffle the sound to begin with. In all cases do not hold the clicker close to the dog's head or ears - try it on your own ears to see how loud it sounds.

Below is a step by step training routine. However, you should remember to not go on for too long. Always stop while the dog is still interested and hungry.

Step 1 - Arm yourself with a clicker, a supply of very palatable titbits in a container and a hungry dog.

Step 2 - Now you need to teach the dog what the click means, and that it means the same wherever you are. To begin with give a click, (just once) and give the dog a treat. Repeat this until it is clear that the dog is making a connection. Lots of dogs achieve this very quickly (within 10 clicks). Others will take longer, maybe a few minutes or even a few sessions. Just like us, dogs are all different so keep going, the dog will get the idea sooner or later, assuming the reward is interesting to him. A good test that he is making some association between the clicker and the reward is, if he is looking away and looks back to the food when you click.

Step 3 - If you were to continue giving rewards every time, the dog would not have to work hard to get his reward, and therefore would cease to try very hard. So the next step is to space the timing of the reward a little, this is called randomising. To do this, click, wait a few seconds, and then reward. Next do the same, but add a few more seconds and reward. Then click and reward immediately. The secret is to not be predictable. Once you have reached the stage where you click and the dog looks attentively at you, in any circumstance or environment, you know the clicker has become a 'conditioned reinforcer'. You can now start to use it to train, reinforce or 'shape' a behaviour.

Step 4 - To start the training, it is a good idea to train a fun exercise, because although the exercise is not important, it helps you to relax and learn. You have a choice of how to go about this:
(a) Find a way to get a behaviour to occur naturally.
Put the dog in a situation where you know he will give you a behaviour without your interference.
Or
(b) Wait for a behaviour to occur naturally.
For example, the dog may take up a position of his own accord.
Or
(c) Induce the dog into doing something.
You could use a titbit up over his head to induce a sit.

Or

(d) Use something the dog already knows and build on it.

If the dog already knows the down position you could use this to develop a roll over.

When the dog is doing what you want, or is working towards it, click. It is important to click when the dog is actually doing what you want, not before or after. Remember you cannot expect the finished exercise straight away. For example, if teaching a roll over from a down, the first step to click on is the down, next a slight movement to one side, then a little more and so on. Once a progression has been made, stop clicking on lesser behaviours. Keep working on this step until the behaviour seems to be stable and complete.

Step 5 - To extend the duration or gain the repetition of a behaviour, withhold the click for extended times or until the dog has given you more than one repetition of the behaviour but, build up by the second for the best results.

Step 6 - Continue to click on good behaviours but sometimes withhold treats. In other words the click is motivation enough but remember to keep randomising - sometimes rewarding sometimes not and varying the time the dog has to wait.

Now you have reached the stage where you are not giving a treat for every click. If you have trained using treats before, you will now be giving far less food than you used to do, and your dog's performance should have actually improved.

Getting Behaviours Under Cue (Command, Signal or Sound)

The word 'cue' is the technical jargon used for the command, signal or sound you use to trigger the behaviour, e.g. the word 'sit', once trained, becomes the cue for the dog to take up the sit position. It's like taking your cue on stage. The basic principle of getting things under cue is simple.

The cue should be given only once and presented in a clear, precise, non-threatening manner. Each time the cue is given, it should be identical. This is sometimes more difficult when moving from training to working at a distance or in competition, demonstration or work – but in order for the dog to have a clear understanding of what is required, the cue introduced in training must be progressed to the performance later. Therefore, you should give thought to what the cue will be and how it will be given, before you start.

Step 1 - Develop the behaviour that you want by using the clicker as a conditioned reinforcer as discussed above. You should be reasonably sure of achieving the behaviour every time before putting on the cue.

Once you have this, give a word, sound or signal that will mean you want that behaviour to occur and, at the same time induce the desired behaviour. For example say 'sit' and lure the dog with a titbit into a sit. Click as the dog sits. To be sure the dog understands you should achieve 20 - 40 correct repetitions (over time) in a variety of environments.

Step 2 - Once you can do this you should cease to click for the behaviour unless it occurs when you have given the command or signal, the command or signal becomes 'the cue'.

The behaviour will then become less attractive to the dog, unless he is given the command or signal, i.e. he will want to do the behaviour 'on cue'. After this the occurrences of the behaviour will dwindle down to the naturally occurring level although he may go through his repertoire when trying to fathom out a new task.

Step 3 – Once the dog is competent add distractions and changes of training area over time.

Telling The Dog He Is Wrong

You can actually develop a signal to the dog that tells him when he is wrong and, as a consequence, he will not be reinforced. The words 'no', 'try again', 'oops' or 'wrong' could be used. Each time the dog does something other than what you want you could give a negative word or signal that is never rewarded. This word should not sound hard or angry, but should be a simple signal to tell the dog that he is not correct and should try again. Consider the word you use carefully - if you have used the word 'no' in a harsh manner in the past, then it is not the best word to be used in this instance.

Time Out!

Occasionally a dog will not respond in the correct way to something he has already learned. Before doing anything about this, you should be sure that the dog has disobeyed, rather than simply misunderstood. It should be remembered that distractions, new environments, and even minor changes in you can confuse the dog and lead to incorrect behaviours. If this could be the case simply start again at the beginning and guide the dog through the procedure.

However, if the dog really does disobey, the worst punishment is to withdraw totally, taking your training treats with you. Give your dog and yourself time to cool off, and then start again repeating the command or signal given previously. Usually this gives a quick response. Withdrawal can be repeated if the dog is still disobeying, but most dogs are devastated by the lack of handler and rewards and really try to comply, if they truly understand.

Extending Exercises

Some more experienced dogs can learn that the sound of the clicker is an intermediate bridge and means 'keep going - what you are doing is good'. However, more often the click will signal the end of a behaviour (terminating bridge) and the dog will come back for his reward when he hears the sound. Therefore, it is a good idea to establish a signal that means 'keep going'.

Often gentle praise, or a food reward without the click will tell the dog that he is correct and to continue. Another way is to repeat the command as you click. Start with an easy exercise such as sit, and work close to the dog so that you can keep the dog sitting using your training aids. You should then introduce a terminating signal and/or command. Use this command along with a procedure that will break the position. For example, introduce the command 'that'll do' and move the dog off the spot by putting your hand in this collar and easing him onto his feet. You probably don't need to reward this behaviour much as it is self-rewarding, but you can click on it. Once the dog is getting the idea, you will be able to do it without the contact.

Without a signal that the exercise is finished, the dog will make up his own mind and this may not coincide with your ideas! A good clear signal will leave the dog feeling confident and motivated and will give you better overall control.

Some Old Rules Still Apply

Like all training you should not go on for long periods of time. Little and often is best, with lots of variation. You may find that you reach a point when little progress is being made, this is the same in all learning and is called a 'plateau'. Just keep going you will find success is around the corner.

If the dog starts to go wrong simply go back to basics and start all over again. It is far easier and less confusing for you and the dog, than trying to correct problems. Dogs trained by correction can stand out, because they often do things incorrectly and then correct themselves believing that this is what the handler wants. Be careful that the dog does not think that parts of the shaping process are meant to be in the end product.

If you are training more than one dog, they need to be controlled so that they can't interfere with or distract each other during training. It is best if they are not in the same room or area, at least to start with. However, once the dogs are competent, working in front of each other may make them more keen to come training. If they are in the same area, put them in a crate or tie them up. If they become too noisy or obviously distressed, it is best to put them out of sight and hearing of the training until you can work on this issue as a part of the training process - you may need help for this.

If you make a mistake just play with the dog, smile and start again.

Alternatively, go and have a cup of tea and come back to training when you have 'got your act together'.

Clicker Training at Dog Club

Many trainers worry about their dog's reaction to other people's clickers. However, you will find that this is not normally a problem. Even in a class full of handlers all using a clicker, the dog very quickly comes to understand which click is his, ignoring all others in favour of the sound of his own handler's clicker.

Some very sound sensitive dogs can become distracted, especially if indoors in a room that echoes - if this is the case it is better to allow the dog time to get used to the noise by sitting on the side lines and not training for a while.

Condition the dog at home or in an environment where there are no distractions. Don't try to introduce something new in an environment that is distracting. Once he is very confident, introduce him into smaller groups to start with. It is perhaps better to start outside where the acoustics will not play a part in confusing your dog's very sensitive hearing.

Target Training

Target training is generally seen as an offshoot of clicker training. However it can be used on its own. Used in conjunction with the clicker training concept it works very well. A target is simply something the dog learns to touch or follow. Your fingers can be used as a target to the dog, especially in exercises where the dog follows your hand. However, your hand does many other things and using it as a target can be confusing unless you are very careful and focused.

Most trainers use a wooden stick painted black on the main body but with a white tip, rather like a magic wand. Alternatively you could use a telescopic lecture stick, put a little white electrical tape on the end to make the end stand out. In the absence of any of these you can use a piece of wood from a tree. The stick should not be too long, about 2 feet (60cm) maximum and around 1/4 inch (10-12 cm) diameter.

The dog is taught to touch the end and then, this becomes a very positive target that can be used to encourage the dog into correct positions or places, to train or perfect a variety of exercises/behaviours.

The dog can be taught to target to other items too. A marker or mat on the ground is a good way of teaching the dog to go to a set point.

Teaching The Dog To Target

Step 1 - The dog must be taught that when he is correct he will get a reward, clicker training is the ideal way. As with normal clicker training, you may find it better to have your rewards in a pot, away from your person so that the dog is not simply watching your hands for the food. If you have already conditioned the dog in this way, he will find this next progression easier to comprehend.

Step 2 - Hold out the stick, many dogs will immediately go towards it because it is new and interesting. Click as soon as his nose touches the stick (it is usually best to hold the clicker in the same hand as the target stick but, be careful as the vibration/sound travelling down the stick may worry some dogs). If he is not interested be patient, move the stick around a little, and tease with the reward. You can click any movement towards the stick and/or touches near to where you want the dog and then, shape towards the right place, as you would shape other behaviours. To start with it does not matter if the dog touches the main body of the stick or even attempts to hold it, click on any move towards the right behaviour. Keep repeating until the dog has made a connection.

Step 3 - Move the stick away from the dog a little and continue to reward each time he touches the stick, ignore any other behaviours. If he gives the stick a good or very positive touch give extra rewards. He will now have to actively move to the stick.

Step 4 - Once you feel the dog has the idea, introduce a targeting cue word, for example 'touch'. Say this word and then invite him to touch. When he touches reward.

Step 5 - Cease to reward any touches that are off cue.

Step 6 - Generalise by changing the environment.

Step 7 - Use the stick to encourage a behaviour. A good one to try is to get the dog to put his paws up onto something. Start with the stick within easy reach and then gradually move it back so that the dog must reach forward and finally get his paws up in order to touch.

Step 8 - Get the new behaviour under cue. 'Paws up'. Gradually hold the stick in place for shorter periods as the dog's confidence grows in the new command.

Step 9 - You can now teach the dog to 'touch' other objects too. Once this is done you can have a variety of targets with a wide ranging number of applications. Put the target stick onto the item and encourage the dog to touch the two together, then as the dog becomes confident, connect a word to the item and then gradually, withdraw the original target stick. This will leave the dog targeting to the new item.

Application Examples for Targeting

Heelwork - The dog follows the target to perfect the desired heel position. You can start with the stick held out at arm's length and then gradually bring it in closer to your side. Ultimately, hold the stick so that the end is just

Teach a touch to the hand

Then bring the hand into the heel position – guiding the dog in with it

As the dog gets the idea gradually raise the hand – use your touch command to maintain the position

Over time raise the hand to the correct position

(Photo sequence J Midgely)

beyond the position that you want the dog to hold his head. You can also work on the dog's gait by having him trotting around at arm's length to the target, and then when you are happy with the gait, put a name to it then bring this closer and closer to the heel position.

Instead of (or as well as) using the target stick you can also teach the dog to target to the hand for heelwork, especially with medium or larger dogs.

Recall - The target is held in front of the handler, (or to heel for the recall to heel), to encourage the dog into the correct present or heel position. You can also use your fingers as the target, hold them in the right place to get the dog to come to the centre of your body for the present or in the heel position for the recall to heel.

Retrieve - The dog can be shaped to retrieve from the beginning, by teaching the touch and then shaping a gradual progression. Rewarding a touch, then open mouthed touch, then hold and so on. The behaviour can then be placed under cue. Next it can be generalised to other articles by starting at the beginning again. The dog will learn rapidly on new articles if you start at the beginning each time.

Scent - To hold a scent cloth or article correctly. The dog's behaviour can be shaped in the same was as described for retrieve.

Sendaway - The target is stuck in, or placed on the ground and the previously conditioned dog readily goes to the target by using your touch command. Distance is built up gradually. Targets can be varied to cover the diverse range of sendaway markers. The dog can also be trained to ignore other targets and go for the named target. This will help the dog to through position/box markers to a back marker.

For sendaway train the dog to the target and then add the down (UK obedience) or stand (FCI obedience.) (Photo J Midgely)

Preparing for the Ring

It is sometimes difficult to get into the swing of constructive training especially after a break or at the beginning of the season. A dog show, Crufts, going on a course or even reading this book will serve as a boost to the motivation, but we still need a plan of action to whip us into match fitness! It easy to go out and practice the same old things and not make any real improvement.

To attain the best results in the ring, the exercises need to be broken down into sections and each of these needs to be trained to as near perfection as we can achieve. Read the various sections to get techniques and tips on the actual training procedure. So, assuming you understand the technique for training, here's a reminder of what to do at your next training session.

General Attention

Getting Attention – Use a good value reward to make sure the dog wants to pay attention. Use the reward carefully so as not to bore the dog – short high value sessions are best. Always make the dog aware that there si more reward to come.

Maintaining Attention – Keeping the dog's attention is always the most difficult thing to achieve, especially with excitable or reactive dogs. Work on getting the rewards in at just the right time, before the dog looks away, and work with distractions of other handlers/dogs etc., to ensure your dog understands that you are fun even when others are around.

Heelwork

Position – Maintenance of a good position is key to good heelwork. Bring the dog into position often, reward the correct position and guide the dog into maintaining it. Do exercises to help him focus on the correct position.

Start and Halt – Don't forget to work on the starting point of heelwork and the end. Work on straight sits and smooth execution.

Turns – Train the turns at each session – it is tempting to just do some heelwork and throw in a few turns, but if you train the turns individually at each session you will avoid faults creeping in.

Straight and Curves – Work on building the distance that you and your dog can maintain in both straight legs of heelwork and with curves (circles and weaves). Build the distance gradually. Remember to work in all directions.

Posture and Footwork – Practice your own footwork and work on keeping an upright posture, looking in the direction that you are going to ensure your turns and straight stretches are tidy and you don't have to think about where your feet need to go.

Recall (Novice)

Even if you are out of the lower classes it is work working on the novice recall as you still need the components for retrieve and scent.

Speed and Accuracy – Work with high level incentives to ensure that the dog wants to get back to you without deviation or distraction.

Presents – Presents should be taught on the spot from immediately in front of you, from a distance and from angles.

Finishes – Work on accuracy, speed and work to avoid jumps, wides and crooked sits.

Recall to Heel

Wait and Call – The dog needs to focus on where you are going to ensure a good accurate recall, but should not be so keen that he anticipates.

Pick up and Heelwork – The pick up and heelwork must be smooth and precise but the dog needs to be accustomed to you taking a turn just prior to the pick up point which may mean he has to change direction at the last minute.

Stays

If the dog breaks the stay position you need to consider what motivated him to do so, and then work on preventing this rather than correcting or chastising.

Positions - Work on each position individually. Short sessions reminding him of what is required.

Distractions - Consider what the dog has to deal with in the ring situation and try to introduce ways of working against the possible problems.

Distance – Build up the distance that you leave the dog in stages, rewarding the dog for good stays.

Retrieve and Scent

Wait – The dog must be stable in the wait position prior to the send, in the present and at the finish.

Pick up, hold, carry and release – Each part of this is trained separately and then linked together.

Variations – Practice the training technique with a variety of articles once he is confident on one. Choose a variety of materials and textures. Include work on a cloth for scent.

Marking – The dog needs to look where the article is thrown for retrieve.

Searching – Work on nose use in a variety of situations to help the dog generalise finding a scent. This will help build confidence. Introduce decoy and neutral scents that are not easy to pick up (e.g. on boards or tiles).

Sendaway

Speed and Accuracy – Motivation is the key to speed and accuracy – the dog must have a high desire to get to the spot. Use motivators, enthusiasm and fun to achieve this.

Control – The wait, down and recall on command all need to be worked on individually to ensure they are stable and immediate.

Distance Control

Positions – Work on each individually remembering to use commands or signals, as they will be used in the ring.

Wait and Return – Train the dog to be accustomed to being left and returned to in any of the three positions.

Distance – Build distance gradually a position at a time before linking them.

General Ring Preparation

Set Up - Go through the set up of exercises, as you will in the ring. Consider the judge and steward's part in this and prepare for it. Add in links to other exercises – in the ring you will not repeat something you will go on to the next, make sure your dog is accustomed to doing this.

Distractions – For example, other dogs, (in the next ring, in the stay ring, outside of the ring), people, judge, steward, children, clapping, food smells, crowds, tables, ring ropes, ring furniture, rain, wind, heat, cold, cars, public address system, dog equipment stalls, tents.

Also consider the dog's general functions he will not work so well if you have not allowed for freedom from hunger, thirst, pain, discomfort, stress, fear. Some dogs need more time than others to take in the environment and feel comfortable enough to concentrate on working – make sure you allow that time.

Fitness – Your dog needs to be fit, healthy and have a good diet in order to perform well.

Preparing Yourself - Remember to prepare yourself well so that you feel as comfortable as possible when competing. This includes fitness and mental preparation but even includes things like feeling comfortable with the footwear and clothes you are wearing.

Forward Planning

At the end of your training session consider what you have achieved and what you need to do next time. It sometimes helps to keep some brief notes to remind you of what you need to do to ensure that you make progress. Analyse both yourself and the dog – consider quality, precision, enjoyment, confidence and any other issues that affect you both.

Conclusion

Competitive obedience for most people is a hobby. For a few it is a way of earning a little extra, and a minority of people are fortunate in that they have managed to turn their pastime into a business and are able to make their living from the sport or its ancillary branches. Whichever section we fit into, we should all remember that the dog is with us because we so desire, he has no say in the matter, and does not have the choice to walk away.

The dog may not always perform in the way that we might like, but at the end of the day we are the teachers, he is but the pupil, trying to make sense of a foreign world.

Planning for the future will make your training easy, aim high but keep your daily targets lot. Don't achieve accuracy at the cost of enthusiasm, you will need both to win tomorrow.

Training is about preparing yourself and your dog, about understanding your pupil's needs and abilities, about enjoyment, and about building up a life long partnership, a bond of trust.

Winning is a great feeling, but we must also feel good about ourselves and about the way we achieved that success.

Happy Dogs - Happy Winners

Control the games, have fun with your dog and when it all goes wrong just laugh and try again!

Another day another dog show!

Appendix
Useful Information

Obedience Competition Rules
Up-to-date copies of the rules for the UK are available from:
The Kennel Club, 1 Clarges Street, Piccadilly, London W1Y 8AB.
Tel: 020 7518 1016. Or you can order on line - www.the-kennel-club.org.uk
Rules for the rest of Europe are governed by the FCI Federation Cynologique
Internationale, 13 Pace Albert I, B-6530, Thuin, Belgium.
Tel 071/59.12.38 (Fax 71/59.22.29).
USA - The American Kennel Club (AKC), 51 Maddison Avenue, New York, NY
10010.
Tel 00 1 212/696-8200 (fax 212/696-8329)
Other Kennel Clubs will have their own rules and guidelines.

Other Useful Obedience Information
Dog Training Weekly – weekly magazine covering show reports, adverts,
and information on Obedience and HTM/freestyle.
Print House, Parc Y Shwt, Fishguard, Pembrokeshire. SA65 9AP.
Telephone 01348 875011 - www.dtwmagazine.com
Kennel Gazette – monthly magazine featuring lists of shows and other
Kennel Club events.
Telephone 020 7518 1016 Email kennelgazette@the-kennel-club.org.uk
Courses with Angela White on competitive obedience contact Angela on
01427 753918. PO Box 1044, Haxey. Doncaster. DN9 2JL.
Email angelawhite@connectfree.co.uk
Clickers
Clickers are available direct from Angela White at the above address.

Common Obedience Abbreviations

ANT - Anticipation
ARO - After a run off
ASSD - Positions in heelwork
Aus - Australian Shepherd Dog
Aussie – Australian Shepherd Dog
B - Bitch
BC - Border Collie
BEG – Beginner
BS - Body signal
BSD - Belgian Shepherd
C - Clear (nothing lost)
Ch - Championship show
CP - Crooked present
CR – Crabbing
CS - Crooked sit
DC - Distance Control
D - Dog (male)
Dev - Deviation
DR - Drift (from heel position)
Drop - Drop of article or cloth
DS - Double sit
DTW – Dog Training Weekly
(Magazine)
Erat - Erratic
Ex - Exemption show
Fin - Finish
F - Full marks
GR - Golden Retriever
GSD - German Shepherd Dog
Hang - loss of position
Heinz 57 - Mongrel
HES - Hesitation
HF - Heel Free (off lead)
HOL - Heel on lead
HS - Head or hand signal
HTM – Heelwork to music
HW – Heelwork
1L - Presenting to one leg
J – Jump
KC – Kennel Club
L – Lagging
Lab – Labrador

Leo - Leonberger
LO - Laying on
LOP - Loss of position
Lt - Limit show or class
M – Mouthing
NOV – Novice
Ob - Obedience
Ob Ch - Obedience Champion
OCP - Off centre present
OOS - Out of sight
Op - Open Show or class
OW - Obedience Warrant
Pre – Present
PSD - Pyrenean Sheepdog
POS – Position
POT – Potential
PU - Pick up
REC - Recall
RET – Retrieve
RO - Run off
RW - Ring work
S - Slow
SA – Sendaway
Sc – Scent
Sheltie – Shetland Sheepdog
SpSp – Springer Spaniel
SS - Slow sit
Surge - Surge out of position
Terv - Tervueren
TT - Temperament test
VCP - Very crooked present
W - Wide
WAT - Wide about turn
WF - Wide finish
WLT - Wide left turn
WPU - Wide pick up
WRT - Wide right turn
WS - Working Sheepdog
WT - Wide turn
XB - Crossbreed
XC - Extra command

Index

Other Books by Angela White

Everybody Can Train Their Own Dog,
A - Z of Dog training and behaviour problems for all dogs owners.
Endorsed by a founder member of the British Institute of Professional Dog
Trainers, and with the ASPCA seal of approval, this easy to follow book
gives advice in a handy, fully illustrated format. A must for every dog
owner.
Published 1992 TFH ISBN 0-86622-524-2

Happy Dogs Happy Winners (Revised Edition Published 2004)
Complete manual of obedience training. Endorsed by top obedience
champion handlers, this book is ideal for complete beginners and more
experienced handlers alike. Each exercise is covered with a step by step
approach to enable the discerning trainer to work their way from the
beginner class right through to championship level competition.
First published 1993 Rainbow Publishing.
Second revised edition 2004, Rainbow Publishing.
ISBN 1-899057-05-6
Price £14.95 Plus £1.50 P&P UK, (£2.90 P&P rest of the world).
Also available in German Translation Price £14.95 Plus P&P as above.

Puppies Your Successful Guide To Dog Ownership,
This definitive work covers every aspect of puppy care right through to
adulthood. How to chose a pet, how to look after it, why it behaves in the
way it does, how to train it and much more. This book is not just for new
puppy owners but, is an ideal book for all who have interests in dogs.
Published 1997 UK, TFH/Kingdom ISBN 185279023-7
Price £19.95 Plus £3.00 P&P UK (£4.50 rest of the world)

The Leonberger,
Essential reading for anyone interested in this most majestic of breeds. This
spell binding, beautifully illustrated book includes the fascinating history
of the breed, how to train using kind, humane, motivational methods, and
even the breeding of this giant of the dog world. It is most definitely a
user's guide to owning the most magnificent of breeds, the Leonberger.
Published 1998, TFH/Kingdom ISBN 185279064-4
Price £24.95 Plus £3.00 P&P UK (£4.50 rest of the world)

Dog Training Instructor's Manual

This much acclaimed instructor's 'bible', is a comprehensive book which includes all you need to know to teach others the art of dog training. From setting up a school, organising classes and courses, how to keep the pupils attention and how to conduct yourself. It includes advice on puppy groups, problem dogs, specialist training as well as standard pet dog control.
Published 2000, Rainbow Publishing ISBN 1-899057-02-1
Price £12.95 Plus £2.00 P&P UK (£2.90 rest of the world)

Book and Booklets Available Direct From Rainbow Publishing
Clicker and Target Training - Teaching for Fun and Competition
Author Angela White. Published by Rainbow, 2003. £4.50 Plus 50p P&P UK
(£1.00 P&P Europe, £1.50 P&P rest of the world)
Order 10 or more copies 10% discount
Other Booklets by Angela White.

How To Be Top Dog
How to recognise, deal with and treat dominant dogs in a domestic environment. From puppy growls, to viscous attacks, this booklet helps owners to avoid confrontations and get the behaviour under their own control.

Home Alone Canine
Getting dogs used to being alone, how to combat stress. Dealing with the problems owners and their dogs face when they are left alone. Including chewing, barking, urinating, defecating as well as associated behaviours.

Training Your Dog
Basic techniques for getting control of your pet. All based on kind, motivational methods of training that work with the dog's own desires. Includes: sit, down, stand, come back, walk on a loose lead, leave and don't jump up.

Above 3 booklets published by Rainbow, 2003. £3.99 inc. P&P UK (£1.00 P&P Europe, £1.50 P&P rest of the world)
Order 10 or more copies 10% discount

Dog Training Instructor's Manual
by Angela White

A comprehensive book including all you want and need to know to teach others the art of good, motivational, humane and positive dog training. The books includes:

Canine & Human Psychology
Problem Behaviours
Social Development & Training
Puppy, Pet & Specialist Training
Clicker & Target Training
The Art of Good Teaching
Setting Up a Training School
And Much More....

Ideal book for those wanting to learn more about dog training, embark on instructing or brush up on new methods and instructing skills.
The author Angela White has been a dog trainer, obedience judge and instructor for over 20 years and has experienced many areas of dog training at a professional, competition and pet level. She presents courses on instructing, problem behaviours, counseling and competitive obedience in the UK and world wide.

Available by post price £12.95 (P&P £1·50). Send your cheque for £12.95+P&P payable to 'Rainbow' Books will be dispatched within 21 days. (Usually sooner).
Send to: Rainbow Publishing, PO Box 1044, Haxey. Doncaster. DN9 2JL. Telephone/fax 01427 753918.